A SEA WITH MANY ISLANDS

A SEA WITH MANY ISLANDS

by

MICHAEL F. PAGE

Illustrated

ROBERT HALE LIMITED
63 Old Brompton Road, London, S.W.7

First Published 1952

*The names of all ships and persons mentioned
in this narrative have been changed*

PRINTED IN GREAT BRITAIN BY RICHARD CLAY AND COMPANY, LTD.
BUNGAY, SUFFOLK.

To
MY MOTHER
for the years of encouragement

CONTENTS

LIST OF ILLUSTRATIONS

EMBARKATION AND THE GATEWAY TO THE EAST

I

WE WERE VERY LUCKY in our weather: all the way from Hong-Kong we had nothing but calm seas and gentle winds, and we came up-Channel in weather that was smooth with spring. When we had turned the corner and entered the North Sea we recognised the familiar landmarks, like old friends who had been awaiting our return: the wallowing red hull of the Sunk lightship, the gull-circled drifters off Grimsby, the massive bulwarks of Flamborough Head. "Canny old Flambro' Heid," said the Third Engineer approvingly, and "'When you get to Flambro' Head, pack your bag and dump yer bed,'" quoted the Chief Officer. We encountered the squadrons of grubby colliers bound southwards from the Tyne, glimpsed Lindisfarne, gazed on the green-and-lavender downs of the Lowlands. And then in the still of a late afternoon we were steaming between the fortified islands of the Forth, with the smoke hovering unstirred above Burnt Island and the great bridge straddling across the western sky.

For me, it was the end of a long voyage; one which had begun nearly two and a half years before, and in the course of which I had sailed in five ships. As a radio officer in the Merchant Navy, I had been to Singapore, to Batavia, to the Andaman Islands and the Mergui Archipelago—the 'sea with many islands'—and to Bombay and the barren opulence of Abadan. I had spent a month in hospital in Japan, and another month on the sacred island of Miya Jima, and six months under the lee of the island of Hong-Kong.

It had all begun on a January morning in Liverpool, whose streets were washed with strange cold light which is like the reflection from an ice-field. I had returned from leave by an early train, and made my way to the office of

my company through the red-nosed, collar-clutching crowds
en route to work. With a part of my mind I envied them,
about to spend the day in their snug jobs and returning at
night to their own homes ; with another part I was thankful
that I was not condemned to the drab monotony of the city's
toil. I did not know, yet, where I would be going, or to
what ship I would be appointed ; within a week I might
be bound for the brown rivers of Africa or the sea-ports of
Brazil, the trumpeting towers of America or the vigorous
Antipodes.

Every step I took upon the frosty pavements brought me
a little closer to that unknown destination, to the exchange of
the hurrying and preoccupied faces about me for the brown
and mournful crowds of India or the arrogant Argentinos ;
as I entered the drab hallway of the office I knew that I was
once again a unit of that service which takes its ensign
wherever a ship can sail.

I reported myself to the staff-clerk, expecting to be told to
wait for orders, but it seemed that Fate had everything
worked out for me that day.

" Ah, Mr. Page," he said as I entered. " We've got a
ship for you, Mr. Page. We're sending you out to Singapore to join the ' Bengal '. You'll be going out as passenger
in the ' Phoebe '. Here's your letter of appointment, so if
you'll just take it down to the owner's office they'll see about
getting you signed on, and fix up your passage and the rest
of it. You can come back here and draw your expenses
when they've got you fixed up."

The individual to whom I reported at the ship-owner's
office seemed to be quite unimpressed by the fact that I was
to sail for Singapore. He examined my credentials through
his glasses, and with the most ponderous deliberation
replaced them by another pair in order to sign some form.
He took these off and carefully stowed them away, only to
produce a further spectacle-case and another pair of glasses
through which to examine me.

" M'ph," he commented at last, and then, " These are
yours."

He handed me a steamer ticket, and an envelope which I
discovered to contain a fascinating variety of labels, tie-on
and stick-on. Some of them merely advertised ' Red

Funnel Line ', others rebuked ' Not Wanted on Voyage ' or just said ' Cabin ' or ' C '.   There were enough labels there—including the long ones which proclaimed ' Singapore '—to camouflage my baggage with gaudy paper.

The official rose, again changing his glasses as he did so. " We'll go to the Shipping Office now," he ordained, and I sprang to my feet to follow him.

I thought that his dignity would at least require a taxi, but soon discovered that we walked. Hurrying past the pillars of the Overhead Railway and through water-front streets decorated with cabbage-leaves and greasy newspapers, I asked him about my ship, and he told me in a condescending manner that the ' Bengal ' was a tanker of about two thousand tons, at present chartered as a fleet auxiliary oiler. She was apparently to be based on Singapore, and I was to report to the naval authorities there as soon as I arrived.

We entered the Ministry of Transport offices, formerly the Board of Trade office, but always, to merchant seamen, the ' Shipping Office '. My escort walked around behind the long counter, while I waited on the seamen's side. The usual group of clerks was laboriously employed behind the counter, the usual woe-begone bunch of lascar firemen was chattering apprehensively in one corner, and the usual argument was going on between a Union delegate and a vociferously resistant seaman in another.

" I tell y' I 'ave paid me doos," he reiterated. " 'Aven't they dedooced 'em on ev'ry bleedun' ship I been on ? "

The Union man looked scornfully incredulous. " Go on, then, prove it," he said. " Where's yer receipts ? "

" I tol' yer an' tol' yer I were torpedered lars' week o' th' war," said the seaman triumphantly. " Lorst everythin' I 'ad—receipt's included. Anyroad, I couldn't pay yer now. I gotta buy meself a pair o' overhauls."

My escort beckoned me towards the counter, where he and the Shipping Master had been exchanging anecdotes during the past five minutes. The latter surveyed me wearily.

" You understand that these Articles you're going to sign are just to cover the voyage out to Singapore, and that as a passenger you agree to accept any type of messing or accommodation on board, sleep in a hammock if necessary, and transfer to any other ship or join any ship you may be ordered to, on the way out ? " he asked.

I felt that he spoke through force of habit, since there was nothing that I could do about it, anyway. So I nodded assent, and in a moment was putting my name to the Articles of Agreement—' THE UNDERSIGNED agree . . . to serve for a period not exceeding two years, on a voyage to any port or ports between the limits of 75 degrees North and 60 degrees South,' etc. As soon as I had signed, my sponsor changed his glasses, requested me to be aboard the passenger ship by two that afternoon, and bade me a casual farewell.

I had plenty to do before I went aboard. First, to the offices of the wireless company, where I collected my travelling expenses. These were ten per cent of the passage money to Singapore, ninety-eight pounds some shillings, which struck me as a considerable sum to pay for transportation of myself and chattels, especially if I had to sleep in a hammock. I began to spend it immediately, on the purchase of various articles which I thought that I needed.

By the time that I had laden myself with packages, and lunched frugally on Guinness and sandwiches, it was past noon, and a sudden panic seized me that I should miss the ship. I hurried to the station and withdrew my bags from the left-luggage office, and with the aid of an enthralled porter opened them up amongst everyone's feet, and stuffed my newest purchases into them. I suddenly recollected the envelope of labels which I had been given, and with our tongues working overtime the porter and I plastered my bags with them. They looked very gay and provocative in the grey light of the sordid terminus.

Although the name of the ship was unfamiliar, the idea of a passenger-ship combined with these variegated labels had led me to expect something pretty big. When the taxi which had brought me through the Mersey Tunnel pulled up at one of the Birkenhead wharves, I was somewhat taken aback to see a ship's bows with the name of my ship painted upon them. They were by no means high, nothing massive or wave-spurning about them at all. They were very humble and unassuming bows, belonging to just such another meek and unassuming little freighter as those in which I had spent most of my sea life. The first thing I did after paying off the taxi was to rip most of the labels off my bags, for I could too well imagine the kind of wise-cracks I'd have to endure if I boarded such a ship with my luggage looking like a film-star's.

But I was not the only passenger, and the taxi had inserted itself into the midst of an extremely vocal and flashily dressed assortment of them. They were focused upon a colossal pile of baggage, every piece of which was fastened with a Houdini intricacy of knots, and two or three lorries were discharging more. Every passenger wrangled at the top of his high-pitched voice, gesticulated furiously, hawked and spat at frequent intervals, and generally behaved as though he had been robbed of his last copper. They were all Chinese, two complete ships' crews being repatriated to Malaya.

No one else was in sight. I lingered on the outskirts of the throng, wondering whether the Articles which I'd signed would compel me to berth with these unruly citizens, and if so how long it would take me to learn the use of chop-sticks and to prattle Cantonese. Then the consciousness of white supremacy asserted itself, and I struck out for myself, fought my way to the gangway, and was stopped at the top by a small man in a felt hat and a raincoat.

" What do *you* want ? " he enquired, in a tone expressing that whatever it was I wouldn't get it there.

" Well, as a matter of fact, I'm supposed to be a passenger in this ship," I explained apologetically. " This *is* the ' Phoebe ', isn't it ? "

" Have you passed the Immigration ? " he asked fiercely, and I shook my head.

" The Immigration ? " I asked dolefully. " Who're they ? "

With a sudden flashing smile, as unexpected as it was affable, he exclaimed, " Oh, well, I don't s'pose it matters very much. Where's your gear ? "

When I told him, he led the way down the gangway to fetch it. He was at once submerged by the Chinese pas-sengers, who squealed and twittered questions at him which he answered with bawls of " I dunno ! I don't-bloody-well-know! Lemme get by! Give over, will you?" and flailed his way through them to my bags.

"Caw, they don't 'arf create, don't they?" he asked, as he helped me to carry my gear aboard.

He led me to a cabin just off the saloon, which he said was mine.

"Now you're all right," he said. "Nothing to do but sit tight until the ship sails."

I prepared to do so, while the confusion of a vessel preparing to sail whirled about me. In a very short time I was caught up in it, when a prying Customs officer discovered me and started off by asking me how much gold, jewellery, or money I might happen to have concealed in my baggage. The scornful laugh with which I greeted this question prompted him to further enquiries, and before long he had discovered that I had not been passed by the Immigration authorities. I was subjected to an invasion by a number of mackintoshed individuals in shapeless hats, shepherded by the Customs officer. In no time at all they disclosed the fact that my steamer ticket did not bear my name, but that of someone called Nankivel, and I was escorted into the saloon for further investigation. That small apartment was jammed with men in uniform and out of uniform, all wrangling and jostling with apparent incoherence; the tables were smothered with forms and booklets in which other men were busily scribbling, or upon which they were solemnly thumping rubber stamps. I was jostled through the throng to stand behind a small man in a teddy-bear coat and a large man in golf-cap, who were already answering the questions of one of the officials.

"D'Arcy is the name," said the small man, with a kind of fuming impatience. "Shall I spell it for you? Look, there it is on my passport. My God! this bloody Government . . ."

His larger companion chuckled deeply, and good-humouredly gave his name as Haig.

"John Haig," he said, and chuckled again.

When my turn came, they discovered a discrepancy between the name on my steamer ticket and that on my Seaman's Identity Card, which appeared to be just the sort of thing that they were looking for, and they all began to ask questions at once.   Who had sent me to the ship ?   What was my full name ?   Where was I going ?   Why ?   Why hadn't I got a passport ?

A rotund man licked his pencil and scribbled in a notebook, glancing up at me from beneath his brows.   He was apparently undecided whether I was an escaped war criminal or a Communist agent, or merely a Tory fleeing the Welfare State.   The Chief Steward, a sharp-faced and worried little man with white hair and a Bootle accent, was unable to improve matters, since I was down on his passenger list as Nankivel.   At last someone entered the saloon, pushed his way through the crowd with an air of considerable secrecy, and bent down to whisper to one of my inquisitors. He nodded in grudging comprehension, and then spoke to me curtly.

" It's all right.   We've been on the 'phone to your office.   It seems that you're taking the place of someone who went sick, and they forgot to change the name on the ticket."

Dump-thump went his stamp on the inking-pad and on to my identity card, and he returned it to me impressed with the triangular hieroglyphic of the Immigration office.

After all that, sailing down the ink-dark flood of the Mersey on a winter evening seemed something of an anticlimax.   I stood out on deck for a while, watching the shadowy mass of the docks and the waterfront slide past us beneath the evening mists, and the lights which shone from the shore with the sadness of all lights which shine whilst you are departing.   A steamer coming out of the locks gave three blasts on her siren, and the sound undulated dolefully out into the deepening night.   This was the moment in which all the regrets for whatever you may have surrendered cohere into a useless melancholy, for it is too late to turn back.   The voyage, and whatever it may hold for good or ill, is all ahead of you, and there is nothing to do but to enter upon it with a good heart.

That night I became acquainted with my travelling companions, in the shabby little saloon with its notice saying ' So many table-cloths have been spoiled by officers' carelessness with cigarettes that if this continues they will no longer be supplied '.   There were only two other ' first-class ' passengers besides myself, Haig and d'Arcy, but in addition there were nine or ten engineers being sent to the East to join ships of the same company as the ' Phoebe '. Also, of course, there were the hundred-odd Chinese passengers, who were clamorously accommodated in the 'tween decks of the ship, so that together with her own officers and crew she literally swarmed with people.

" I've been lucky, anyway," grunted d'Arcy that first night at dinner. " I told m'wife that I'd have to share m'cabin with someone who was seasick all the time or someone who'd booze their way to Singapore. Never thought that I'd run across you again, Johnny old boy."

Haig chuckled contentedly. The two men were old friends, and were each of them in their own way cultured and charming old gentlemen. They had both spent their adult lives in Malaya, and, although they had retired before the war and had never expected to return there, d'Arcy was returning to piece together business holdings ruined by the war, and Haig to reorganise the Government department of which he had been chief.

Haig was exactly the type of man envisioned in the term ' a ripe old age '. In his youth he must have been a magnificent figure, and was still upright and sturdy, and was constantly good-humoured, tolerant, and kind. I never heard him say a cross or unkind word, even during our political affrays, and anyone less like the liverish and overbearing Colonial official of tradition can hardly be imagined. But d'Arcy was of a different type altogether. Much the same age as Haig, he gave the impression of being at once older and younger. A small man, he had a kind of semimilitary bearing, a dapper pungency of manner which impressed one more than his constant plaint of age. His resentment at growing old he expressed with a bitter and cynical humour, a mordancy with which he would slash at himself as bitingly for his own incapacities as he would slash at the Government or at any other person or thing of which he disapproved.

" What a thing it is to be growing old," he would snarl. " Nothing behind you but regrets for the chances you've missed, and nothing ahead but a slide down a hell of a steep hill, with death waiting for you at the bottom."

In d'Arcy, however, we were blessed with a polished *raconteur*. His tales of the ' early days ' in Malaya, before the First World War, gave a fascinating glimpse into a world populated by mem- and pukka-sahibs, remittance men, lonely planters, wasters, and faithful native boys—a world as three-dimensional, and yet as curiously arrested in space and time, as that in the pictures viewed through an old-fashioned stereoscope; the figures tiny, archaic, rigid, and yet somehow alive, imbued with life by one who had survived them. A picture of a colony over which the Old School Tie still waved, in which people would cycle for miles along jungle tracks in order to play bridge at a club with a dozen members, and would send for the girl at home when they had made good.

His gift for story-telling was a welcome one on the long voyage, for conversations on shipboard, where there is not very much else by way of entertainment, are apt to be as lengthy as those reported in ' Pilgrim's Progress '. As the ship wallowed and lurched her way out into the Atlantic and down into the wintry Bay of Biscay, we began to shake down into a routine in which d'Arcy's anecdotes played an important part. Conversation became our main pastime, for on the overcrowded little ' Phoebe ' we had no room for deck games, no one officious enough to organise entertainments, and no women. We had plenty of liquor, and after dinner in the evenings the little saloon became the arena for cards and dominoes. I don't quite know how the passion for dominoes began, but every night a cluster of intent faces would be brooding over the angular patterns of black and white against the green baize cloth. We were as absorbed as were the Chinese passengers in their eternal mah-jongg. Up the companion-way leading to their temporary quarters there came at all hours of the day and night the clack-clack of the mah-jongg tiles, the scrape of their shuffle over the bare table-tops, and the chattering wrangle of the gamblers. The ship's doctor, who was himself a Chinese, told me that they were playing with wads of pound notes, and that already one or two of them had lost their savings of years away from home. He was a little elderly man, the doctor, with a brown, humorous face adorned with rimless spectacles. He dressed invariably in a

II

The floating town, the self-sufficient and enclosed community of the ship, passed the serrated brown hills of Spain and the battleship-grey bulk of Gibraltar and entered the spiteful gloom of the winter Mediterranean, to roll and plunge her way towards the sea-level coastline of Egypt and the toll-gate of Port Said.

For a place so tinged with romantic implication, Port Said must be the tawdriest sham on earth. The gateway to the Orient, the wickedest city in the world, and other such colourful synonyms have been attached to it, and it falls short of them all. It is, of course, the gateway to the East, and yet there is about it none of the sultry glamour which one would associate with such a term. Its atmosphere is one of transience, as feverish and temporary as that of a railway terminus, so that it is always surprising to realise that people actually live there.

The mixture of influences which have contributed towards this atmosphere, of French bureaucracy and Colonial exploitation and Egyptian decadence, tinged by the austere dogma of Islam, is most apparent in its architecture. From the sea it is an Egyptian town, with ochre and saffron, citron, pink, and orange blocks of tenements arising where the fringe of the desert meets the sea. Once you have entered between the long breakwaters and steamed past the graceful little sailing-craft at anchor and the verdigrised statue of de Lesseps, it is impossible to say what it is. The Canal offices are housed in a kind of bogus mosque; a delicately aspiring minaret arises out of blocks of offices and shops; there are great ugly hotels like an Edwardian architect's conception of the Orient; many of the buildings are a kind of compromise between flat-roofed Moorish and the Riviera villa. The commercial section of the town contrives to appear at once massive and frivolous, cafés in the Latin style spread their tables all over the pavements, while advertisements for K.L.M. and Johnny Walker rear above the harbour. A short walk from the night-clubs, whose dim lighting is kind to the French cocottes, lie the sprawling slums of the native quarter, where lamp-lit wooden stalls display obscene edibles.

It would seem that Port Said's reputation for wickedness must have been built upon petty commercial immorality. The main impression which the average traveller will take away with him is of having been assailed from start to finish by dusky hawkers and touts, either working independently or as agents of bumboatmen who trade under such names as George Robey, Indian Joe, and Squinting Dick. Apart from the more obvious vendors of flimsy clothing, trashy and gaudy souvenirs, and half-cured leather-work, there are any number of mysterious individuals who contrive to pick up a living from seamen and travellers. There are the sellers of cognac which turns out to be cold tea, of the Turkish Delight which old sailors aver to be made from boiled rats, and of eggs reputed to include those of the snake, lizard, and alligator. There is the magazine merchant, whose real stock-in-trade is dog-eared copies of ' One Night in a Harem ' and ' The Amorous Duchess ' ; the vendors of ' feelthy ' pictures, imitation Damascene, aphrodisiacs, and lucky charms. They have developed the art of salesmanship to a high degree, emphasising not so much the virtue of an article as the fact that it is forbidden.

" Psst, Johnny ! " is hissed from behind a grubby palm. " 'ere—come 'ere ! Roun' a corner. Look ! I show you ! " A package is produced from a recess in grimy rags. " Keep it dark ! Genuine ! From Paris, I tell you ! How much you gib, eh ? "

The traveller who goes ashore will find himself the focus of a swarm of touts, pimps, guides, hawkers, and mendicants as persistent and as heedless of remonstrance as the flies of Egypt.

" Johnny ! " they shriek, plead, implore, command, suggest. " Johnny, baksheesh ? Johnny, you wan' nice girl ? My sister, very clean, very sheap, very sweet. Johnny, you want beer ? I savvy good place. I take you, Johnny. Johnny, you gib me . . . Johnny, mister, I show you, what you want see ? Nice girl, shoppin', everythin' got. You buy necklace your wife, silk stockin', dirty pos'card ? Everythin' got, very good, very sheap. . . . Johnny—Johnny ! "

Filthy little boys in ragged striped nightgowns, gaunt, frenzied individuals in longer gowns and the tarboosh, arrogant elderly gentlemen in lounge suits and cracked patent-leather shoes, they pursue the hapless wanderer with their pleas and lamentations and commands.   Compared with them, the London spiv is but an apprentice to his trade.   If you are foolish enough to buy something from them, and produce a note to pay for it—" Orright, gib it 'ere, I got change—English money ; gib it "—and that's the last you see of it.

" I speak you, price one pound," protests the dusky spiv energetically.   " I no got change.   Wot you speak, change ?   Orright, call p'liceman ; I don't care."

Undiscouraged by the argument, which you have lost before it starts, the rest of the party follows you onwards. With immense secrecy and precaution, one of them produces a battered dollar watch, from which most of the gilding has long since worn away.

" Look, Johnny . . . stolen from passenger on 'merican ship.   Gold !   I sell you very sheap—look out, p'liceman ! —'ere, lissen, I whisper . . . only twenny-five quid ! "

It is as futile to lose your temper as to flail at the heedless flies.   Taking a seat at one of the café tables may get rid of some of them, for the waiters will chase them away, and they will disappear with howls of, " Muckin' bastard, Johnny . . . stinkin' Englishman."

But the waiter has his own friends, and in a few moments a couple of shoe-shine boys will be dabbing at your shoes with their brushes, trying to smear them enough to make a polish necessary.

" Photograph, sah ? " inquires a courtly gentleman laden with apparatus, and a curly-headed urchin approaches your chair and accosts you in the accents of the Gorbals.   Before you can recover from your surprise at the Glaswegian ribaldries emitted by his shining, coppery face, he is addressing you with the jaunty plausibility of the Dubliner, followed by the sing-song of the Rhondda.   Such talent should be rewarded, you think, but before you have time to grope in your pocket they are all dispelled by a tall and hawk-nosed apparition in flowing black robes.

" Go 'way ! Get out o' this ! " he cries.   " Bad mans ! Leave shentleman alone, will you ? "

As they retreat he looks at you with a soft cunning, and

murmurs, " Better you don't buy anythings from those bad
mans. . . . Now me, I gotta something to show you . . ."
Squatting amongst the swirl of his robes, he extends a
sinewy, sensitive hand, snaps his fingers and cries softly,
" *Gulli-gulli ! Gulli-gulli !* "

His empty palm is all at once holding two or three
cheeping, fluffy chicks.   They disappear as quickly as they
came, and then the yellow balls of fluff are appearing from
everywhere : from your trouser-leg, from your pocket,
falling one by one from his empty palm on to the table-top,
to run cheeping for a few seconds before he makes them
vanish again.

" *Gulli-gulli, gulli-gulli,*" he exhorts them wheedlingly as
they appear and disappear, and with a sly glance upwards
explains, " I am *gulli-gulli* man."

He softens you up with a few small tricks with cards and
with the bean under three thimbles, and then proceeds to
coins.

" Now, you lend me a couple of moneys," he asks
casually.   " No—must be silver moneys ; coppers no good
this trick."

Your two half-crowns lie upon his open palm ; he sweeps
the other one across it and cries, " *Gulli-gulli!* "   They
have changed to ha'pennies, and you couldn't be such a bad
sport as to complain at being so taken in.   As you walk
away, you hear the commencing howls of his argument with
the waiter, who is already demanding his commission.

The wanderer who wishes to test Port Said's reputation
for wickedness in the more conventional sense of the word
will doubtless end up in one of those famous brothels, the
Golden House or the Constantinople.   The advent of a
patron turns out the guard with the celerity of a crack
regiment, and the *filles de maison* line up in giggling, anxious
ranks for inspection by the intending purchaser.   He is
accompanied by Madam in person, lending her word of
stately recommendation.

" This one very nice guaranteed girl.   Or Cleo, she's
good.   Knows all the tricks."

If this is wickedness, then how excessively dull wickedness must be !   But the average traveller via Port Said,
when he comes to reckon up what he has spent with what

he has gained for it, will have experienced wickedness enough.

The 'Phoebe' remained two days there, taking on bunkers, a process which in Port Said is usually carried out with a despatch which is the more remarkable in that it is all done by man-power. The coal-lighters, laden so deeply that the water is lapping over their gunwales, tie up along-side, and out of them is erected a flimsy scaffolding up the ship's side. From one stage to another of this the coal is passed in little baskets from the lighter to the steamer's deck, where a constant stream of coolies trots with them to the bunker hatch. Through long practice the workers maintain such a fluent rhythm, with the basket-fillers in the lighters, the passers on the stages, and the carriers on deck all working in such close co-operation, that the coal pours into the bunkers as rapidly as from a chute. While they work, the coal-passers often keep up a deep-voiced chant, with a rhythm as monotonous as their work. The turbaned wretches delving in the coal, naked but for a clout of knotted rags, and their coppery bodies smeared with dust and sweat, the women on the stages in their matted sack-cloth robes, their sinewy arms raising and lifting in an effortful ballet, the fellaheen in their striped night-gowns trotting across the decks, all harmonise in a dismal concordance of toil. It needs no vivid sense of imagery to hear in it the song of the under-privileged, as tuned to the sombre themes of hunger, weariness, and toil as are their dreary lives themselves.

Probably they sang in the same way when they were digging the Suez Canal, which must be one of the world's monuments to coolie labour. And, whether or not Port Said is the wickedest city in the world, there is not much doubt that the Suez is about the dreariest of all the great engineering spectacles. There is not even anything par-ticularly romantic about its story, regarded simply as an engineering phenomenon; the digging of a great ditch through the desert, from Port Said to the Bitter Lakes and thence to the Gulf of Suez, is a history of dogged hard labour and endurance rather than any novelty in procedure or design. As a monument to hard work it is indeed something to be marvelled at, though the race which raised the Pyramids by hand is no stranger to such grandiose feats of toil.

We entered the Canal on a hard, bright morning scoured by the vehement north-easterly wind which possesses Egypt in the early months of the year.

At breakfast-time d'Arcy promised, " Well, if there is one thing I refuse to do, it's look at the Suez Canal.   I've seen it too ruddy often, and I never thought that I'd have to see it again.   Someone let me know when we get through."

He retired to his cabin, and I strolled out on deck.   I was immediately accosted by one of the four boatmen which the ship takes on, together with their boats, to tie her up in case it is necessary to let another ship pass her in the Canal.

" Johnny," he wheedled softly.   " Mister . . . you want Turkish Delight ?   Map of Canal ?   Pitcher pos'-cards ?   Want a good wallet, Johnny ? "

After shaking him off, I turned my attention to the passing scene.   There is not very much to see, and throughout the twelve hours during which the ship is in transit the passenger's gaze is blunted by endless shimmering vistas of buff or tawny desert.   It is diversified, mainly on the western bank, by angular control stations built of cinder-coloured brick, an occasional clattering train, gaunt camels and their attendants, distant groves of some coarse ever-green, and impatient groups waiting at the ferries and floating bridges for the ship to pass.   Saltpans glitter whitely on the horizon, and great triangular sails appear to drift away over the desert as the dhows sail along the Sweetwater Canal, which runs near to the Suez for a part of the way.

The ship's wash creates a constant curling wave which sweeps along each bank of the Canal as she passes, and only vanishes when she enters the Bitter Lakes, about half-way through.   They make a refreshing change from the barren utility of the Canal, since many of the Canal staff and their families live there at the little town of Ismailia, whose buildings are half-hidden among green belts of trees.   But this oasis is soon left behind, and the ship passes through the winding chain of lakes before entering the final section of Canal.   More desert follows, with a range of reddish hills glowering across the horizon, until you reach the Red Sea terminus of Port Tewfik.

Suez itself is a mile or so along the coast, a dirty, clotted town composed mainly of ochre stucco tenements and disreputable cafés, while Port Tewfik is a comparatively clean and orderly little place, with shady avenues along the Canal banks and the dock installations behind the town. With great excitement the boatmen are lowered into the Canal in their boats while the ship is still under way, and with cries of " Ya'Allah! Cast off boat-rope! Wa'Allah! Leggo boat-rope! " row frenziedly alongside until they are clear of the ship.

In a few hours you have crossed the link between two continents ; have passed from the Mediterranean into the Red Sea ; left behind the remnants of the West and become definitely committed to the East.   It is a change which is as much psychological as physical.   You have taken the highway of Empire, and the theme-song is now that masterpiece of wishful thinking :

> " Take me somewhere East of Suez,
>   Where a man can raise a thirst,
>   Where there ain't no Ten Commandments,
>   And the best is like the worst."

CHAPTER TWO

INTO THE TROPICS

I

THE CAPTAIN, A STUMPY, elderly man with a highly seasoned stock of prejudices and a slight Cockney accent, said at lunch-time, " Don't bother to change for dinner, gentlemen. We're quite informal here in the hot weather."

Although we hadn't had the least idea of doing so, nor had done so since leaving home, we murmured our thanks and looked suitably impressed. We had begun to wear tropical clothing that morning—another change as much psychological as physical. I had also commenced sun-bathing, and had been pelted with all the old familiar predictions concerning death by sunstroke. But, since it was January, the Red Sea was fairly cool, and we slid smoothly along through a lustrous sea.

It took us four days to reach Aden, where we were to spend twenty-four hours, and d'Arcy was anxious to improve the occasion by ordering a stock of hand-made Egyptian cigarettes. It was his pre-war practice to have them sent to him from Aden, wherever he might be, and he said that they were of far better quality than those actually made in Egypt. He invited Haig and me to accompany him, and we went ashore in the late afternoon in a long-boat rowed by Somalis with mops of frizzy, hennaed hair.

Aden is a fantastic place. It possesses a magnificent harbour in the form of a deeply curved crescent, at each horn of which is a tortured mass of rock. The smaller, on the northern horn, is an extremity of the horrific coastal ranges which border the Red Sea, and the larger is Aden. It resembles not so much mountains as mountain-tops ; the peaks of some gigantic eruption which once smashed itself up out of the earth. The jagged and chaotic summits, chasms, and peaks, in savage shades of black and grey and bronze, rear themselves upward with a kind of stony snarl, a gesture of arrested defiance at sea and sky.

The settlements of audacious man upon this rock are separated into two parts : the crescent of houses and shops along the harbour front, curved round a little park of miraculous greenery, and the town upon the Indian Ocean side of the rock. This is about five miles away, and is reached by a road which swoops up and down through a slit in the sheer cliffs, and is known as Crater. It is a sizeable town of flat-topped buildings, holding a large Indian settlement, and has the advantage of some breeze from the sea. Here we proceeded in a taxi hired after much haggling—a low, rakish vehicle with wire wheels and a canvas roof.

I once stayed two midsummer weeks in Aden, and spent much of the time in riding about on a battered bicycle, hired from the fattest man I ever saw. This was an occupation which, I suppose, should be added to the list of the Englishman's tropical insanities, but I saw most of what there was to see. I recognised it again as we sped along the harbour road, past the barrack-like native quarters of cinder-coloured brick, past the dhow-building yard where craftsmen construct replicas of the vessels which carried Hiram's apes and peacocks ; past the R.S.P.C.A. compound with the lack-lustre camels tethered to a stake, and whirling upwards to the pass through the cliff. Here an English regiment has defiantly painted its crest, and the period of its garrison duty, upon the rock face, and it used to be the high spot of my rides. The exhausting push up to the pass was well rewarded by the magnificent swoop downwards, on to the roofs of Crater in its bowl beneath the snarling peaks.

This time I was being carried in greater dignity, listening with youthful respect to the discourse of the two old gentlemen. We found the establishment where d'Arcy was wont to order his cigarettes, and were welcomed with grave attention by the Greek proprietor. He gave us coffee and small talk, and several varieties of cigarette, after the order had been made, and then showed us his factory. I had always been at a loss to account for the production of the neat cylinders which we burn so casually, and was now fascinated by a small chattering machine which turned out one a second. Doubtless it was an antiquated affair, a very Rocket amongst cigarette machines, but I was as impressed

by it as was the turbaned child who was its attendant.   He
solemnly fed it with handfuls of shredded tobacco, while
an endless strip of paper ran over rollers, one edge being
gummed by a little wheel revolving in a glue-pot before
it entered a groove which began to curl it round, then
under the tobacco hopper, out of sight for a moment, and
then chunk-chunk-chunk as the completed cigarettes were
guillotined into a basket.   I suspect that that small boy was
the envy of all his contemporaries.

His business concluded, d'Arcy was anxious to take us to
see the Gardens.   He had already assumed a proprietorial
air over the whole rock, would hear nothing against its
virtues and advantages, and spoke enthusiastically of its
social life.   We entered the car amongst a straggling swarm
of Indians who were coming from a football match, and
whose countenances displayed the proportions of gaiety or
despondency common to football crowds everywhere.
Supporters of the winning team shouted and flashed their
teeth and waved their flags at us as we hooted slowly along
the street, until we were clear of them and could speed along
the road round the Indian Ocean side of the rock.

We were halted at a point where Customs officials were
examining an inward-bound camel caravan ; a dozen or so
of the shaggy, dusty creatures standing in a motionless file
with an air of supercilious disinterest.   Among the bundles
which the last one carried tied to his wooden saddle there
perched a boy of about ten years old, his skin a glossy black
in the sun and with a red cloth around his head.   The butt
of a rifle protruded from amongst the bundles beside him,
and he gazed down at us with an expression of wondering
disbelief.

We now embarked upon a lengthy drive across the sandy
isthmus which connects Aden to Arabia, and along a road
which bore us through country like a desolated Netherlands.
Instead of canals there were angular ditches, and instead of
tulip-fields great glittering flats of salt, but the authentic
note was struck by the many skeleton windmills, which are
used to pump salt water along the ditches and into the pans
for the sun to evaporate.   But there was nothing even
remotely Dutch about the village of Shaikh Othman, through
which we presently passed : a straggling column of flat

houses upon either side of the road, and populated by a milling throng of Arabs, Indians, and Somalis, with their camels, donkeys, dogs, and goats.   The buildings were all of the monotonous tawny yellow of the surrounding desert, and it is this monotony of colour—unless you have the eye which can delight in infinite variation upon a few basic tones—which must be one of the worst things about living upon the edge of the wilderness.   But even to the most subtle appreciation I imagine that an endless modulation upon the themes of amber and umber, charcoal and ochre, rust and copper, would eventually pall.

Perhaps it was some bygone administrator, sighing for the drenched sweetness of a Shropshire dale, or perhaps some sun-dried sheikh anticipating Paradise, who conceived the gardens at Shaikh Othman, but now they stand as a refreshing if somewhat pathetic oasis in a perished land. Their main growth seems to be a kind of convolvulus, twisting itself thickly about the boles of the palms and over the ground, and providing a dense greenery which, together with a sounding trickle of water, makes the desert seem temporarily remote.   On our way back I noticed that the same creeping plant had been trained over the barrack huts of the garrison, to provide a living awning against the sun. And I was glad that my time abroad was not to be spent there, to waken each morning to the heat-waves flickering over the tawny plain, and with the savage mass of Aden simmering between the desert and the sea.

II

" Well, now we are really committed to the East," gloated d'Arcy gloomily, as we rounded Steamer Point and turned to head south-eastwards into the Indian Ocean. " No turning back once you leave Aden.   No more fresh breezes—nothing but heat and stinks."

As far as I was concerned there had been no turning back ever since I had signed the Articles of Agreement, but I looked forward with tolerable contentment to whatever might lie ahead.   At any rate it would all be new to me, and I continued to divert myself as the 'Phoebe' steamed placidly towards Colombo.

Things were as before: dominoes and whisky in the saloon at night, and endless conversation at all hours of the day. Most of our discussions had degenerated into politics, and I had reached the point where I would sit up in my bunk expounding Trade Unionism to Haig as he was shaving. He and d'Arcy, who were both the staunchest of Tories, had a powerful ally in the Captain, who had a battery of prejudices and intolerances which could obliterate any opposition. Shipmasters, who are accustomed to having the last word upon any subject from mermaids to merry-go-rounds, develop an authority of pronouncement which impresses by sheer weight of manner. The French were bastards, he said; and as he passed judgment—in a slight Cockney accent—the pomp and glory of Gaul receded like a dream. The Americans were bastards, and the entire potential of the United States was relegated to somewhere beyond the horizon. The Spanish and Italians were respectively dago bastards and slimy bastards, and Socialists, Jews, Australians, the working classes, and the coloured races of the world were branded with the same bar sinister, and dismissed the consideration of honest men. His first action upon entering the saloon at meal-times was usually to turn off the radio.

" Anybody want it ? " he would enquire, turning it off. " There, that's better. Hear yerself fink now. Mind you, I like a nice sympathy concert, but I can't stand those bastards yaw-yawing all the time."

Every Sunday he invited Haig and d'Arcy and me to join him in his cabin for a drink before lunch. He regaled us with gin-and-bitters and stories of how he had scored off one bastard or another, and proudly displayed to us the results of his hobby. This, incredibly enough, was the drawing of young women in various stages of undress.

The weather grew steadily warmer. I sun-bathed, read a lot, exercised my tongue in endless clapper-claw. The days passed quickly, one after another as similar as a string of glittering blue beads, and almost before we were ready for it we were due in Colombo. We expected only a short stay there, but found that the local coolies were indulging in a kind of slow-down strike, which kept us for several days bunkering in the overcrowded harbour. But there are far

c

worse places in which to spend a few days than Colombo. It has numerous advantages over many Eastern ports, chief of which is that it lies well opened to the sea, instead of being crouched behind a muddle of docks and slums, like Bombay, or being up some abominable river, like Rangoon or Calcutta. Also it seems to be unusually clean and neat and well-organised, to be quieter and less teeming than the cities of India, to be altogether more spacious and more westernised. Not westernised in the sense of colossal ugly buildings, clanging street transport, and commercial frenzy, but in the sense of civic order and organised sanitation. One does not feel, there, that at any moment something barbarically unpleasant is about to erupt through its crust of civilisation.

I went ashore with three of the engineer passengers on the first morning. There are no docks in Colombo ; every visiting ship must anchor in the wide harbour, and the boatmen who ply for hire make a good thing out of this.

" Five rupees," said the adamant owner of the boat which we hailed, as the opening gambit in one of those bouts of haggling which help to make Oriental existence so infuriating.

The price was eventually fixed to the satisfaction of neither party, and we were rowed down the length of the harbour to the landing-stage. For a while we wandered about the town, which at that time was a-swarm with British and Dutch naval sailors of both sexes, and eventually took refuge in the Merchant Navy Club. After lunching there we decided, since we had brought the equipment for it, to go for a swim, and piled into a taxi, which we directed haughtily to the Galle Face Hotel.

Whence this establishment derives its peculiar name I don't know, but as such it ranks with the Taj, the Raffles, and the Peninsula Hotels as the Empire-builder's landmarks to the East. It is a sprawling building in an unlovely shade of terra-cotta, whose cliff-side disposition and architecture make it look as though its builders had added haphazardly to its original plan. Since a good many people had been enjoying the war within its shadowed halls, it was still fairly stiff with gold braid and brass, and our taxi nearly ran over some kind of an admiral as we drew up to the steps. We had taken precedence of his car, which drew up behind us with an angry hoot, and he surveyed us with an insolent wonder as we climbed sheepishly out. I felt that I ought to touch my forelock, or make some other kind of recognition of such a legendary creature, and apologise for having the effrontery to be a human being.

Of course we had come to the wrong entrance, as a supercilious creature attired as a sultan rapidly made us aware, and we slouched away round the corner of the building to the swimming-pool entrance. For fifty cents, outsiders are privileged to use the hotel's fine swimming-pool, an opportunity of which most of the local garrison seemed to have availed itself. All the same, it was fine and cool under the high roof, with the noise of the waves breaking lazily on the rocks below. Quite often there was room for a swim, and the intervals could be filled with speculations concerning the occasional female dabbler.

We spent most of our time in Colombo at the Galle Face, and our evenings at one or another of the cinemas. We had neither the time, inclination, nor money to venture farther afield, though we did make one excursion as far as Mount Lavinia. This was due to no initiative of our own, but because the M.N. Club ran a truck out there every Wednesday and Saturday afternoon. It was one of those covered wagons, open at the rear and with benches fitted down the centre and sides. Its native driver, encouraged by his cramped and sweating cargo of merchant seamen, fled through the streets of Colombo and along the coastal road like the proverbial blue-assed fly. He only drew to a skidding halt near the Galle Face, to pick up a Second Mate who seemed to be a familiar feature of the excursions. Seated well at the rear, he engaged himself in the singularly futile pastime of making alarming gestures at the driver of every vehicle we passed—and we passed everything on the road. Pointing at their front wheels, he would waggle his hands significantly from side to side, and it never failed. 'Buses, private cars, service vehicles, commercial transport— they all drew hurriedly into the side of the road, to disgorge puzzled drivers who poked and prodded at wheels and radiators. Our passengers treated this as a colossal joke, joining in one by one until a cargo of shrieking and gesticu-

lating seamen threw terror into the hearts of every driver
on the road.

"A-h-h-h-h!" they screamed happily as the driver
wrenched at his wheel and the truck flung itself off the highway and into a side road. It lurched in and out of a deep
gutter, and tore onwards through a maze of narrow lanes.

I spent most of the journey with my eyes tightly closed,
and didn't open them again until we reached the Mount
Lavinia Hotel. I didn't notice any neighbouring mountain to justify its name, but it is an extremely pleasant
place. Bowered in palms, it stands upon a slight eminence
at one end of a long, shallow crescent of white beach, also
bordered by palms. It would be a most romantic spot if it
were not also bordered by the railway, along which trainloads
of goggling Tamils pass every few minutes. Nevertheless
the blue sea broke in creaming surf upon the beach, and it
generally fulfilled every promise of what a tropical beach
should be.

Naturally it was well populated—about as well as Brighton
at Whitsun. It seems that there was some prudish rule
about undressing on the beach, so intending bathers had to
cram themselves into a dank concrete receptacle beneath the
hotel, and struggle out of their clothes in an atmosphere of
feet and wet swim-suits. But the result was worth it, and
we spent a long afternoon there before being whipped back
into Colombo by the same devilish driver.

Our time was nearly up, and the Captain at last lost
patience with the procrastinating coolies. We had enough
coal to carry us onwards, and one afternoon just as the golden
light was mellowing into dusk we passed out between the
horns of the breakwaters, and on to the final leg of our
journey.

CHAPTER THREE

ARRIVING AND WAITING

I

TRAVELLING BY SEA IS a little like going to the pictures. You take your place, and in due course a variety of scenes are displayed for your observation. Once out of sight of land there is slight sense of movement or of progress—unless you happen to be a navigating officer, plotting the ship's laborious crawl across the white wastes of a chart. For everyone else the ship is an island, and day after day its inhabitants scan the same exact circle of sea and the same canopy of sky. They know that it is a different section of sea and sky each day, but apart from the vagaries of wind and weather, it always looks the same, and for all that it shows in positive disproof might just as well be the same. Until one day a piece of land protrudes above the horizon and the sense of movement is regained. Another scene is rising to fill the screen of the empty sky.

Scene I of the act of transit from Colombo to Singapore is a conical mountain of lush greenery, its lower slopes covered with what looks from a distance like smooth green turf. This is the northernmost tip of Sumatra, the main seaward frontier of the Malacca Straits, and in itself a link in that great necklace of islands about the throat of Southern Asia. They sweep down through the islands of the Mergui Archipelago along the Burmese and Siamese coasts, through Sumatra and the clustered green jewels of the Rhio Archipelago about Southern Malaya, curve round through Java, Sarawak, Borneo, the Celebes, and the rest of the fabled groups of the East Indies, on to the Philippines and up to Formosa and the savage islands of Japan.

Once around the tip of Sumatra and into the Malacca Straits and you have entered the Far East. The climate changes abruptly. Yesterday you were hot, but with a sun-drenched warmth; there was usually a breeze somewhere about the ship, and the sea danced brilliantly. To-day the sea is a sullen mirror to the milky sky. The mangrove swamps along the horizon tremble upon a miasma of heat ; thunderstorms brood and grumble amongst the distant blue ranges of the mainland, and launch themselves upon the straits in a brief fury of rain, and when they have passed, the air once more clings languidly to your perspiring form.

" We're not quite sure about the effects of a humid climate, in a lot of ways," a doctor was later to tell me in Japan.

Perhaps the truest comparison of its effect would be to that of a vampire. You awake each morning feeling as though the sap had been drained out of you during the night, and begin each day feeling already irritable and tired. The legs feel boneless and the head woolly, like a slight hangover, and a constant succession of such hangovers are doubtless to blame for the traditional tropic irascibility. Tempers are apt to simmer upon the edge of explosion, and are sparked off by a trivial irritation. The vampire, besides energy, has robbed you of patience, tolerance, and good humour, and about the only time you get all your energy back is when you are spurred on by a bad temper.

But we had not yet been in it long enough to really feel its effects, though d'Arcy was already snarling at the impossibility of sleeping in such a misbegotten climate. Besides, we had the anticipation of arrival to keep us cheerful, and before long had dropped anchor in Singapore harbour. It is a superb natural harbour, a wide bay whose approaches are protected by a chain of islets blossoming with lettuce-green foliage. We arrived in the morning, and having spent most of the previous night in packing, were all ready to disembark. But, after some brief formalities with immigration officials, our arrival was met with stony disregard.

We spent the day in wandering restlessly about the decks and around the huge pile of baggage by the gangway, while d'Arcy sat under an awning and regarded the barrage of buildings along the water-front with a bitter satisfaction. At last, in the late afternoon, a boat arrived to disembark passengers : a ramshackle craft like a discarded Mersey ferry-boat. It took nearly an hour for the passengers and their baggage, particularly the Chinese baggage, to be

loaded aboard, but amongst a chorus of sardonic farewells
we were finally on our way.

It seemed that I was suddenly odd man out. Haig and
d'Arcy had been met by a mutual friend, the engineer
passengers by a Ministry of Transport official, and the
Chinese by a variety of exotic individuals. D'Arcy, however,
persisted in defining me as the most fortunate amongst us.

"You'll be snugly aboard your ship to-night," he
opined. "God knows what's going to happen to the rest
of us—God knows!"

Our craft drew nearer to the water-front, until we saw
more clearly the succession of portentous buildings which is
its main feature—Union Building, Ocean Building, the
Municipal Building, Fullerton Building, and so on. Above
them, a black and ragged cloud was advancing rapidly over
the sky.

"A typical Singapore welcome," sneered d'Arcy, as the
first drops of rain began to fall.

As the ferry bumped against the landing-stage we were
given another welcome, by the swarm of porters, pedlars,
and anonymous Orientals who struggled aboard.

"You'd better get a porter, quick," advised d'Arcy.
"One of those fellers in the red turbans."

Our hands went round in a hurried circle of farewells—
"Cheerio . . . g'bye . . . best o' luck . . . take care o'
yerself . . . see you again sometime"—and I pushed after
my porter into the crowded gloom of Clifford Pier, the great
covered landing-stage projecting from the centre of Singapore water-front. Chinese women in black trousers
squalled at me to buy bunches of bananas, newsboys flapped
at me with the *Straits Times*, and a white-robed Indian
enquired whether I wished to change any money. I
exchanged the remnants of my English money for Straits
dollars, saw my luggage into the Customs office, and passed
through the barrier into the street.

The rain had stopped, and I walked out on to a parking-
square fenced off from the thoroughfare by white posts, and
occupied by lines of Service transport and strewn with
banana-skins, pineapple-peel, and cigarette packets.

"Can you tell me where Naval headquarters is?" I
enquired of a dawdling sailor, and he looked at me curiously.

" Right there in front o' yer," he replied, waving his hand, and I looked up to see a huge White Ensign flying over the biggest of the buildings across the road.

I approached its overpowering bulk somewhat timorously, and entered a vestibule thronged with sailors and marines. I collided with an over-stuffed Wren officer, received an affronted glare in reply to my apology, and pushed my way through to a desk marked ' Enquiries '. The young sailor who occupied it had no idea where I might find the officer to whom I was to report, but after some discussion decided that I might try the A.F.O., third floor—or ' deck ', as he called it.

I went up in the lift, and found the office I wanted. Within were three desks, two empty and the other used by a gaunt and bespectacled lieutenant-commander. He was surrounded by a complication of radio apparatus, and was speaking confidentially into a hand-microphone.

" This is Singapore Twenty-eight, Twenty-eight," he explained to it. " Tarantula, Tarantula, this is Singapore Twenty-eight. Come in, please ; come in, please ; over."

The loudspeaker buzzed and clicked, heralding a heavy Scots burr exclaiming, " Twenty-eight, Twenty-eight ; this is Tarrrantula. Nothing for you, nothing for you ; over."

Singapore Twenty-eight and Tarantula conversed for a little while, before he put down the mike and looked coldly at me.

" Well ? "

" Er—good afternoon. I'm the new R/O for the ' Bengal '. I just arrived this morning, an' they told me to report to the S.N.S.O. when I got here, but——"

" The ' Bengal ' ? " he interrupted incredulously. " What've they sent you here for, then ? She's in the Cocos Islands, isn't she ? Was when I last heard of her, anyway."

I looked at him miserably. Disembodied voices chattered distantly on the loudspeaker, carrying on an ethereal conversation.

" Don't expect to get any answer from him on a Saturday night, do you ? " asked one of them, and was answered by a horse-laugh.

" I dunno," sighed Singapore Twenty-eight. " There's always something. Well, all I can tell you now is that you'll have to stay in Singapore until we can find out where she is. I dunno if she's coming here, or whether you'll have to go somewhere else to join her. Let's see if we can fix you up with somewhere to live."

He picked up his telephone, and after a series of increasingly acrimonious conversations—"Yes, I know it's Saturday evening, but I can't help that, can I?"—he was able to offer me a choice of accommodations, out of which I chose the Singapore Marine Hostel.

This is another of the massive buildings in which Singapore abounds. It stands on a cross-roads not far from the docks, and a plaque upon it will tell you that it was financed by a legacy of forty-eight thousand dollars from a Scottish engineer. His executors were apparently bent upon getting as much building as possible for their money, and the great hollow square of masonry is a monument to their success. A pamphlet published in 1948 notes that " During the war the premises were used by the Japanese as a prison and a sailors' club . . . the Hostel came out of the war badly scarred . . ."

I can testify as to the latter part of the statement. As to the former, I was informed during my first meal in the place that it had been used by the Japanese Navy as a brothel, and within the next few days must have been told so a score of times. The statement was always couched in the form of a rhetorical question :

" You know what the Japs used this place for, don't you ? "
" No. What ? "
" A brothel ! "

One's informant seemed to derive a lascivious triumph from the fact. But before long I began to wonder whether popular report assigned the Japanese any other use for large buildings. One had only to mention the Raffles or any other hotel, or the barracks, or the better-known clubs, for the same knowing, prefatory look to come over one's companion's face. The atom bomb began to seem rather redundant.

No sooner had I unloaded my bags from the truck which had brought them from Clifford Pier than I met some friends—the ones to whom I had said farewell less than an hour ago. They were the engineer passengers who had travelled out in the ' Phoebe ', and they greeted me without pleasure.

" 'Strewth," they said.   " What've you come here for ? "

" Ker-yst," said one of them gloomily.   " You never saw such a dump.   Wait'll I show it to you."

He led the way into the main hall of the Hostel, whose grubby stone floor was cluttered with roughly carpentered tables and chairs, all somewhat less than normal size.

" See ? " he asked.   " All Japanese size.   They even cut the legs off the billiard tables, only there aren't any billiard tables.   Not any more, anyway."

They accompanied me while I registered, and with an air of sombre triumph followed me upstairs to my room.   I found it to be a large and airy apartment, but somewhat simply furnished with a wash-stand and a bed.

" See ? " they asked.   " See ? Ker-yst, I hope our ship doesn't waste time getting here."

But we had yet to discover the worst.   The Hostel was a place of lofty, stone-floored rooms, with wide, unglazed windows.   The doors and corridor walls were all of slatted wood, topped by a wire grille, which was an admirable arrangement for ventilation, but no defence against the slightest sound.   Downstairs, the great, high-arched apartments which had once been the cinema and dance-hall, lounge, billiard-room, and so on, and the present officers' and ratings' dining-rooms, were equally immune from sound-proofing, and the whole building echoed and thundered continually.   There was plenty to make it do so.   Outside, a river of Army trucks rumbled and roared to and from the docks, and inside the lower floor was used every evening as a Fleet canteen.

At about seven o'clock the place would begin to warm up, and by eight would be crammed with exuberant naval ratings and merchant seamen.   Theoretically, each rating was allowed two bottles of beer a night, and was issued with two coupons to exchange for his ration, but of course most of them managed to corner a good many more.   The befuddled A.B. leering over a table tight-packed with tins of beer had bought or scrounged the coupons from his more temperate mates, and I even heard rumours of an enterprising combine which had stolen the ship's stamp of a wrecked landing-craft, and was printing and stamping coupons for sale to thirsty mariners. In any case, it is certain that the determined drinker was never at a loss for sufficient refreshment.

As it began to take effect, it sometimes seemed to those on the floor above that the building was about to take off, so solid was the blast from below. Each of the battered little tables was occupied by a noisy quartet, singing or arguing or merely conversing at the top of their voices; ' Nelly Dean ' mingling with a discussion of the comparative merits of Chinese and Japanese women or reminiscences of the last ship. They were watched by a naval picket, belted and gaitered and lounging gloomily against the streaked walls, prepared to move into swift action to check the fights which invariably developed towards the end of the evening. Sometimes they were minor affairs, sometimes full-scale battles between the Navy and the Merchant Navy, with the pickets wielding their batons indiscriminately and bottles exploding against the walls like hand-grenades. The residents in the officers' quarters usually made a point of staying out of the building in the evenings, but often returned to find the last struggling combatants being hustled out by the pickets, their caps knocked off and shirts crimson with fresh blood, and the broad stairways littered with broken glass.

Even after the canteen was closed it took a long time for the building to simmer down into placidity. The rating's dormitories were apt to resound until all hours with the noise of distant strife, and in the officers' quarters the occupants of the various rooms would be having small private parties, or chatting over a quiet glass of beer. Every sound was audible: the interminable rambling arguments, the long, low mutter punctuated by a sudden guffaw, the clip-clop of someone walking down the stone passage-ways.

Around midnight those who were trying to sleep would begin shouting, " Quiet! Pack it up, can't you! Let's have a bitta peace ! "

The subsequent arguments would be heralded by the angry clash of a slatted door flung open, purposeful footsteps down the hall, and a tattoo at one or another of the complainant's doors.

" Look here, mister . . . get out, go to bed ! " . . . " Man can't have a quiet drink " . . . " Do you think you are in the fo'c'sle ? . . ." " I tell you, I'll make as much noise as I like ; I've as much right as . . ."

At last there would be quiet, broken only by the scuffle and hiccup of some late reveller and the echoing crash of his closing door. Our clamorous existence was unlightened by few of the creature comforts. The beds were furnished with a single sheet and a coarse blanket, the bathrooms were either devoid of water or overflowing with it, the long and garbage-littered grass which filled the building's compound was prolific with mosquitoes and with cow-voiced frogs, which moo'ed delighted anthems to the rain. During the first night I spent there I cursed the herd of cattle which I believed to be pastured nearby, and was somewhat taken aback to discover that the deep-voiced ululations came from frogs. Whenever it rained, as in Singapore it does frequently and with Wagnerian authority and orchestration, many of the rooms were flooded by leaking drains. The whole establishment had that air of depressed resignation which follows long maltreatment, and was not improved by the languid efforts of the house-boys.

All these things seemed to be nobody's concern, and most of us had experienced worse on one ship or another. The thing which aroused most grumbling was the food, which consisted mainly of tinned stew and biscuits, and we were finally goaded to march in a body upon the Ministry of Transport and make a formal complaint about it. The Hostel was run by a Ministry superintendent, with the unofficial aid of a Catholic priest, and I did not envy them their task of keeping housed, fed, and happy anything between fifty and a couple of hundred M.N. officers and seamen. Since most of them were waiting for a passage home, they passed their days in a fuming impatience which found its climax on a sailing day, when an uproarious crowd would pile aboard the trucks which were to carry them to the docks.

The building was almost as noisy during the day as at night. The corridors and landings were apt to be lively with men playing darts or hand-ball, or just playfully scuffling; shadow-boxing, calling upon each other with much clashing of the slatted doors, or wandering about gossiping, singing, and arguing. When it was not raining, the broad, flat roof was a popular rendezvous. We rigged up a deck-tennis pitch there, and it was well occupied besides with strollers, sun-bathers, and men craning over the parapet to whistle at passing females.

The whole place seemed to me to have much in common with the sponging-house in ' Vanity Fair '. There was the same variety of characters being kept there against their will, and with the same need for distraction to while away the time. We were glad of anyone who could amuse us, even the political fanatic who could apparently talk for hours without ceasing, once he got going. He was a little man with wiry arms and glassy, pale-grey eyes, and we would stand around him in an admiring group while he waved his arms and the words spouted out of him in a practised stream ; capitalism, the workers, the right to happiness, the elemental dignity of labour :

" Take the ship-owners, now—are they any different from you an' me ? Was a ship-owner born with three arms, or something ? Does he eat any diff'runt, does he breathe any diff'runt, is he any diff'runt when he's dead ? Only diff'runce is he can sit on his bottom in a padded chair, while you an' me's sloggin' it out at sea, so's he can rake in the moncy wc makcs for 'im. Or take money, now. What is money ? Can you eat it ? Can you wear it ? Would it keep you alive on a desert island ? S'posin' you was in a lifeboat, same as I was, an' the water-breakers was filled with tanners, could you drink 'em ? Answer me that ! "

We stood around him and listened, arms folded, sweating a little, winking at each other : the bearded Scots cadet who had done six months in jail for anarchistic activities, the pompous-bellied Lancashire Purser, the Birmingham engineer who told me dreamily, " You know, I've got a lovely wife " ; the Second Mate with the wound-scar on his right cheek, the Second Mate who hated to wear his false teeth, the Second Mate who had had all his hair cut off and was worrying whether it would have grown again by the time he got home ; the Radio Officer whose plaster leg-cast was scribbled over with ribald comments in indelible pencil. The group varied from time to time, as some of them went home and their places were taken by others waiting their turn, and the pale-eyed little man was replaced by an even more articulate Welsh Nationalist, and he by a massive-featured Fourth Engineer who was obsessed by the iniquity of the seamen's unions.

It soon became apparent that it was a group of which I was to be a member for some time to come, since the news that the ' Bengal ' was in dry-dock in Bombay, and that I was to await her arrival in Singapore, had destroyed my hopes that I was to have only a few days ashore. I set about making myself comfortable; watching my chance, I appropriated a marble-topped table, a chest of drawers, a couple of chairs, from one or another temporarily vacant room, to supplement the meagre furnishings of my own apartment. I bought a hundred-watt bulb on the black market, to replace the twenty-watt one which dispensed a pinkish glow. Books I obtained from a local library, and occupied myself mainly with reading, writing, gossiping with the other residents, and exploring the island of Singapore.

CHAPTER FOUR

THE TWO SINGAPORES

I

THE PRIEST WHO HELPED in the administration of the Hostel was a tall, gaunt man, whose dark eyes seemed to express a kind of nervous patience. Although I did not personally like him very much, I could not help feeling a baffled admiration for whatever inspiration it is that enables such men to live in a way which is outwardly so drab and barren. For he had nothing: a few books, a plaster image, his ill-fitting clothing, were the sum of his possessions. Whatever else he needed he begged or borrowed, and amongst other things he had obtained the loan of a Naval bicycle to take him about his duties. In a little while I was also borrowing the bicycle—his ' two-wheeled jeep ', as he called it—from him, and was using it to aid my explorations. My memories of Singapore are inextricably woven into that of the bicycle; the green-painted upright, heavy and ungraceful, whose hard saddle transferred its brown dye to the seat of my sweat-damp shorts.

All the same, there is no finer instrument than a bicycle for the dissection of a town, conferring the intimacy of walking without its jostling weariness, and combining ease of transport with an unrestricted view. Even as it was, I could do little more than find my way around the labyrinths of the congested town, the sprawling green suburbs, and the quiet inland by-ways of the island. Although the whole island is only about the size of Greater London, it must be amongst the costliest and richest islands of its size in the world. On its southern coast lies the fabulous city itself, and on the north, separated from the mainland by the narrow Johore Strait, is the hitherto profitless naval base. A much less suitable site for a naval dockyard can hardly be conceived, standing as it does on a winding strait one entrance to which is blocked by the Johore Causeway, and although it would be arbitrary to say that the millions which

47

have been spent on it have been wasted, it has yet to prove its worth.

It is connected to the city by two main roads, one of which winds and swoops over the comparatively high ground in the centre of the island and passes through little villages of thatch-and-bamboo huts. The other is the road from Johore, which passes over the Causeway and takes the more level route, but still winds and undulates over the rolling ground and the steep hillocks which characterise the island. You are never out of sight of habitation as you travel along them, from the bamboo shanties to the utilitarian oblongs of Chinese shops and dwellings along the roadside, the ramshackle wooden factories of Chinese business-men, and the white bungalows of Europeans. These inland approaches to the city, often so sordid and depressing in the cities of Europe and America, are here redeemed by the springing virility of the greenery amongst which they stand; everywhere the vivid leafiness of the foliage which riots unchecked wherever it can gain a hold, the bright green of the lalang grass and the rifle-green of the great trees and the dark glossiness of the palms. All the colours here are struck by the white flame of the sun into an aching definition, sharp and unshaded; the raw redness of turned earth, the white of buildings amongst the eternal green, everything illuminated into a hard persistence of its smallest detail, until you long for the soft diffusion of an autumn evening.

To enter the city from inland is to plunge into a confused congestion of traffic, to glimpse littered streets thronged with dissonant crowds; to enter from seaward is to gain an impression of mercantile pomp, from the solid front of masonry which the city presents to the sea. Business offices, the law courts, stores, hotels, and public buildings have been built around the curving shore-line, in the most favourable position to catch the breeze from the sea and block it off from the rest of the town, and the level of buildings falls only as you proceed inland. These two separate Singapores—that of commercial grandeur and orderly administration and of the sprawling, incoherent ferment of the East—exist awkwardly together, and to view the city from the eminence of one of the larger buildings only seems to add to the confusion. Thence you can see that the square modern erections and the isolated, yellow-stucco buildings in the more graceful Colonial architecture of last century arise out of a field of curved and red-tiled roofs, curving gently over the undulating ground and unexpectedly decorative and charming and of a definitely Chinese flavour. Then you can see that it is in Singapore that East meets West, and, if you see it first after you have been in Singapore for some time, it is with something of a shock, and the thought that, after all, the city might be as romantic as its associations imply.

For it is far from seeming so at first. It is devoid of the scenic advantages of Hong-Kong or Penang, and its architects seem to have been obsessed with the idea of cramming as much as possible within the available space. Great ugly blocks of masonry, undistinguished and over-bearing, occupy a large part of the town, from the pompous public buildings of the water-front to the ramshackle native tenements. The eye is so overshadowed by them that it is, at first, difficult to appreciate the many attractive examples of earlier Colonial architecture, for, like many a city at home, the graces of a more leisured age have been swamped by industrial expansion, by the tangible expression of a bloated civic consciousness, and by the kind of latter-day American influence which expresses itself, in Singapore, by the truncated skyscraper of the Cathay building. During a prolonged period the city has had too much money and too few ideas, like a Midlands city of the late nineteenth century, and the result has been much the same. Even the Cathedral is Gothic and unwieldy, looking as though it had been lifted *en masse* from some industrial parish. But perhaps the most impressive thought which Singapore inspires is that anyone, in the devitalising lethargy of the Malayan climate, should have had the energy and initiative to construct these hotels and cinemas, these overcrowded miles of streets, these offices and tenements, these hospitals and department stores and banks.

The Singapore of Conrad and of Somerset Maugham has gone. It is no longer the wide-open town whose *demi-monde* was as international as Port Said, nor the base for shady adventurers of the Eastern seas. To-day it is a

D

" How good it would be to be aboard a ship again "

Johore Bahru

tropical replica of any medium-sized seaport the world over, cleaner than some, dirtier and more equivocal than others.   The British section of the community are mainly suburban expatriates, with all the caste distinctions and petty jealousies and innocent, respectable amusements of suburbia flourishing under the sun.   They work hard and play hard, as they themselves would say, with the more fortunate living in suburbs with such nostalgic names as Swiss Cottage and the others paying inflation prices for apartments.   Most white women in Singapore seem to look flustered and blowsy, and most white men to bear a look of suppressed desperation.   Despite the clubs and entertainments and functions at which they strive to recapture the atmosphere of a more spacious day, their lives are restricted, monotonous, and repressed.   Perhaps the type who is happiest in Singapore is the hearty extrovert who finds complete satisfaction in hard work and play, in heavy drinking and heavy-handed humour.

Only sometimes do you catch a glimpse of the ' romance ' of the East, as when you enter a little street and find it devoted to the making of paper lanterns, from those the size of an apple to gaudy monsters like wine-jars.   Colour, noise, and confusion, added to dirt and smells, substitute for any more genuine glamour.   By far the greater part of the population is Chinese, and their painstaking cunning and laborious rapacity have long since conquered the barbarically Utopian existence of the Malays.   They have been settling in Malaya for well over a century, and by this time have attained such a superiority in numbers that they claim—rather oddly when one remembers the timeless chaos of China itself—that they ought to have the predominating vote in the government of the country.

Together with their love for colour and decoration, they have also brought their bestial disdain for cleanliness and hygiene.   Looking down a road lined with Chinese shops, the vista is bizarre with the gold, black, red of the vertical signs which each of them displays, their eccentric characters extolling the wares and virtue of their owners.   Most of these streets of shops are built in such a way that the upper stories overhang the lower, forming covered walks along the pavements and giving useful protection from sun and rain.

These shady arcades are raised a little above the road, and the deep monsoon gutters which run by their sides are used by the Chinese as deposits for every kind of garbage. These gutters are essential to trap the heavy rainfall, but the stinking refuse with which they become choked makes them traps for the unwary as well, and on hot days they are far from an asset to the amenities of the town.

Above the street a myriad of ragged banners droops beneath the sun, for from every upper window there protrudes the family washing, on bamboo poles thrust through the arms or legs of the garments. Every sight and sound proclaims a life of the streets, vivid, swarming, intense, for it is in the streets that the main drama of life is enacted for the thronging peoples of the city. Nerve-jolting firecrackers explode to celebrate a birthday or betrothal; red paper joss-signs warn the devils away from doorways. The sidewalks throng with surly, bearded Sikhs and portly Chinese merchants; with fragile Chinese girls like strutting waxen dolls; with black, bony Tamils and waddling Hindoos; swarthy Parsees, ox-eyed Eurasians, jaunty Mohammedans, jostle the gentle-featured Malays. All the castes of India leaven the lump of Chinese; orange-robed Buddhist priests precede French nuns in their striped, billowing gowns and sculptured headgear; dawdling groups of soldiers in jungle-green gape at the maidens in their gay pyjamas. The *lingua franca* of Malayan is spoken by men from the parched plains of India, the silent jungles of the East Indies and Siam, the exhausted territories of China.

The medley of races, colours, costumes is an antidote to the drabness inherent in most cities. The sprigged, voluminous sarongs and starched white jackets of the Malay women contrast with the mauve, orange, and purple scarves of the Indian dandies; the snowy robes of the orthodox Hindoo with the black pyjamas of the Chinese craftsmen. Chinese housewives, with their sleek hair coiled into a gold-pinned intricacy, in black silk trousers and white cotton tunics, clatter along on wooden sandals; the female coolies in their shabby uniforms of red and blue hurry along in urgent files. Native clerks in flashy tropical suits are elbowed by guffawing junk sailors; the old men with their coppery, ironic faces sit gossiping in the doorways, and naked children squeal amongst the legs of the passers-by.

In these littered streets the hawkers stand beside their barrows of glowing fruit, or squat beside their baskets of odorous dried fish, wilted vegetables, or black, earth-stored eggs. Women and children crouch on the pavements with their trays of cigarettes, matches, and sweets ; the sellers of boiled noodles and rice-cakes emit throbbing, mournful cries which rise above the chatter of the crowds. The shops spill their goods out on to the pavements and into the streets ; workmen drag their tasks out of the dark interiors to toil over them in the sunlight of the streets. Here are two coolies sawing a great roll of newsprint, like a trunk of one of the trees from which it came, into sizes to fit the presses ; there a bicycle repair-shop has strewn wheels and cogs and tools amongst the feet of the passers-by. Outside the police posts hang the great brass gongs once used to strike the hour, and an expressionless audience is gathered about the Chinese equivalent of a Punch-and-Judy show, clangorous with drums and cymbals. Coolies, like creatures formed from bone and sinew, force their fleshless bodies along under the weight of a pole which bears two great loads. The trotting rickshaw coolie gives his high-pitched warning cry —a cry which is fading as he is being replaced by the trishaw, a bicycle with a sidecar decorated with scenes from Chinese mythology, and whose pilots make the streets even more unsafe for pedestrians. Street kitchens displaying anonymous tit-bits are lined with patrons solemnly gobbling out of china bowls ; Malay policemen immaculate in white uniforms direct the crossroads traffic.

The Chinese is a confirmed jay-walker, and with complete detachment strolls or gossips or labours amongst the streaming traffic ; the glittering American limousines of the rich merchants, street-kitchens and high-piled barrows being trundled along by their owners, a myriad cyclists, trishaws, rickshaws ; antiquated tramcars, ramshackle taxis, over-flowing private buses, and contraptions of which one can only say that they have four wheels and an engine. Trans-port built from the remnants of a dozen different vehicles does yeoman service in the hands of the Chinese, whose genius for improvisation is nowhere more apparent than here. No one else would think of converting an Austin 7 into a lorry, but scores of them may be seen about Singapore, laden with anything from ducks to a football team. With patient skill the Chinaman builds a pyramid of goods upon his truck, secures it with a cat's-cradle of rope-ends, and sends it forth to brave the perils of the streets. Even pigs are carried in this way, with each pig in a two-piece, capsule-shaped basket of which one half fits over the other, so that two or three layers of resigned swine may be carried through the streets. I never witnessed the operation of inserting the pig into the basket, but with the pig's objections combined with the not dissimilar palaver of the Chinese, I imagine that it must be an extremely vocal one.

How the Chinese ever gained his reputation for inscrutability I cannot understand, since his every action is accompanied by a violence of expletive and gesticulation which would shame a stage Spaniard. Everywhere the ear is filled with the drawling, plangent, guttural, sibilant, explosive tones of the dialects of China. They are an intensely articulate race, even the meanest of them seeming to find his deepest pleasure in yarning, gossiping, wrangling, or otherwise expressing his views at vehement length. Perhaps the most impressive things about them are their callousness and their humour; the way in which they look unmoved upon scenes of misery and disaster, and their constant lively laughter, which seems to find inspiration in the slightest cause. But perhaps the two are related; a race which has known such centuries of misery as have the Chinese must at last become insensible to it, and develop a broad humour by way of consolation.

In the streets there is always something new—a funeral procession led by a brass band; a paper dragon whose snarling head and gold-and-green body weaves above a score of sinewy legs, to head a wedding entourage; a shaggy and bewildered group of Tibetan holy men, who have walked the length of Asia to sell their amulets and charms. It is, above all, this brilliant incoherence of the life of the streets which is typical of Singapore—or indeed of any Eastern city. Life goes on at so many different levels, can be seen from so many angles, all of which are completely opposed. There could be no greater contrast than between

the life of the Raffles Hotel and that of the swarming
rookeries of the native slums, and the chasm is almost as
wide between the shabby-genteel existence of the Eurasian
petty official and that of his European superior. The
hungriest coolie might be nearer to understanding the
flamboyant opulence of a Chinese tycoon than would, for
instance, the British manager of one of the department
stores, for he would be nearer to him in philosophies,
traditions, heritages—everything.

Singapore, like London, is not one city, but scores. The
city of incredible wealth and unimaginable poverty, in which
Chinese millionaires fill their gardens with painted concrete
scenery, and tubercular families of seven or eight are
crammed into one tenement room. The seaport city, of
great liners and the cargo-carriers of the world, and of
mediæval junks which navigate by methods old when
Christ was born. The city of gay colours, lights, and
sounds, and of the brooding, sombre vacancy of the Orient,
as dispassionate and oppressive as the sky above an empty
sea. The city in which one finds night-clubs, Parisian
dressmakers, jewellers, all the tinsel clutter of sophisticated
life, and drowsy alley-ways haunted by the tones of a
bamboo flute. It is a city which seems to be lacking in
cohesion, to be without self-confidence or solidarity. Too
many races mingle there, too many influences clash ; the
atmosphere is at once languid and irritable, sensuous and
constrained. After a time the mind becomes obsessed with
a vague and indefinable apprehension, a discomfort of the
senses which urges one to go, to seek another place where the
air does not quiver with the sun and with the smouldering
violence of the East.

Perhaps the most profound influence towards this atmosphere is the city's geographic position. One degree,
twenty minutes North—eighty miles above the Equator.
It lies within the humid equatorial belt, in which there is
never more than a few degrees variation in temperature.
There is no cool season, and although there are technically
dry and rainy seasons, that only means that it rains more
during the wet period. The whole year round, the weather
alternates sun and rain, and even when it does not rain, the
air is laden with moisture, so that it feels always clammy

and oppressive. The languor which this induces is tinged with the keyed-up irritability which one feels when waiting for a thunderstorm to break, but without the subsequent release of the storm's passing and the clearing of the air. In Singapore the storms pass without relief, since they are followed only by the relentless sun.

The rain is one of the most consistent and energetic things about Singapore. Out of the Straits a purposeful cloud will arise, its mauve-and-saffron contours toppling over the city as it grows like the geni out of the bottle. And from inland there hurries to meet it a black and ragged regiment of cloud, glinting with lightning and ominous with thunder. In a little while the whole sky is obscured, and the daylight gloom is split by a lavender glare of lightning and a tearing, metallic crash.

Then, the rain. The first great blobs are followed by vertical spears, rattling on to the roofs of cars, and in a few seconds by apparently solid sheets. The buildings across the way almost disappear, the ships in harbour are hidden behind shifting grey curtains, the sky flings itself down upon the earth. In your suddenly darkened room your ears are filled with its hissing roar, you look out at it with awe and astonishment as the thunder cracks directly overhead, and watch the wavering course of some drenched creature running blindly for shelter. Sooner or later it will cease almost as suddenly as it began. The sky is blue again, the flooded streets begin to steam and to drain away into the monsoon gutters, and over the Straits the tall and saffron cloud still stands, a silent witness to the whole affair.

II

I was often caught in these downpours as I cycled or walked about Singapore, but even on dry days I would be, like everyone else, almost as wet with my own perspiration. Alone, or with one or another of my temporary companions at the Hostel, I discovered whatever amusement fell within my scope ; the NAAFI clubs and canteens, ENSA shows of variable quality, the swimming-pool at the Tanglin Officers' Club, the ambitious and well-attended concerts given by the Municipal Orchestra, the crowded cinemas. One could always find something to do, even if only in staring about the streets, and usually find something of fresh interest. The Raffles Museum, perhaps, with its fascinating display of East Indian trophies and specimens. Or the War Crimes Trials.

These were going on all the time, and were regarded, somewhat callously, as being good entertainment. One was constantly being urged not to miss them. I attended several sessions, until I became weary of listening to the mannered arguments around seeming unimportant details and the monotonous unfolding of sordid, irrefutable evidence.

There was something bizarre about the defendants, who ranged from privates to generals, and some of them, spectacled and studious, looked in their shoddy uniforms like members of some Oriental amateur dramatic society. They gave an air of unreality to it all; it was difficult to conceive of their participation in such gruesome tales as were unfolded by the prosecution, and to which they listened with such outward indifference. About some of the others there was an aura of vicious brutality which could not be wholly accounted for by one's knowledge of their history. In their roped square in the centre of the court, and surrounded by their fresh-faced, insouciant young guards, they seemed like trapped animals, and one could feel from them a caged beast's barely restrained hatred. The Japanese have often been compared to apes, but these appeared to me to be more like some hybrid between simian and feline, with the capricious sadism of the cat joined to the blustering hysteria of the ape. The impassivity of their features was belied by their eyes; barbarous, enigmatic, and sullen.

They sat erect upon their hard seats, and did not speak or make any sign. Most of their talking was done for them by their lawyers—Japanese officers who spoke in low, polite voices—but the central character of the court, the man upon whom attention continuously focused, was the interpreter. He was a plump, youngish Chinese, neatly dressed and wearing rimless glasses. Sitting in his raised chair with fingers interlaced, he concealed whatever feelings he might have behind a slight, bland smile, and unwearyingly parroted every word which was spoken in the court.

From Japanese into English, from Chinese into English into Japanese.

The Japanese were still very evident in the Singapore of that time. Docile and over-polite, they were employed mainly in clearing up the mess which they had made. They had a kind of drab, patient uniformity, like a slave class in a Wellsian fantasy, and one became too used to their trudging columns to pay them much attention. Curious details of their equipment caught one's eye : their antique water-bottles, or the two-toed shoes, which gave them a sinister hint of the cloven hoof ; but apart from that they seemed as featureless as so many fish.

This impression of them I preserved until one day after I had joined my ship. She was then up at the naval base, where there was also one of the repatriation ships to take the Japanese home. Fairly early one morning I was ashore, and was walking through the almost deserted dockyard, when I saw the head of a column of troops enter the long, straight road which stretched before me.

These were no longer a resigned and formless mob of defeated men. They marched in column of fours, as smartly as they knew how, in what must have been best uniforms preserved for the occasion. Their boots crunched rhyth-mically on the asphalt, their officers, in white shirts and well-pressed uniforms, strutted erectly at their head. At least a couple of battalions strong, they marched in silence, and as their dark-green ranks passed me, and the sombre, primitive eyes beneath their long-peaked caps surveyed my solitary form, it was easy to picture their march the other way : when they were equipped and armed, with Singapore lying prostrate to their sword, and when with rape and fire these savage men brought their New Order to the East.

CHAPTER FIVE

THE SHIP AND MEN

I

ONE STILL AND SULTRY noon I returned to the Hostel feeling lonely and oppressed. There had just been a great exodus of officers and men, and with envy in my heart I had watched them carry out their baggage and seen the noisy truckloads depart for the docks and home. Their time abroad was finished for a while, but mine, it seemed, stretched endlessly ahead. All the acquaintances I'd made had gone, and I'd have no one to talk to but the priest. A seafarer's life is too largely compounded of such broken friendships, of saying " Cheerio—see you soon ", to shipmates and to friends made ashore, but of rarely, if ever, seeing them again.

The hostel seemed very quiet and deserted, and I was just debating whether to have a shower before lunch when the desk-clerk called, " The telephon' is for you, Mistleh Page."

I gaped at him for a moment, before running to grab it out of his hand.

" Hullo ! Is that Page ? " a casual voice enquired.

" Y-y-yair . . ."

" Hullo ! How are you ? Well, that ship of yours is coming in to-morrow. D'you think you can be ready to join her ? "

It was three months since I had left home with that intention, but it did not seem up to me to make any comment. I gabbled some kind of assent.

" Okay, then. I'll send a truck to pick you up at two to-morrow, and the duty-boat will take you out. Cheerio for now."

" But when's she sailing—where's she going ? " I asked hurriedly, and there was a moment's buzzing silence before the voice answered, with a faint accent of surprise :

" Going ? She's not going anywhere, 's far as I know. G'bye now."

So I was joining a ship which wasn't going anywhere. And the next afternoon, long before two, I was waiting for the truck, and at last was speeding over the scintillating harbour towards the actuality of a ship.

The many ships already anchored there formed a forest of masts and funnels, a barricade of hulls, which at first denied her to my eager eyes. Then, suddenly, there she was, tautly poised upon the water, her slightly raking funnel and the flare of her bows bespeaking ready speed. A yacht, a perfect model of a ship, a small jewel of a craft. It seemed to me already that it was going to be good to sail in her.

As we came alongside I noticed appreciatively the polished stanchions, scrubbed gratings, and white side-lines of the accommodation ladder. The blue-grey paint and enamel of her hull and housing had a cool glow in the sun ; there was the efficient gleam of brass and the shimmer of varnished panelling. How good it would be to be again in a ship ! And how especially good to be in one like this, instead of some cluttered, wearily laden tramp.

A gentle-eyed Indian Quartermaster made the boat fast and came down to carry my gear. " Capitin i-shoreside, saab," he said in answer to my question. " Chiefy officer foreside, top deck."

I walked forward from the gangway, and on the small deck-space for'ard of the bridge found a group of men reclining in deck-chairs under the awning.

" Good afternoon," I greeted them. " My name's Page—the new Sparks, you know."

" Blimee, are you Mr. Page ? " asked one of them. " We'd about given you up for dead. They told us you'd arrived here when we were in Bombay. What'd they want to send you here for ? We've been refitting in Bombay for two months. Paddy'll be glad to see you—he's the man you're relieving, you know. I'm the Chief Officer. This is Mr. Macleod, Third Engineer, Mr. Jackson, Third Officer, and Mr. Erikson, Fourth Engineer. Everyone else is asleep, I expect. The Old Man's ashore, but he'll be back before dinner."

He was a stocky, strongly built man of about thirty-five, with cropped fair hair and eyes which looked very blue in his sunburned face.

" Sit down, won't you ? " he said.   " What's Singapore like ? "

" Bloody awful," I said conventionally, mopping my face dry of the excess of heat and excitement.

He gave a triumphant chuckle, turning to the rest.   " I told you so.   'Strewth, what a place to be stuck in ! "

I peeled off my shirt, and asked, " How long's she gonna be here ? "

He gave what I was to discover was his characteristic short, cynical laugh.   " Huh ! God knows ! Be here for months, prob'ly.   Bunkering duties, that's all we know. Fill up with oil from the shore, pump it into ships, fill up again.   Packed full of thrills.   But here's Paddy now."

A short, sandy-haired man had come round the corner, and said in a hesitant Irish drawl, " Quartermaster told me Mr. Page 'ud arrived.   How are yer ?   Riley's my name —Joseph Riley, but these guys all call me Paddy.   I've a stack of mail in my cabin for you.   Would ye like to have a look at the wireless room now ?   I've told 'em to bring you a cup o' tea."

I rose to follow him, and he led me down a steep companion-way into a kind of vestibule, with cabin doors opening from it.

" Phew ! Is it always as hot as this ? " I asked.

" All the accommodation's below decks on this ship," explained Paddy.   " There's not much ventilation at the best of times.   Wait'll yer at sea in 'er, an' you have to keep all the port-holes closed or get flooded out.   An' you've got the engine-room right in the midst of you, so when she's steaming—Oh boy ! " He gave an expressive whistle, and led the way aft along the starboard alleyway.   " Here's the bathrooms, an' here's my cabin—your cabin now—an' here's the engineers' cabins, and here's the wireless room."

We entered the small compartment, within which there was just room for the two of us to stand amongst the thicket of apparatus.   I gazed around me at the gleaming bakelite panels, wire-mesh safety doors, shining copper aerial connections ; the various meters—Feed Current, Oscillator Filament Volts, Rectifier Filament Volts—on the transmitters, the clock showing G.M.T.   I felt on familiar ground.

" Looks in pretty good shape," I commented. " What's it like to use ? "

" Och, shewer, she's not too bad. You c'n get along with 'er. But ye've got plenty o' time to find all that out. Come along now, an' I'll give ye yer letters."

We returned to his room, outside which my cases had now been piled. The remnants of their labels were still plastered over them, and ' Singapore ' leered mockingly up at me as Paddy opened the cabin door. It was about the size of a railway compartment, and already over-occupied by the bunk, a short settee, a tiny chest of drawers with a glazed bookcase fixed above it, and a twelve-inch wardrobe.

" Ye've got to come outside to change yer mind," said Paddy, with his slow grin. " But ye won't be spending much time in yer room this weather, anyway. She's that small, d'ye see ? The ship, I mane ? "

Small she certainly was ; the smallest ship I'd yet been in. She carried two thousand tons of oil, which is about a quarter of the burden of the average deep-sea tanker. Built in 1916, she was still in first-class condition, and indeed from outside was as smart a model of a ship as you'd wish to see. Within, however, she betrayed the days when a ship's crew was regarded as more of a necessary evil than anything else. The cramped and comfortless accommodation was all amidships, about her engine- and boiler-room, and separated from them only by the fore-and-aft alleyways. This was a convenient arrangement for the engineers, who could step straight out of their cabins and across into the engine-room, but it was a privilege which in hot weather they would willingly have foregone.

" Here's yer mail," said Paddy, and handed me the three months' accumulation of letters which had been waiting for me. " I'll leave ye to it, an' give ye a shout whin the Owld Man gets back."

At all events, I thought, it was a change from the Marine Hostel.

I read through my stack of mail, and began to unpack, and a couple of hours had passed before Paddy returned to tell me that the Captain had returned.

I put on my shirt, and with the feelings which probably assail any ship's officer when about to meet his new captain—

a blend of curiosity, apprehension, and resignation—went up on deck. I turned the corner of the lower bridge and found him sitting in a deck-chair, and approached to introduce myself.

My first impression was of a strong, quizzical, deeply sunburned face. If it is indeed possible to judge character from the features, then these bespoke a man firm and self-confident, disciplined but not narrow, kindly but without weakness, and of one who would bring to his dealing with others the tolerant irony which is the very plasma of experience.

He introduced me to the officers whom I had not met before, and they regarded me stonily whilst I answered his questions. I was on sufferance until I had been accepted or condemned, and was very conscious of the fact.

It was six o'clock, the beginning of the twilight hour. There would be no twilight, none of the long tranquillity of evening which is the blessing of a northern summer. But during the space in which the sun dropped steeply into the sea there would be a kind of stillness, a slackening of the tropic pulse, as though it awaited the transition from the brazen clamour of the day to the drugged languor of the night.

Ashore there would be still heat, dust, irritability. The first merry-makers would be swaggering into the Fleet Canteen. Here there were clean decks and a cool awning, a little breeze off the sea, the sense, however intangible, of being at home. A tinkling of ice and glass foretold the approach of a steward with a loaded tray, which he set on the low table in our midst. In a few moments I heard the exhortation which was to be so frequent during the coming two years—" Have a drink, Sparky ! "

II

The crew of the ship was of Indian seamen, fifty of them, of whom twenty-one were engine-room ratings, nine cooks and stewards, and the remainder sailors. They were mostly Mohammedans from the Ratnagiri district of the Bombay Presidency, apart from the cooks and stewards, who were Portuguese Indians from the tiny colony of Goa. These

Goanese, who for some reason seem to be invariably argu-
mentative, reluctant, and morose, are all Christians, and so
will cook and serve pork, bacon, beef, and the other foods
which Mohammedans believe to be unclean and an abomina-
tion.   For this reason they are always carried in ships with a
Mohammedan crew, to whose conscientious cheerfulness
they form a sharp contrast.

Our stewards were headed by a lanky individual with a
very black skin, a cunning expression, and a thatch of frizzy
grey wool, invariably known as ' Uncle Tom '.   Anyone
less like that benign and saintly character can hardly be
imagined, but in his capacity of Chief Steward to nine
constantly complaining sahibs he no doubt thought that he
experienced martyrdom enough.   His equivalents in the
deck and engine-room departments were the two Serangs.
The Deck Serang was a tall, neat, smiling man about thirty-
five years old, who had a sixteen-year-old son amongst his
sailors, and the Engine-room Serang was a dignified, elderly
gentleman who was very conscious of his position.   He also
had one of his sons at sea with him, and in fact the whole
crew seemed to be linked together by some kind of relationship.   The two Serangs were very much the leaders of the
clan, and under the wise administration of their senior
officers maintained a happy crew.

Mohammedan crews are usually a contented and well-
behaved community, and bring to sea with them not only a
tradition of good discipline but also a strict regard for the
demands of family and religion.   It is their religion which
dictates many of their habits and customs ;   their strict
personal cleanliness, sexual modesty and morality, honesty
and sobriety, all stem from the rules for personal behaviour
laid down by the Prophet Mohammed.   The strict
Mohammedan prays five times a day, but on the ' Bengal '
most of them joined only in the evening prayer, which is
offered only after the suppliant has bathed and donned
clean clothes.   In red fez or embroidered skull-cap, baggy
white trousers with shirt hanging outside them, and bare
feet, he stands upon his prayer-mat and faces towards
Mecca and goes through the ritual attitudes of prayer.
Our most orthodox believer was the ship's carpenter, or
' Mistri ' ;   a light-skinned young man of about twenty-two,

soft-eyed and unassuming, who spoke perfect English and who loved nothing better than to discuss the similarities between the Koran and the Old Testament; the prophets which are shared by both creeds and the fundamentals of truth, honour, and decency upon which both Christianity and the code of Islam are founded.

For about two months after I had joined the ship we remained in Singapore Harbour, so I had ample opportunity to get to know both officers and crew. It began to look as though the dismal prophecies of the Chief Officer—usually known as ' Choff '—were well-founded, and that we were to stay there indefinitely. Our only employment, as he had foretold, was to take on a cargo of fuel-oil from the oil-tanks ashore, return to our anchorage, and wait for orders to supply some ship with two or three hundred tons of oil-bunkers. If she was smaller than we were, she came alongside us; if she was larger, we weighed anchor and went alongside her. My own work was cut to a minimum, since all I had to do was to keep in communication with the shore on the radio-telephone, and perform whatever small maintenance tasks might be necessary.

I was the newcomer to the ship, and so took my place amongst the others comparatively slowly. Outwardly I was accepted, but I knew how long it really takes to become one of a community. Especially on shipboard, where men who are often of diametrically opposed temperaments are confined together, and have to work, eat, live, amuse themselves, and do most other things in each other's company—a feat which, even with mutual tolerance and good humour, it is not easy to accomplish without stress. Such minor points of character as would, ashore, pass as unnoticed as the colour of a man's eyes, on shipboard assume the degree of a major irritation, and this is particularly true of such ships as the ' Bengal ', which stay abroad for long periods. And when, like the ' Bengal ', they spend much of their time lying in port, the opportunity for studying your companions is excruciatingly prolonged. When the port is Singapore, and the climate that of the equatorial tropics, and the quarters are so close as those in the ' Bengal ', you rub shoulders so often that they quickly become sore.

Perhaps it is surprising that we usually got on so well.

Snake-charmer, Singapore

A Street in Johore Bahru

We learned too soon the ways of going against each other's grain, and, except in moments of spite, avoided them. It might have been better if we had not; if, instead of allowing resentments to show themselves in sarcastic courtesy, or in venomous gossip when the subject was elsewhere, we had allowed them more often to explode and consume themselves.

Except for the Captain, the Chief Officer, and the Chief Engineer, we were all of us under thirty. The latter was a lanky and sun-dried Australian, who seldom spoke except to make disconcerting remarks at unexpected moments. He had an able assistant in his Second Engineer, Freddie Strong, who was a forceful and direct Yorkshireman. He was short and over-weight, with peculiarly searching eyes beneath heavy brows, and had the pallor of those who spend their lives amongst machinery. Engines, in fact, seemed to be his main reason for living, and he slaved at his until they ran 'like a sewing-machine'. Unlike many single-minded men, he was amiable and sociable, and at the end of the day liked to find his relaxation in good company and good liquor. About the only things which could jolt him out of his equanimity were when someone either tried to break up a party or to disturb the equilibrium of his engine-room.

His juniors, Sandy McLeod and John Erikson, were both Scotsmen, but that was their only likeness. Sandy, the Third, was not sandy, but slim and dark, his nickname being the Scots diminutive for Alexander, and was a neat and canny young Aberdonian. Erikson was an orange-haired young giant of a Glaswegian, a pleasant and un-demanding companion, ready for whatever project was on hand and full of cheerful energy.

Choff was, I think, our most valuable asset. With the extroverted cynicism which typified him, he condemned our mode of existence as demoralising and enervating. " Hanging about like this, in this weather, we'll all go bloody mad if we don't find something to do. We've gotta get organised. Get a bitta exercise, get some parties going, invite people aboard, take an interest in life. Anything you like. Tell you what, I'll have the dinghy put overside for a start, and we'll do some rowing and sailing. Anybody on ? "

E

He would look about him with his challenging blue stare, and was always foremost, with the same vitality and drive which he applied to his work, in the kind of organisation which he recommended. He worked as hard as a canvassing politician to secure co-operation in whatever he had in mind, but there were many obstacles in his way. Most of the time we lay three or four miles from the shore, and, since the Indians were not held to be responsible enough to handle the boats alone, whoever wanted to go ashore had to arrange with someone to pilot the boat in with him—and to fetch him back later at night. I often went in charge of the launch or the smaller motor-dory, especially to carry the mail in the daytime, but it was not a popular job at night.

Choff's two juniors, Michael Gough and Jimmy Jackson, for varied reasons were not much assistance to him in these schemes of his. Michael Gough, the Second Officer, was something of an intellectual, and looked like a younger and slimmer Charles Boyer. He had an easy charm which kept him from seeming aloof, and a pleasantly cultured voice in which to make his excuses, but he seldom joined in our more energetic pastimes. I think that he sometimes suffered from his own lack of tact, since he persisted in discussing the liberal arts and the more gracious aspects of living in company which was not interested in them, and would then be baffled by its lack of interest.

Jimmy Jackson was a complete contrast to him. A foxy, agile Cockney with a sharp face and a crest of sandy hair, he had all the townsman's need for gaiety and diversion, and the monotony of our existence provoked him easily to irritation. He loved the bright lights, jumping music, laughing women; and his efforts to manufacture substitutes for them sometimes became almost pathetic. It would seem that he would have been a perfect companion for Choff in his plans for our entertainment, but unfortunately he developed the idea that the older man's attempts at ' organisation ' were overbearing and over-riding, a covert endeavour to use his seniority off as well as on duty.

However, there was always one pastime in which it was never difficult for Choff or anyone else to secure co-operation. Every night, from six o'clock onwards, three or four or more of us would be joined in consuming whatever NAAFI had yielded us that month. A bottle of gin between us before dinner would whip some life into heat-dulled appetites, and afterwards there would be yet further anodyne against futility, for as long as anyone cared to partake of it. It did, at least, serve to bring us together; to make us feel some of that warmth of comradeship which was often lacking. In the small hours of some mornings, lolled back in our chairs and chanting some such old favourite as ' I'm the Foreman of the Gang, Gorblimee ', we would indeed feel that no company could be more congenial. We were the best of pals, a principality of jolly good fellows.

But on the next day, when to the usual tropical languor had been added a bird-cage mouth and a tom-tom head, the moment's coherence had gone. We were once more nine units squeezed together by the economic pressure of wage-earning, which was nevertheless not strong enough to abrade each personal knob of character. We were still nine separate and distinct units, and we looked at each other, and what we saw was sometimes good, sometimes bad, but it made no difference. The only thing that could make any difference was for the company to disintegrate; for each of us to go his own way to the home which formed the constant background to his mind.

CHAPTER SIX

BATAVIA AND CECILIA

I

I DON'T KNOW WHO first mentioned Batavia. The galley wireless had got hold of it in its usual mystic manner, and the buzz passed quickly around the ship.

" What's all this about Batavia ? " asked Freddie Strong one day.

" Ah, Batavia ! " snorted Jackson. " This bastard'll never go to Batavia, or anywhere else. Who wants to go to Batavia, anyway ? "

" I-ship go Batavia, saab ? " one of the quartermasters asked me wheedlingly, and I shrugged.

" I dunno. You like ? "

" Oah yiss, saab. Verree good place, Batavia."

" How about a drop of Batavia, eh ? " asked Choff buoyantly. " Make a change, wouldn't it ? "

A little later, during the sundowner, he asked casually, " Anything in this yarn about Batavia, sir ? "

The Old Man smiled quizzically. " I wouldn't know. Nobody ever tells me these things."

But soon the portent followed the prophecy. " ' Prepare for a voyage to Batavia,' " uttered the dispassionate voice from the R/T loudspeaker. " I spell: Baker—Able—Tommy—Able—Victor—Item—Able. I say again, Batavia. Sailing date . . ."

The ship had been in Singapore for two months, with every prospect of remaining for many more. This was only to be a brief interruption, but we entered upon it in holiday mood. There were few preparations to be made, for as usual the ship was ready in every respect for sea: manned, fuelled, provisioned, her only restraint a few fathoms of anchor cable. Early one morning the windlass drew it clanking over the bitts, with Choff leaning over the rail to see the anchor a-weigh. The telegraphs clanged, and

68

there was a long hiss of steam, as though the engines were drawing breath for the effort ahead.

It is only a two or three days' run from Singapore to Batavia, and the climate and terrain of Malaya and Java differ less than do those of Devon and Scotland. But for us it was an excursion whose mood was reflected in the increased vigour and purpose of all aboard ; the contentment of having something to do, somewhere to go. We were only to be there for a month or so, on the same duties which occupied us in Singapore, but whilst we steamed through the milky jade of the waters of the Straits we had no thought for the morrow.

Java was approached through the outposts of a hundred tiny islands, like green garlands adrift upon the sea, and revealed itself to us as a bar of dark coastline across the horizon. Low and featureless it seemed, beneath a pearly haze of humidity, and the whole time I was there I thought of Java as a low, flat country. Until on the very last day the haze lifted, and left a sky as clear as a baby's eyes, and against it there loomed the peaks and cones of the great inland ranges, blue and purple before the delicate sky.

We discovered that our station was to be at Tanjong Priok, the port of Batavia, and at some miles distance from it. It is an artificial harbour, with two long breakwaters like outreaching arms to protect it from the sea, and with room for a good many ships to lie alongside the wharves. As we made up to our berth we were surprised to find that the others were all occupied by busily loading ships, for we had almost imagined that the dock area would be besieged by mobs of insurgents. However, the only revolutionary touch to this commercial scene was a scrawl of ' Property of the Republic of Indonesia ' across one of the warehouses.

Some of us went ashore for a look round soon after we had berthed. The warehouses were stacked with bales of pungently reeking raw rubber, and we had to dodge trolley-loads of it propelled by sweating coolies. They were much like the Malays : short and sturdy men with smooth muscles rippling beneath hairless skins, and round, deceptively bland features.

The dock gates let us out on to a road which was very Dutch in its regularity and straightness, and in the avenue of trees which shaded it.   It was crowded with people strolling to and from the village towards which we turned, and with gaily painted little pony-carts, tinkling with bells, trotting amongst the sauntering throng.   Under their fringed awnings there sat coyly smiling native families, the women plump and sleek in their white jackets and voluminous sarongs, and holding owlish, milk-chocolate babies.

" Some lovely bits of careless rapture amongst that lot," grunted Choff as we trudged on down the road.

A little farther along it was lined with unpainted, tin-roofed shacks and stalls, but the remnants of Dutch order showed themselves even here.   The village was divided up into blocks with numbered alley-ways, and each hut bore a neat blue-and-white enamel number.   There was even a canal through its centre, leading to the sea.   A green and slimy stretch of water, but straight and clear-cut and in-dubitably a canal.

The goods in the shops were the same as anywhere in the East, and no more attractive.   Brilliant piles of vegetables and fruit, tawdry curios, amateurish leatherware, lengths of gaudy cloth, and a clutter of oddments like the unsaleable stock of every bagman in the world.   There were numerous drinking-shops whose shelves were stacked with brightly labelled bottles, but each of them bore a placard blaring ' DANGER OF DEATH !   NATIVE LIQUOR IS POISON ! '

Frayed curtains swayed aside as we passed one group of shacks, and daubed, giggling faces watched us pass.

" Sai-loh-man ! " called piping voices after us.   " Hey, sai-loh-mans !   Eengleesh sai-loh-mans !   You wan' nice time ?   Look !   Hey, look !   Lookee here !   Look ! "

A giggling girl was thrust out into the street, ducking her head from side to side, and attempting to cover her breasts with the hands which a grinning hag held down by her sides.

" Look !   Very chip !   I promise you !"

" Ker-yst ! " snorted Choff.   " All the comforts of home. A cheap dose, I s'pose she means.   They ought to hang a Danger sign on her as well."

A company of Dutch soldiers advanced slowly up the road, shuffling in the dust and singing in weary rhythm.

They brightened up at sight of the little whore, who dodged back inside again before their wolfish cries. English sailor-men she may have been ready for, but not Dutch soldiery.

Clothes-drenching heat, intrusive dust, the tang of woodsmoke, exuberant foliage, the flamboyant, alien crowds —there was nothing different here.

" Another day packed full o' thrills," sighed Choff over his last cup of tea that night. " Ne'er mind, we'll soon get something organised."

" Sarongs ! " snorted the Third Mate viciously. " I'll never go to see Lamour again ! "

" Sure, th' Dutch girls'll be better," said Erikson cheerfully. " I wonder where they'll be at ? "

We found them at the swimming-beach, about two miles along the coast. Choff organised expeditions there at four every afternoon. For the sake of exercise, we were to row ourselves there in the dinghy, until after a few such outings the engineers began to sigh at the waste of energy. We tried sailing the dinghy instead, but the wind was so erratic that we would take a couple of hours to get there, and spend half the time with the dinghy's bows flirting with the rock-fringed shore. But whether we got there by sail or oars, or —as after a good deal of argument we eventually did—by launch, the swimming-place provided some pleasant variety. It could hardly be described as a beach, since the sand was confined behind a low sea-wall, but for some reason it was supposed to be always free from sharks. Consequently it was usually crowded with swimmers, and we had plenty of opportunity to observe the Dutch girls. Fine, plump, milky-skinned creatures they were, too, but always vigilantly guarded by their escorts, so that we didn't get much closer than observation. Our boats made a handy focus for the swimmers, and would often be laden to the gunwales with scantily clad Hollanders of both sexes. Most of them spoke good English, but our attempts to impress our personalities upon whatever peach-skinned, Rubenesque females chanced to be in the boat were always thwarted by a throaty command from their swains, whereupon they would plump obediently back into the water.

Our Sunday mornings there were usually the best. The

wind did not rise until the afternoons, and the sea was a riffled mirror to the intense blue sky. There were more people than ever there, for truck-loads of them were brought in from the crowded refugee camps inland. Out of these, we met Cecilia and her family. She was a petite, olive-skinned Eurasian girl, with half a dozen brothers, and they clambered into the launch in a chattering cascade.

" Out to the wreck ! " she commanded without pre-liminary. " Is goot schwimming out by dere—less go ! "

The wreck was one of the many Japanese transports, wooden vessels of a couple of hundred tons burden, which either by accident or design were impaled on the rocks off the shore. We chugged out to the nearest one, made fast, and explored the canting decks and peered down into the dank gloom of the hold. There was certainly good swimming around it, with inviting depths like cool, trans-lucent jade probed by the quivering fingers of the sun.

Cecilia sky-larked about with innocent abandon, her close-cropped hair bouncing over her ears. She was as cunning as a cormorant in the water, but at last I dived and managed to grasp her by the thigh, by the yielding, supple waist and sturdy arm, and crushed her against me so that we both sank into the emerald shadows. When we surfaced again I still held on to her, and she asked, " Lissen, how old you t'ink I am ? "

" About fourteen, I s'pose," I answered honestly, and she said :

" Well, I'm twenny-one ! "

Thinking of her brothers, I rapidly let her go.

She shouted, " Follow me ! " and I scrambled after her up the splintered woodwork to the top of the bridge, forty-odd feet above the glittering sea. " Goot, eh ? " she asked. " Now, yump ! "

She took a run and jumped, in a compact ball of arms and legs, and hurtled down to plunge through the flashing surface of the water. I took a run, too, but at the last moment didn't jump.

" Yah, Sparky ! " they heckled up at me, and soon she clambered panting back again.

" Whaffor you didn't yump ? You scared ? "

" Too right I was scared."

" I don't believe it," she answered staunchly, which saved my face but didn't alter the situation. And ' How Sparky wouldn't jump after his girl,' was thus added to the annals of the ' Bengal '.

We sat side by side on the sloping woodwork, feeling the sun soaking luxuriously into our bodies and watching one of the native fishing-boats making for port. Her sail hung limp in the glowing air, but her crew was paddling her, and she sped rapidly towards her haven. They stood ranked along the bulwarks, each man aiding the power of his arms by a leg curled about his long-hafted paddle. Their blades flashed rhythmically as they left the water, and the grunting chant of the sailors drifted across to us.

Sun-scorched and salt-rimed, we returned to the ship for a feast of curry and a siesta through the flaming afternoon. Sundays were the only days we had curry, since Europeans were only allowed a minute allocation of rice, and it was a noble dish : eggs, meat, prawns, or salmon in a thick, red, buttery sauce, flanked by snowy rice and garnished with dried fruits, chopped eggs, chutney, and Bombay duck. The sauce itself, the detonator of the compound, was made from cummin seed, chillies, turmeric, cardamom, mint, black pepper, ground ginger, and ghee. When we had had our fill we would wander towards our bunks, momentarily too stunned even to think.

Our month in Batavia passed too quickly. There were no real advantages over Singapore, but somehow we could find more to do. Almost every evening there were cinema shows in one of the empty warehouses, and the fact that the velvet night would often be torn by a distant volley, or that the air would sometimes shudder with a far-away explosion, did not jar our absorption in the pictured scenes. They seemed, somehow, to be closer to reality. And we were used to the shooting ; near or far throughout the night, the thudding of gunfire came from somewhere, though no one could ever explain it to us.

Even Michael Gough found companionship in Batavia to suit his taste. They were a group of Intelligence officers, and they and Gough spoke a language beyond our ken ; in languid tones discussing counter-point, the true significance of jive, the correlation of Huxley and Proust. One of them, a lofty and gangling Etonian, had a fine collection of gramophone records, of which he brought a selection one night to give Michael a treat.

Michael received his guests with the gracious aplomb of a Mayfair hostess. We had not exactly been invited to join the party, which was to be held in our little mess-room, but, since it was going on, were attending anyway. The shabby little apartment, with its two tables, half-dozen chairs, and cushioned seat lockers, soon became filled with the soaring rhapsodies of violins, with tobacco smoke, empty bottles, the subdued comments of the uncivilised and the cultured palaver of Michael and his friends.

" I love this part where they seem to hesitate for a moment, as though they were waiting for the flutes to step in," said the Etonian critically. " Trouble is, I don't think that Stankastovitch has got 'em entirely under control."

" No, there is just that prestissimo of the whole orchestra at the wrong moment."

" I think that he's coming down a bit too heavily on the brass, too."

" The third violinist's breath smells," cackled the Third Mate happily. " Fill 'em up again, b'ys."

As far as we were concerned, the entertainment ended in its usual manner, with quavering renditions of the lesser-known part-songs. I don't think that we were heard too critically by Michael and his guests, who had retired to his cabin to continue their discussion.

It was almost our last night there, and soon we steamed out between the breakwaters' stony arms.

" An' so we say farewell to Javver, island of colour an' ro-mance," intoned Sandy nasally, in imitation of the well-known travelogue. " An' as its waving palms vanish beneath the horryzon, we turn our eyes to-wards the Narth, an' the stinkin' swamps of Seen-ga-paw."

II

Whilst we were in Batavia, and during the trip back to Singapore, we had laid plans for something ambitious in the way of parties upon our return. We decided that we had been too conservative in our entertainments, and that what we needed was a run ashore to shake us up a bit, and never mind the expense.

When it came to the point, only four of us went, the rest abstaining for one reason or another. Choff, as a married man and the father of a family, decided that his time for such festivals was past, but offered to take us ashore and to collect us at midnight, and to return for any stragglers on Sunday morning.

News of the expedition got around, and four or five others from various sister-ships arranged to join with us. We had determined that it was to be none of your sweat-rag and sandshoes affairs, but as formal as we could make it. Freddie Strong even suggested that we should wear dinner-jackets, but as he was the only person who possessed one, he was vetoed, and we compromised on white jackets and grey flannels.

The appointed hour was eight o'clock on a Saturday night, and we set off in good spirits. We had to collect the others from their ships, and there was much anxiety as to the smudging of white jackets as they climbed down into the launch. One of them, who had to clamber down a pilot ladder over the stern of his ship, called up, " All right—let 'er go now," into the darkness out of which he'd descended. Two bottles came swaying and tinkling down on the end of a line, and he grasped them anxiously. " I've got a flask in me pocket, too," he assured us. " D'you think it'll be enough ? " For in view of the prevailing price of liquor ashore, we had arranged to take our own stores with us.

Our last call had a destroyer alongside her, and we could see our guest hopping feverishly about the deck of his ship in his white jacket. " Won't be a minute," he bawled as he saw us appearing out of the night. " All dolled up, eh ? Just gotta cast off this fella, an' I'll be right with you. Leggo fore an' aft ? Aye-aye . . . leggooo fore an' aft——"

He skipped away over ropes and pipe-lines to chase up his crew, whilst we lay off. The destroyer hummed smoothly away into the darkness, diminishing into a clump of lights as we bumped alongside.

" Buck up, Pete ! " we shouted impatiently, and he gave a mellow chuckle as he climbed down into the boat.

He was a cheerful young bull of a man, like a fair young Falstaff with yellow curls and small, jocund blue eyes.

" Here we go, eh ? " he greeted us.   " Full ahead for the lures of the mysterious East.   Let 'er go, Choff."

The chattering boatload of us pounded towards the shore, passing down the columns of anchored ships with their lights quivering out over the placid sea.   It took us nearly an hour to reach Clifford Pier, where I had first landed in Singapore, and now seeming unnaturally quiet with its daylight throngs departed.   We walked through the wicket-gate and piled into the nearest taxi-cab.

" Where're we going ? " asked Pete.   " The Great World ? "

" Nah, the New World ! "

" Wotcher mean—New World ?   Happy World, driver, chop-chop ! "

" Oi ! New World galow——"

We wrangled for some moments, like so many celestial aspirants, as to whether we were bound for the Great, the New, or the Happy World, although there was little to choose between them.   They were each of them a kind of combined fun-fair, market-place, and amusement park. Within their large compounds were enclosed side-shows, outdoor cafés, small cinemas, Chinese theatres, boxing and wrestling booths, shooting galleries, stalls of every kind of goods, and the usual sucker-baits of such amusement concessions.

We decided upon one of them at last, and the taxi set us down before the gaudily painted plaster archway over the entrance.   For some little time we strolled about gazing at the sights, or taking a drink here and there at the cafés ; mingling with the crowds which drifted aimlessly between the booths and side-shows.   The star-glittering sky was obscured by the harsh glare of arc-lights, and the night filled with sound : the undulating clash and thump of a Chinese orchestra, the spit and clang of shooting ranges, nasal bellowing of sideshow barkers, brassy insistence of canned music, multi-toned chatter and laughter of the crowds.   We peered in at the door of one of the Chinese theatres, and in the white glow of a spotlight saw a figure in a

green-and-silver-figured robe posturing and chanting before
we were driven away.

" Ach, c'mon," said one of our guests.   " We're wasting
time an' money—let's away to the dancing."

His name was Sam, a heavily built man with aquiline
features, and he led the way to the huge dance-hall by the
entrance.   It had a corrugated-iron roof and wire-mesh
sides, and except for the far end, where an ear-splitting band
mangled the popular tunes, the dance-floor was surrounded
by chairs and tables too heavy to use in a fight.   In an inner
circle to these were the benches of the dance-hostesses, for
the privilege of whose partnership you paid a dollar for three
dances, or twelve dollars for an hour's companionship.   A
dollar is worth two-and-fourpence.

We put two tables together, and Sam ordered lemonade.
" Gotta get glasses to drink out of," he explained to our
raised eyebrows.   " Gotta be civilised in this joint, y'know.
Hey, look, there's our Second Mate——"

He pointed to a tanned and burly young man, who was
dancing obliviously past in firm control of a clinging half-
caste girl.

" ' White   Cargo ! ' "   guffawed Sam.   " C'mon, less
dance."

" Bottles under the table," reminded Pete.   " Turn-
about in watching 'em.   I'll stay first."

Thereafter the evening followed the old familiar tune.
Dance after dance with one gum-chewing, inarticulate
hostess after another, who held out a mute hand for your
ticket before getting up to dance, and grimaced at the smell
of liquor on your breath ; round and round the floor up to
the blaring band and back again to our table.   Our jackets
were soon sodden with sweat, and discarded to hang over
chairs ; about half of us soon gave up dancing and began to
wrangle dazedly about some half-forgotten exploit, and one
slid slowly and inevitably to the floor.

" H'ist 'im up again," roared Sam as he capered past.
" He's in amongst them bottles, don't ye see ? "

Most of them were empty, anyway.   I had done my share
in killing them, and was almost at the point in which I
wasn't sure whether I was dancing round the floor or the
floor was dancing round me.   At long last the band stopped,

and stammered out a few bars of the National Anthem.   It
was time to go, and in a tangled knot we wavered towards
the exit, all talking at once about what we should do next.
We had two women with us: a plump Siamese in a candy-
striped evening gown and a toothy Chinese girl, but somehow we lost them at the entrance to the park.

There was the usual mob of drunks and semi-drunks,
pick-pockets, prostitutes, pimps, panders, rickshaw-wallahs,
beggars, and hangers-on eddying round the garishly lighted
gates, and we became separated.

I found myself with Pete, who was still holding a bottle,
and he said, " C'm on, I know where to go.   Let's grab a
trishaw."

" Get in, then," he ordered me when he'd obtained one,
and I looked dubiously at his bulk.

" Both of us in one o' these ? "

" Sure, go ahead ! "

I take up about as much room as a whittled matchstalk,
but squeezed myself into a corner of the seat.

" All set, less go ! " he yelled, and plumped himself down
beside me.

The little sidecar with its attached cycle began to lean
over backwards, slowly and gracefully at first and then
suddenly accelerating to tip us on our backs in the road.
Its owner stood by, grinning helplessly.

" Still got the bottle, anyway," said Pete, brandishing it as
we untangled ourselves.   " Told you these things were no
good.   I'll get another, an' you follow me."

I followed him on a bell-tinkling dash in and out of side-
streets and ominous alleyways, in and out of one cockroach-
haunted dive after another.   We sang in doleful harmony,
plunged in and out of hysterical elation and maudlin
reminiscence ; quarrelled and made up, embraced in eternal
friendship ; slandered everyone we knew in rambling con-
demnation.   We wagged our fingers at each other across
stained little tables, watched by groups of nervously grinning
Chinese.   We were on a bender, a night out, a spree.
Having a wonderful time.

CHAPTER SEVEN

GEORGETTE AND JOHORE

I

THE RISING SUN FLASHED in through the open window, and cast a flaming square across my face. I opened my eyes, and shut them again immediately. For a tortured interval I willed sleep to return, but the anæsthetic had worn off, and it was time to return to life again.

I began to wonder, vaguely, where I was. In jail? There should have been bars in the window for that. I opened my eyes again and stared up at the ceiling, which was covered with soiled calico. A lizard, hanging upside-down upon it, returned my gaze with an unsympathetic stare. I turned my head, gently.

I was lying on a low, wide bed, uncovered, in a tiny room of which it was the sole furniture. Except for my clothes, heaped on the matting floor. The open door gave into a little yard washed dazzlingly by the sun, and while I looked a shadow fell across it. It was that of a Chinese crone in threadbare black pyjamas, holding a cracked cup in one hand. Unperturbed by my lack of clothing, she offered it to me.

" Kaffee ? " she enquired, and gave a gap-toothed grin.

I sipped reflectively, then, spurred by a sudden thought, reached for my clothing. I found that whatever money had been in the remnants of my once-white jacket had departed. There was about fifty cents in a trousers pocket, and no more. I dressed slowly, except for the one shoe which I couldn't find anywhere, and peeped around the door. The yard was empty, though from the house of which my cell was an appendix there came a sing-song chattering. The yard gate was invitingly ajar, and in one dash I was across the yard and out of it and down the alley it entered, clop-plop on my one shoe and one sock. There was a trishaw standing in the road I came to, and I shook its Sikh driver awake. " Clifford Pier—*juldi karao !* "

79

"Two dollars," he said when we got there, and I gave him my fifty cents.

I walked away from the subsequent discussion with as much dignity as a one-shoed man can muster, and found sanctuary on a bench at the end of the pier. I waited there for what seemed like several hours, until I saw the launch approaching.

"Boy, are you a life-saver," I told Choff as I climbed down into it. "Never no more, boy. That's the lot."

He didn't make any of the customary wisecracks, but as soon as we were well away began to talk excitedly. "You know last night? After I'd put you ashore? Did y' notice that bunch of women waiting about on the pier? One of 'em came over to me an' asked how could they get back to their ship—that big Frog, you know, the 'Cap St. Pierre.' 'Course, I said I'd give 'em a run out. Lissen. They're all right. French Army women going to Saigon, they are, an' they've invited me—us—to go over for a drink 'smorning. You'll come, eh? Y'know what the others are—need a week's notice before they'll go anywhere."

I watched him wearily. "Lissen, you know what day it is?" I asked him. "Sunday. Day of rest. An' that's what I'm doing when I get aboard—turning in. S'posing Betty Grable had asked us over for a drink, I'd be turning in."

"Ah, be a man! What's a few drinks? Cor beggar me, I dunno about you young fellers nowadays. Why, when I was your age—— Lissen, they're peaches. No kid. They're all right, boy, take it from me."

"I've had enough women to last me the rest o' me life," I growled, as sudden memory assailed me.

But he was obdurate, and we wrangled until by sheer weight of personality he wore me down.

"Dunno's I've got a clean shirt, anyway," I said weakly at last, and he replied firmly:

"I'll lend you one."

So, after shaving and showering and changing I helped him to pretty up the launch with cushions and canvas seat-covers, and we departed, accompanied by Sandy and Freddie Strong.

"Where did you get to last night, afterwards?" asked Sandy, to which I replied truthfully:

" How the hell should I know ? "

The ' Cap St. Pierre ' had a kind of battered magnificence as we approached her.   She was an old liner, still bearing the white paint, green stripe, and Red Crosses of a hospital ship, but all sadly smirched with rust and oil.   She was now being used as a French Army transport, and we could see her passengers crowding the rails as we came closer.

" Good God ! " exclaimed Choff in shocked accents. " They're all women ! "

Very conscious of our audience, we brought the boat smartly alongside the accommodation ladder, and nervously followed Choff up on to the main deck.   I was convinced that he would not recognise his hostesses amongst so many, but I need not have worried.   They were waiting determinedly for us at the gangway, and surrounded him in a vivacious group.   I admired him ; he was quite at his ease, and strutting like a bull-terrier amongst so many poodles.

We began to get sorted out.   " This is Freddie *et* Sandy *et* Sparky, and *ici* Paulette and—er—Georgette and —*et*—Suzette *et*—what ?—er, pardon ?—oh, yes—*ah, oui*— Marianne *et* Madame *de* Pompom and—*er*—yes, well, how are you all to-day ?   *Comment allez-vous*, that is ? "

" Oh, but why do we stand 'ere—you mos' com' an' 'ave a dreenk ! " cried one of them, and we were escorted between a double line of eagle-eyed females towards the smoke-room.   Most of them followed us in, and sat about watching us at our table.

We began to progress excellently well.   *Fine à l'eau* was a new drink to me, but it seemed to have a remarkably provocative effect, and combined with such a bouquet of femininity it made us into different men.   With their English and our French, we soon became fast friends.

" But picture what a voyage terrible ! " cried one of them. " Two mont's we are comeeng from Marseilles, an' ze— ze—'ow say you ?   To 'ave to eat, onnerstan' ?   Ah, yes, ze food—*c'est affreux* !   Fright-fool !   An' ze 'eat !   And "— she lowered her voice, with an indescribably Gallic flash in her dark eyes—" ze weemin !   So many on wan sheep ! Creeminale, *n'est ce pas* ? "

In a little while our acquaintanceship seemed firm enough

F

for Choff to ask them to lunch, and they assented with delight.

"Bring your bathing-dresses too," he said. "We'll go out in the launch after lunch, and find somewhere to swim."

About half a dozen of them came, and they entered our little mess-room with coos of pleasure. They seemed to be especially impressed with the bowls of fruit and carafes of wine set out in their honour.

"*C'est comme un petit estaminet, à la française,*" said one of them happily.

Lunch was a great success. We had an especially pungent curry, which they ate with little squeals of pretended pain, and I found myself progressing sympathetically with Georgette. She was a tall and sumptuous girl, with a complicated blonde hair-do which was somewhat dark at the roots. But it was very effective with her brilliant black eyes, which added piquant accents to our talk.

"Seex mont's en France, an' you speak lak' un Parisien," she assured me, after I had launched into a particularly ambitious speech in pidgin-French.

That was one Sunday on which we did not bother to sleep off the effects of the curry. Directly after lunch the boat was prepared and we changed into swimming-gear. The girls changed in the Captain's quarters, and the effect as they emerged was more than even Ziegfeld could have desired.

Georgette swayed up to me, smiling sweetly. "Don' you reco'nise me in my costume ? " she asked.

I gulped and nodded, and led her along to the boat. We were bound for one of the little islands which surround the harbour, about an hour's run from our anchorage. Conical, and thickly clad with lush, bright green, it was encircled by a strip of beach which we found changed to mud and stones below the water's edge. But we managed to beach the boat, and piled ashore.

Georgette beckoned to me, smiling happily. "Com'. We—we deescover ze island, *n'est ce pas ?* "

Before the others said anything we were away ; along a winding path which curved around a spur of the island and up the other side, which was not so thickly wooded. It was very still, very warm ; the sun glinting back from the countless facets of the sea, the air drowsy with the bumbling of wild bees.

" Walk beside me," she asked coyly, and tucked her arm through mine. " Now, we shall 'elp each ozzer to climb . . ."

We reached the top, a levelled space upon which stood a white-painted navigational beacon. Thence we could look far out over the sea ; over the panorama of the ship-filled harbour and the distant town.

" Nice view," I remarked conversationally.

She tightened her clasp on my arm, until I turned my eyes to hers. She regarded me solemnly, and whispered, " And me ? Am I not nice, also . . ."

. . . at last we retraced our steps back down the hill. I wondered whether the boat would still be there, or whether they would have thought that we had lost ourselves, and started searching for us.

Just before we came out on the beach, she gently tweaked my ear. " You don' tell anybodee, eh ? " she murmured.

" Of course not . . ."

The sound of shrieks and splashings reached our ears, and we found the rest of the party engaged in a merry game.

" Hullo ! you haven't been long," said Sandy casually, and scampered off in pursuit of a buxom little Parisienne.

We took them back aboard for dinner, and returned them to their ship soon afterwards. They invited us to lunch with them next day, but unfortunately we had a fuelling job just at that time. However, since they had said that they would like to go ashore for some shopping later in the afternoon, I was deputed to transport them in the launch.

Together with a quartermaster and an engine-hand, I arrived prompt to time.

They were already waiting on the accommodation-ladder, and Georgette called, " I tell a few more of my frien's zey can com' in ze boat—is okay ? "

" Sure, you bet. Let 'em all come."

They did. I discovered that the queue which began on the accommodation ladder must have ended somewhere astern. They filed down one after another, with gay little shrieks as they were helped off the platform into the boat,

and making great play with their skirts.   The two Indians
with me rolled their eyes as though they hoped that the
Prophet was excusing them their association with such
immodest creatures.   Big girls, little girls, plump girls,
thin girls, blondes, brunettes, red-heads, and all the shades
between—it seemed that all the female attachments of the
French Army were descending into my boat.   Bedazzled
as I was, I soon realised that we could not carry a tenth of
them.

"*Non-non, non-non,*" I pleaded.   "No more—*pas de
plus—j'ai peur de la bateau*—er—*vous savez*—topsy-
turvy . . ."

They either would not or could not understand, and in
despair at making them do so, I ordered the quartermaster to
cast off.

"Eh, m'sieur!" they wailed, those left behind, and those
in the boat clutched at my knees.   "M'sieur—wan leetle
wan more—my frien', she arrives at ze end . . ."

It broke my heart; I felt like the Gestapo, but I had to be
hard.   As it was, the boat turned sluggishly away from the
ship, and wallowed as though uncertain whether to sink or
swim.   On the way to the shore I delivered to Georgette
and the others the messages with which I had been charged,
and told them of Choff's suggested arrangements for a
rendezvous ashore.   They were complaisant, and at seven
that night we met them at the landing-stage.   We were
once more in white jackets, hastily laundered for the occasion that very day, but had planned a somewhat more sedate
evening than the last in which they had participated.   We
took the girls to the Adelphi Hotel for dinner, and then on
to one of the more Europeanised night-spots.   There was a
Hawaiian band there, composed of Filipinos, and Georgette
desired to dance to it.   She was wearing shoes with high
cork platform soles, which were ill-suited to dancing, and
so she took them off.   Her doing so, and her barefoot
boogie-woogie, created something of a sensation, but she
and her companions soon became restless.

"I t'ink we go somewhere else now, hey?" she demanded, and so we took them to the Great World.

They enjoyed it much better.

"Oh, I lak' it 'ere," panted Georgette, still barefoot,

after we had circled the floor seven or eight times. " Zere is more *couleur*, more—more atmosphere, *n'est ce pas* ? "

Our white jackets were discarded again, and the atmosphere was causing our shirts to resemble wet tissue-paper, but it was impossible not to respond to their vivacity and *joie-de-vivre*.

We returned them to their ship at midnight, and I made a date with Georgette for the following day. It was to be their last, and so they invited us to their ship for a farewell party in the evening. Georgette and I went out to the Botanical Gardens in the afternoon. They are amongst the finest in the East; superbly designed and maintained, with rolling lawns between groves of flowering trees, and winding paths astray through lush, deep-shaded shrubberies. We saw less of them than we should have done ; it was too warm, too languorously scented an afternoon.

" *Regardez, un papillon noir*," she murmured lazily, as a great butterfly with wings like black velvet drifted across our glade.

It was like a fragment fallen from approaching night ; a warning that our time was nearly done. We gathered our things together and strolled silently back into the world.

She came back to dinner on board, and afterwards those of us not on duty returned with her to their farewell party on the ' Cap St. Pierre '. It was held in the smoke-room, and before long we were dancing to the piano which one of them played. I'd often been to dances during the war, when the men were in a majority of about fifty to one, but now for once in a way the position was reversed. We could have danced the soles off our feet if we had wanted to, since the sound of the piano rapidly drew a crowd of pleasure-hungry passengers.

As bars have an unpleasant habit of doing, this one closed just as the fun was at its height, and we were herded disconsolately out on deck. But the anti-climax was resolved by Choff, who began inviting everyone within reach to return with us for a night-cap on the ' Bengal '. Our boat was soon almost as overloaded as it had been on the previous afternoon.

Time, which for us too often crawled through the morass of days, now took to its stealthy wings and snatched the moment from our hands. Too soon we had to take them back again, and wave farewell to their gay figures as we returned alone. The ship seemed empty and dull ; tired as we were, it was impossible to turn in. We sat about on deck, discussing our adventures over one last drink.

It was one too many for me. I sprawled back in my chair, expounding loudly my views upon life ; man's endless campaign against the vacancy which surrounds him on all sides. From that I went on to the art of war, the vicissitudes of love, the intangibility of happiness. Presumably they left me to it. When I woke up I was still sitting there, the sun burning my eyes out and the gong sounding for breakfast.

Choff came round the corner, looking fresh and vigorous as ever. " Breakfast time," he commented.

" Do' wan' any."

He looked at me curiously. " Heard the news ?"

" Uh ? "

" They're shifting us round to the Johore Straits. We're going to work round the naval base from now on."

II

Our days of philandering, such as they had been, were now over. We had complained enough before at our idle and restricted existence, but now we had something to moan about. Instead of being anchored in the wide open spaces of Singapore Harbour, we took up our anchorage in that part of the Johore Straits which lies off the naval base, and found ourselves in surroundings which hardly rewarded the constant contemplation of them which was forced upon us.

" Well, I think it's nice to have a bit of green to look at, anyway," said Choff soon after we had arrived. He stretched out in his deck-chair, and gazed at the long, low vista of dark-green mangrove swamps which was the coastline of Johore. " Better'n having nothing but ships to look at, I reckon."

Johore is on the northern side of the Straits, so that we had two prospects upon which to rest our eyes : either the angular workshops, storehouses, executive buildings and barracks of the base, or the verdant monotony of the swamps, over which we could gaze to the gently rising interior. The tin-and-bamboo huts of fishermen stood by the water's edge, amongst decorative clumps of coco-nut palms; behind them the country was monotoned with jungle and the tree-tops of rubber plantations. There was one salient point, an abrupt hill whose side was scarred with pinkish-grey, marking the quarry from which stone was brought for the building of the base.

Also, of course, we could look at the Straits, which, like a wide and winding river, stretched to east and west. Many small rivers flowed into them through the jungles of Johore, and the naval base and dockyard is situated upon a broad, curving reach. We were fourteen miles from Singapore, and about four from Johore Bahru, capital of the State of Johore. We could see the square, canopied tower of its Government buildings over the tree-tops from where we lay, and for some time thought that it was the Sultan's Palace. The town lies at the northern end of the Johore Causeway, which completely seals the western entrance to the straits. There are spillways through it to allow the tide to flow, and there was once a small lock at the Johore end, but this was blown up during the occupation.

This mile-long erection of granite blocks, with the road and railway running along its top, formed one of the barriers of my existence during nine of the eleven more months which I was to spend in the ' Bengal '. In retrospect, it is difficult to believe that it was so long. I suppose that it is because the days, which were occupied with trivial pastimes, the quest for entertainment, and the sedate routine of the vessel and her work, at last ticked by with the slumberous monotony of a clock in a quiet room.

We had the time, all of us, to embark upon any kind of study or hobby; either to pass the time or with a definite end in view. Two or three of the junior officers did make a feint at studying for their higher certificates, and Choff even sent for the books with which to study for his Extra Master's certificate. They arrived, and lay on his shelf unopened. The climate was partly to blame, I think; the languid heat which lay like a steam-soaked blanket over everything, and which made you too irritable and restless to relax, too vitiated of energy to act. Partly the climate, partly the fact that the less you do the less you want to do.　And the knowledge that there was always to-morrow, and to-morrow and to-morrow, stretching away to the far-off milestone of our relief.　Whatever plans we made for our occupation or amusement were always sabotaged by that realisation ; that they could be as easily carried out to-morrow as to-day, and next week, or next month, as easily as either.　We lived in a lotos-land of undemanding leisure—leisure which men of deeper resources could have turned to valuable account, but which we spent as thriftlessly as a drunkard's pay.

Apart from the various pastimes in which I joined with the others—swimming, boating, walking, and so on—I found my main occupations outside what little work I had to do in writing, looking after the library, and running the canteen.　The need for books, for something, anything, to read being a part of my make-up as deep-rooted and in-eradicable as a dope-addict's for his syringe, the former was more of a pleasure than a duty.　The same could not always be said of the latter.

Soon after I joined the ship, the Captain had asked me to take over the canteen.　The last officer who had managed it had gone on leave before I joined, and since no one else had been willing to operate it, he had done so himself, with the aid of the chief steward.　For the work and respon-sibility involved, he proposed to allow me a five per cent profit—which amounted to about four pounds a month—on all items handled; and, on the principle of trying anything once, I agreed.

The process involved the buying and redistribution, to officers and crew, of our spirits, beer, and tobacco ration from NAAFI, together with whatever else the officers might order in the way of unrationed wines, spirits, and liqueurs.　There were numerous other canteen items, including most of the articles which one would expect to find in a village store, and the turnover varied between eighty and a hundred pounds a month.　The crew accounted for about a fifth of this sum, since they were allowed no alcohol and a smaller cigarette ration, but purchased a good deal of soap, tobacco, matches, and writing-paper.　I attempted to interest them in chocolate, but they wouldn't look at it.

" Chahklit eat, teeth kalass," explained the serang, with a flash of his own perfect ivories. I didn't blame him for wanting to preserve them, but he evidently had no such qualms with regard to gin. " Saab, you sell me one i-small bahtle ginnie ? " he often wheedled softly, until I became tired of refusing him.

" No ! " I exclaimed. " And besides, Mohammed speak that Indian man mustn't drink gin."

" He no speak ginnie, saab," he replied with dignity. " He only speak wine. Ginnie different."

I ran my general stores and off-licence for about three months, but the system did not meet with the approval of Sandy Macleod. He was in favour of the canteen being run on the lines of a club bar, which meant that all officers would subscribe a certain amount to start a canteen fund. After this all profits would accrue to the fund, and when they were sufficient would be used on various projects beneficial to all of us.

The majority were indifferent as to how the bar was run, so long as it was run at all, and I opposed him on the grounds that it would institute an unnecessarily complicated procedure. But by dint of a gentle persistence he talked one after another of us round to his way of thinking, and once Choff's powers of organisation were mobilised in its favour, it was as good as done.

A notice was put on the board to the effect that a meeting would be held to consider the institution of a canteen fund, and with due solemnity we assembled. Everything was done with an unusual formality, and it was something of a *coup d'état*. Doubtless in order not to offend my susceptibilities, a little canvassing had been done behind the scenes, and in no time at all the Third Officer had been elected Secretary, and Sandy the Treasurer, of the new scheme, and I found myself with my occupation gone.

In some ways I was slightly relieved, in others annoyed. The monthly sweat and wrangle over cases of beer and cigarettes, the turmoil of redistribution, and the intricacies of accountancy, were all things I could do without, but I suppose that my sense of humour was too atrophied to appreciate the way in which I had been relieved of them— and of my four pounds a month.

However, it was not to be for long.   Less than a month later, when we had started our voyage to the Andaman Islands, Choff went for an afternoon's shooting with some Royal Indian Navy officers.   We were anchored in a place called Port Mouat, and he returned to the ship at about eight o'clock.   Finding me solitary in the saloon, he insisted on sharing a beer, and over it was loud in praise of his hosts.

"Damn' fine blokes," he assured me earnestly.   "Gotta give a party for 'em—asked 'em all to come aboard t'morrow. We'll have to get something organised—there's about two dozen of 'em coming.   Phew! it's too hot down here. I'm going top-side—coming up?   Blimey, you're always writing, aren't you?"

He departed, and about an hour later I followed him up on deck.   I walked right into the middle of a red-faced argument, which I momentarily disrupted by tipping over the Third Officer's glass.

"You c'n buy me another for that!" he snapped testily.

We had already introduced the more civilised system of selling drinks by the glass, instead of by the bottle.

Peaceably, I signed the chit for him, helped myself to a drink and settled back to listen.   It was something like an altercation between a whippet and a bull; Choff laying down the law with ponderous logic, while Jackson snapped out taunting confutations.   The others sitting there goaded them both with facetious comments, and one could feel the bubble of temper stretching tight between them.   Suddenly, it popped.

"After all," said Choff heavily, "when we started the bar we agreed that one reason for it was so's we could throw parties between us, instead of one or two people supplying all the booze."

"Yair, but this is gonna be your party."

"Everybody'll join in, won't they?"

"I tell you the stocks aren't big enough to give a party like that, for twenty-odd men," stated the Third Officer sullenly.

"That's nonsense.   There was plenty when we left Singapore."

"Oh, nuts!"

Choff leapt to his feet, damson-faced and raging. " **Nuts** to me, young man ! Nuts to me ! Let me get—I'll teach you t'say—you little——"

Someone cackled delightedly, but I put myself in the way as he plunged towards Jackson. I had a distaste for seeing the last rags of our dignity stripped from us by a brawl, and spoke fast along those lines. In a few seconds I found myself deep in their dispute, with Choff invoking my support and Jackson calling out : " We all know why Sparky's shoving his face in—he was makin' a good thing out of it, an' wants it back again ! "

And I got it. The disturbance ended when Choff, as a committee of one, summarily dismissed Jackson from his post, in the same moment as the latter resigned. He ran below and slammed the cash-box—a fancy-biscuit tin—into Sandy's cabin, whilst Choff was canvassing for a new Secretary. Everyone declined the honour until he came to me.

" What about you ? " he demanded, and I shook my head.

" Not me. I'm chokker with the whole outfit. Don't care if I never see another drink aboard."

" You've bloody well got to, old boy," he declared with finality. " There's no one else will do it, so it's up to you to rally round."

At last I agreed, and soon found myself performing the same tasks as before. Sandy discreetly faded out of his post as Treasurer, and for seven months more I held the post of Acting Unpaid Secretary and Treasurer of the ' Bengal's ' Canteen Fund.

presents them with legends combining a charm and fantasy of which he never dreamed.

In addition to these nocturnal voyages to Johore, the daily runs for mail and passengers and its monthly employment as a stores-carrier, we found yet another use for the launch. During a succession of Sunday afternoons we amused ourselves by exploring the many little creeks and rivers which flow into the Straits, and sometimes found ourselves in complicated positions in the way of stranding and so on. The launch was really too big to venture up them, and I enjoyed better the expeditions which I later made by canoe.

Ever since our first arrival in the Straits I had looked enviously at the little rubber or canvas canoes skimming their surface, bearing one or two well-tanned adventurers. They seemed to me to be just the thing for navigating those calm waters, but I couldn't think where to obtain one. Choff didn't seem much interested, and though I often spoke of them, and even suggested that we might build one he paid scant attention. And then at last Sandy said one day :

" I've just seen a couple of those canoes you've been talking about. We were taking some stuff back to the return store, and there's a couple in there."

At once I went to work on Choff again, and, presumably worn down by nagging, he finally indented for ' Canoes, two, recreational purposes for the use of '. My face fell when they arrived, for they were in an extremely battered condition. They were two-man folding canoes, with plywood tops and bottoms and canvas sides supported by hinged struts. I wanted to start repairing them right away, but Choff said that he would put the carpenter on the job. He did so, but other things cropped up, and they were only patched up for a start.

I didn't get the true benefit of the one which I came to regard as mine until after Christmas. I had used them quite a lot in the meantime, but their general crankiness and normal state of being about two inches awash made them uncomfortable craft. At last, inspired by a passion of boredom, I really went to work on one of them. I removed all unnecessary hamper, caulked the seams with white lead and tallow, dressed the canvas sides with linseed oil, and gave the whole four coats of paint.   The final coat was green with red trimmings, and as a final touch I borrowed a set of stencils and christened her ' Mon Amie '.

The launching was a matter of some misgivings, and after I had gingerly lowered myself into her I was delighted to find that she didn't leak a drop.   After that she was my main solace and occupation.   I was out in her between three-thirty and seven every afternoon, and for much longer on week-ends.   Sometimes I went a long way, sometimes not very far ; the main thing was that she provided an opportunity to get away from the ship, the means to drift about completely alone.   Besides, of course, providing for an amateur the most easily handled way of tasting the joys of ' just messing about in boats '.

There was a step for a mast, so I fitted a bamboo mast and a square sail.   It was the only practicable rig ; she was too light in the water, besides having no keel, to sail across the wind, but she would go like a leaf before it.   I often let the wind carry me for so long, for the sheer pleasure of it, that I'd have over-far to paddle home.   I was out in all weathers, and found a crazy exhilaration in being caught in the monsoon squalls of the early part of the year.   I had a canvas cover for the cockpit, so that it was water-tight except for my body, and when the ragged clouds boomed down from the mainland I would clip it into place, set the sail square, and let the howling wind drive me before the curtains of blinding rain.   During the north-easterly monsoon the weather rapidly alternated blazing sun or lashing rain, with sagging, sombre clouds viperish with lightning, and the storms were so abrupt that one had always to be prepared for them. But the rain was harmless and warm, and unless it degenerated into an endless drizzle, its passing left the world for a moment washed and refreshed.   Until the sun reappeared, and sucked back the moisture in drifts of cottony mist over the jungle and swamp.

I did not learn until later how foolish I was to venture into those swamps alone.   They had a strange fascination for me ;   the winding, aimless channels which probed the tangled monotony of the lower jungle, with sometimes a river which, though broad at its mouth, would eventually lose itself in a score of watery filaments. It is an amphibious territory, and the dwellers in it are as much at home on water as ashore. Their houses are built on stilts, and I would often meet them paddling about the highways of their domain, their canoes laden with fish or hardly won firewood, or the ducks which they corral on higher pieces of ground. Or would pause to watch them whilst they netted for prawns.

This is an operation which, like many performed for sheer utility, had a flowing grace and beauty of its own. The fine-meshed net they use is circular, with a thin chain sewn in around its hem, so that it opens out as it is thrown, yet draws rapidly together as it sinks. Balancing upright in his dug-out canoe, the supple fisherman dangles the net like a folded umbrella, and with a sudden fluid motion casts it up and away from him. It opens like a gossamer flower blooming in the air, falls to hit the water with a little plash, sinks, and he hauls it in by the line fastened to his wrist; folded again, and dripping, and perhaps holding but a single prawn. With ancient patience, he casts his net again and yet again, until he has enough to take to market. The succulent river prawns are esteemed by the Chinese, and a basketful will repay all his toil.

But their most profitable fishing is done by means of traps. In the nine- or ten-mile stretch of the Straits which came within my scope there must have been more than twenty of these, mostly on the northern shore. They are sturdily constructed in a way which combines simplicity with efficiency, as all good contrivances should do. About a hundred yards from the shore, and at right angles to it, several score of bamboo stakes are driven into the mud at intervals of about a foot, and the spaces between them filled with a wide mesh of rattan, reeds, or wire. The outer end of this stockade is built in the form of a three-sided square, with its opening facing the shore, and across this is slung the net, readily raised or lowered by means of wooden wind-lasses. These are fixed to the platform on which the fisher-man's hut is built, and catwalks run around it and across the square which is the active section of the trap.

Fishing is done at night, on a rising tide. The net is lowered into the water, and above it is suspended a brilliant

The 'Kyoto Maru'—ex-Japanese Navy Cadet ship, used for repatriating Japanese P.O.W.s

Johore Bahru

light, usually an acetylene lantern. The fish, browsing slowly up the Straits on the flowing tide, come up against the stockade, the mesh of which would be wide enough to let most of them swim through. But it diverts them for long enough to notice, and be attracted to, the overhanging light, and so they swim along the stockade and into the open square.

Crouched on their catwalks above the dark water, the glaring light making them into bronze statues, the fishermen watch the glinting assembly of their prey. There is an atmosphere of slow tension ; the motionless, impassive forms gazing down like the Fates of the foolishly swarming fish, which goggle up at the dazzling light in their skies. They are so fascinated that it would be difficult to scare them, but still nothing is said. The final orders are given in low voices, the figures move stealthily to their posts, and the windlasses creak protestingly into the silent night. But once the edges of the net are above water, and there is no escape for their prey, the tension breaks in a hullabaloo of bawled orders and jests, and the fish leap within the net in flashing arabesques. Slowly the net is raised, sagging beneath its load, and the fishermen start to scoop it out into their baskets. To-morrow it will be in the market of Johore, dull-eyed on the merchants' stalls, or split and drying rankly in the sun.

But it was not such scenes as these, nor anything else about the gentle, hard-working folk of the swamp-lands, which attracted me into them. The scenery was monotonous enough, and sometimes when the falling tide exposed the naked mangrove roots, and the mud-banks in which they grew, it was almost repellent. All the same, there was something placid and soothing about those stretches of polished water, convoluting through the maze of oily green foliage. The dusty heat and clangour of the base, the petty animosities and restrictions of shipboard life, seemed far away. But for the rippling of my paddle, there was no sound, and, if I drifted, the silence was of that intensity which has its own deep resonance—the absolute stillness which enables you to hear the vibrant humming of your own blood, pulsing behind your ears.

G

There was not much to look at, nothing to see but the water, the foliage, and the sky.   Quite often there would be the turquoise-and-orange flash of kingfishers, which lived there in great numbers, and once a large monkey, walking a branch overhanging the stream, paused to stare at me in wrinkled incomprehension.   But that which I found there was more valuable than any brilliant scenes, for it was the deep serenity in which the mind can uncrease itself.

The danger which I was unwittingly courting remained concealed until about a fortnight before I left Singapore. One evening, after a day of rain, I went out as usual.   The Straits were held in a limpid bell of atmosphere, the sky webbed with a pearly haze, the water like a sheet of polished steel.   It was the kind of evening in which a laugh or a little sound travels for miles over the surface of the water. For all its stillness, the air had been so washed by the rain that it felt fresh and cool as I paddled vigorously away from the ship.   I travelled a good way, to the mouth of the river known as the Sungei Terbau, and there I rested.   I was about a hundred yards from the shore on either hand, and the placid opalescence of the evening sky, the absolute immobility of the water and the air, made me feel as though I floated in an element compounded from both of them.

I heard a heavy splash near the shore, and thought it to be a shoal of fish jumping.   Then, about a minute later, there was a sound behind me like a horse blowing through its nose. I glanced around, and was petrified by the sight of the flat, malevolent head of a crocodile, on the surface about a dozen feet away.

With a churning swirl of water, it dived.   Through the clear water I could see the white plates of its belly as it turned, and thought that it would surface underneath the canoe. I have rarely been so afraid.   I had always thought of crocodiles as something like big lizards ; dangerous if they caught you while swimming, but not otherwise.   This one's body alone looked as big as a cow's, and it could clearly overturn me with great ease.

It surfaced on the other side of the canoe, then dived again, but by this time I'd pulled myself together enough to start paddling. My bows were pointing diagonally away from the shore, so I made for a fish-trap about a quarter-mile away. I'd like to say that canoes do not often move so quickly in those waters.

I reached the trap, hurriedly made fast, and scrambled up the bamboo ladder.

There were already two or three men on the platform, including a young Chinese who asked, " What matter ? "

Gasping, I explained, and he laughed politely.

" Dis morning one small boy catch by croc'dile, bite off leg. Boy die," he said, and laughed again. The Chinese custom of laughing at such incidents, instead of showing the crude emotions of distress, is apt to be somewhat irritating at times.

I sat there chatting to him for about an hour. He was the son of the owner of the fish-trap, and with deprecating laughs he told me something of the habits of crocodiles. How they will creep up on someone fishing in the shallows, concealed by the muddy water—as one had done to the small boy that morning ; how they steal chickens and ducks from pens ashore, and will tackle a goat or pig if they come across one, and then drag their prey to their dens in holes under the river-banks ; how they will sometimes surface alongside a canoe and shatter it with one sweep of their armoured tails.

" Dey only break canoe when dey real hungry," he chuckled. " One time, one croc'dile come in dis fish-trap after de fish, get caught up in de net. Ai yah ! I like you to seen dat ! Ev'body shout, yell, t'row knives, sticks, ev'thing. Croc'dile, he don't care. He go 'way by-'n-by, an' take my net with 'im. I never see dat net again."

He laughed again, and I shuddered inwardly. I have too much imagination, and could only too clearly visualise that crocodile snapping at me in the water, and my body lying in some underwater larder. I knew that I should never venture into the swamps again, and when I thought how I might have encountered it in one of those inlets too narrow to turn my canoe, my bowels seemed to turn to water. At last I bade the Chinaman good-bye, and made a

frightened dash back to the ship before sunset.   I hadn't
been out in the canoe again a fortnight later, when I was
transferred from the ' Bengal '.

But all that was after we had returned from the Andaman
Islands.

CHAPTER NINE

TO THE ISLANDS

I

SINCE WE HAD MADE up our minds that we were going to
remain in the Straits for an indefinite period, we were
electrified by the sudden news that we were to make a
voyage to the Andaman Islands. We were assigned to
carry fuel oil, provisions, and other stores to the minesweeping flotillas which were still operating around the
islands and along the Burmese coasts, searching for mines
which the Japanese had sown indiscriminately about them.
We spent several days alongside, taking aboard the stores
and doing the various odd jobs which were necessary before
we put to sea, and it was during this period that I at last
obtained the canoes. We also obtained a piano, which by
endless manœuvring Michael Gough had secured from a
ship ordered home ; a neat little job for which we could just
find room in our mess-room. It was to him what the
canoes were to me.

With the piano, the canoes, the NAAFI rations, and the
rest of the cargo aboard, we were prepared to sail, and at
nine o'clock one morning we slowly backed out of our berth
alongside, steadied in mid-channel, and were full away.
None of us knew anything about our destination, except
for the brief and dry official information, and we were bound
first for the island of Tavoy, and thence across to the
Andamans. Tavoy is off the coast of Burma, and the
Andamans in the centre of the Bay of Bengal, so that our
northward route towards them took us first through the
Malacca Straits. There was nothing new in this ; the
climate was the same ; what little we saw of the shore was
very similar to the environment we had just left.

At sea, my watches were six to eight and ten to twelve
in the forenoon and two to four and six to eight in the afternoon, and on the morning of the third day I completed my
first watch and went in to breakfast without having been on

deck.   As usual, it was stuffy and hot in the mess-room, a
condition which we now hardly noticed, and after breakfast
I sat smoking and talking to the Fourth Engineer.   This
was no longer John Erikson, whose time had expired, but a
sallow and cynical young Scot whom for some forgotten
reason we called Rigor Mortis.

"Aweel," he said at last, " it's kinda warrum doon here.
Let's awa' up on deck an' catch a few ozones———"

As soon as we emerged from the companion-way, the
atmosphere told us that we were well out of the Malacca
Straits.   The north-east monsoon was blowing fresh and
clear, and the sudden impact of its cool, sparkling air was
like a draught of spring water, after drinking over-long
from a muddy well.

"Mah Goad!" exclaimed Rigor, expanding his chest.
" Isna that wonderful ?   An' hey, look, there's an island."

We strolled up forward, breathing deep of that clean,
salty air which seemed to flow into and through our half-
clothed bodies, cleansing them of the stagnation of Singapore.   We stood up in the bows, gazing at the island which
lay ahead and a little off the port bow.   We were approaching it rapidly, and about to pass very close to it.   Rising
out of a sea so blue that it was almost purple, and wind-
stippled with the creaming of small waves ; beneath a sky
wind-cleansed, and traversed by the marching lines of small
regular clouds, it was the perfect picture of a tropic island.
The reefs around it enclosed an irregular basin of sea, which,
in lovely contrast to the dark-blue depths, was of the most
lucent turquoise ; encircling in its turn the concentrics of
white surf and yellow beach, from which the island rose
steeply into two domed peaks like a green, solid cloud of
foliage.   So closely grew the trees, rising one above another,
the leaves of one hiding the trunk of the next highest, that it
was difficult to realise that they had solid base.   Here and
there among them, though, the white columns of blasted
trunks reminded us that the tonic breeze could blow with
hurricane force.

The island's easily comprehended proportions, the simple
contrasts of its colouring, gave it the jaunty, uncomplicated
romance of the islands of young dreams.   Seen like this,
there was no mud-ooze in the mangroves by the shore, no

leeches in the vivid undergrowth, no venom or disease in the insects with which it would swarm. There were only the clean, clear sky and the merry sea; the coral reefs, the surf, the yellow sands, the green woods rising up the rounded peaks.

It was the first of the islands of the Mergui Archipelago, the unfrequented group which parallels the Burmese coast. The dictionary meaning of archipelago ' is a sea with many islands ', and no better description could be found for that part of the ocean which lies between the Andamans and Burma, and from Arakan southwards to Sumatra. There are more than eight hundred of them; none of them very large, most very small, and we were to see a good many of them during the next two months.

From the distances at which we viewed them, they are entirely charming. Scattered so haphazard over such a small area of sea, they have the enchantment of the island dreams of us all. There can be few people, in childhood or even as veterans of the campaign of life, who have not dreamed of such islands as these: remote, serene, unassailable, where one could live in freedom from the vicious assaults of existence; master of oneself and all that one surveyed and in a life natural and at ease.

Whether it is possible to live thus in those islands I do not know. We were told later that there were men on them who did live in that way; beachcombers and derelicts of the East who had found their way to them and taken native wives, and who, with the fruits of their plantations and the harvest of the sea, contrived to live like petty patriarchs. I only know that it was the way that they appeared. Placidly anchored amidst a laughing sea, under a sun and skies always brilliant and warm, they had all the primary colours of the islands of romance. Blue of the sea, white of the crisping waves upon the yellow sands, the foaming green of their trees and the thickets by the shore. If you set yourself to depict the island of which you have dreamed, it would be the image of one of these, and all that was lacking in them was your hut amongst the trees.

Their atmosphere of remoteness from everyday reality seems to have infected whoever first charted and named them, and doubtless prompted him to give them such fanciful

names as Aladdin, Humpty-Dumpty, and Lalla Rookh
Islands; Jolly Boys, Pudding Basin, Cap and Feathers,
Freak and Grim Islands.   Some of the most decorative bear
such pretentious labels as Sir Elijah Impey or Sir John
Metcalfe Islands, probably after bygone potentates of John
Company or the India Office; many have such honest
British names as Peter Scott, Maclaren, Bamford, Griffiths,
Oates, presumably the names of men on ships which
charted them.   There is even a Page Islet, which the Sailing
Directions describe as ' a conical rock, covered with straggly
trees '.   Those who first went there had the chance to
perpetuate their girls' names more effectively than by mere
carving on trees.   It is pleasant to think of the lasses in home
ports who gave their names to those charming fragments of
land, and, since they have all the smiling mystery and casual
loveliness which girls should have, they could not be better
named.   So that amongst all the unaccountable names
which they bear, my favourites were Port Maria and the
Polly Islands; Elizabeth, Daphne, and Rosy Islands,
Sheila Rock, Charlotte Islet, and the Biddy, Violet, and
Marian Islands.

The only information I could discover concerning the
history or population of the islands, such as one can readily
find of almost any territory in the world, was in the ' Bay of
Bengal Sailing Directions ', Chapter One, page 19.   In the
same terse and informative language in which they discuss
currents, climate, and navigational hazards, the Directions
comment that ' the islands are almost uninhabited except
for the Salones, or sea gipsies, who wander from one fishery
ground to another in their boats.   There is an influx of
people to the Archipelago for the pearling season '.

And that ' Hastings and the surrounding islands are
frequently visited by the Salones or Mawkens who put in
there for fresh water.   They live in boats called kabangs
. . . which usually shelter a family of anything up to eight
persons and one or two dogs.   The Salones are of a very
nervous disposition and are terrified of strangers, but after a
little coaxing and kindness they readily become friendly.'

' The most important product of the islands,' continues
the Sailing Directions, ' is the shell of the mother-of-pearl
oyster, for which divers go down to depths of 28 fathoms,

and occasionally 30 fathoms; the season is from September to May . . . green snails and trocas shells are gathered for their mother-of-pearl shell, but . . . the bêche-de-mer is not found in any large quantity. The edible bird's nest of the swift and the eggs of the large turtle are also collected.'

The reader is also informed that the tracks of large animals have been seen on the beaches, and that the islands are also the habitat of the Nicobar pigeon, the flying-fox, monitor lizard, and tree crab. It is somehow reassuring, in this world of domestic uproar and international brow-beating, to consider that in one part of it there are the Aladdin and the Humpty-Dumpty Islands, where the Mawkens only need a little coaxing and kindness to become friendly, where the Nicobar pigeons and the flying-foxes live in the vivid trees, and the important things in life are the eggs of the large turtle and the shells of the green snail; where the eight hundred islands of the Mergui Archipelago lie inviolate on the sea.

II

We arrived at Tavoy Island early one morning, and anchored in the wide strait which separates the island from the mainland. We were nearer to a small, precipitous island off its southern tip than to Tavoy itself, which is larger than most of the islands of the Archipelago, and lay with the islands to port and the coast of Burma to starboard. My previous visit to that country had been to the drab, marshy area about Rangoon and Moulmein, so I was unprepared for the beauty of the coast at this point. Above a band of gleaming beach, range upon range of darkly forested hills rose inland towards the blue of distant mountains, with their ridges threaded by the white filaments of cascades. It was difficult to realise that this was the ominous territory of Burma. It was reminiscent of the background to mediæval Italian paintings, an effect enhanced by the purity and clarity of the air, and the brief evenings, lucent with sunsets of a nacreous tenderness, held a peace and silence which were almost sublime.

We were lucky in the season and weather of our visit, for we had day after day, week after week, of sunshine and sparkling air.　On our first afternoon off Tavoy, Sandy and I ventured to put one of the canoes in the water and head towards the smaller island.　This was our first outing in it, and it began at once to leak slowly but persistently.　Before long we were sitting in a couple of inches of water, and the sea, which had looked so calm from the deck of the ship, seemed to have developed a sinister commotion.　When we were unwise enough to glance around, we seemed to be very far from both ship and shore ; the canoe had all at once become both very frail and very hard to move.　Whenever she lifted to the little waves, I could see them silhouetted through her canvas sides.

" Paddle," said Sandy in forlorn tones, and we dug our paddles in harder.

Soon we began to blame each other for not keeping stroke, since we kept heading away from the smaller island, but at last decided to blame the tide.　Co-operating with it, we began to approach Tavoy Island, and as we came nearer saw a little palm-fringed beach with a hut standing upon it, and several canoes drawn up on the sand.

Our approach was watched by a group of natives who drifted up one by one to stand knee-deep in the water, and when we beached the canoe they helped us drag it ashore. Smiling and chattering, they surrounded us ; we grinned back at them and shook hands all round.　They were short but sturdily made, with flat, cheerful faces and sheening, coppery skins ; the children naked and the others wearing no more than a bit of twisted rag.

They urged us up the beach towards the house, which was built of bamboo and palm-thatch and stood on bamboo stilts.　I don't know whether they were all of the same family, but they followed us up the rickety ladder and into the house, where we were welcomed by a wizened, grinning ancient in a frayed sarong.

We squatted on the rush mats which covered the floor. Two or three women whispered and giggled in one corner, about a smoulder of fire on some flat stones, but the rest of us watched with grave concentration as the old man hacked the husk from two green coconuts.　Frowning and muttering, he hacked at the tough fibres with a great square-ended knife, dropping the refuse through a hole in the floor, but at last reached and pierced the young nuts. He pierced their eyes with a corner of his blade, and offered them to us, and the rest of them broke into a gale of delighted laughter as we tipped back our heads and sucked for the sweet milk. The laws of politeness were relaxed by the absurd sight of white men drinking out of coconuts.

We hadn't a word of each other's languages, but nodded and smiled affably at one another, and smoked the cigarettes which Sandy handed round. A memory from the *Boys' Own Paper* came to me, and I pointed to the headman's knife and enquired " ' *Dah* ' ? "

" *Tah, tah!* " he assented delightedly, and an awed ripple of repetition ran around the staring circle.

They waited for further conversation, but the word for ' knife ' had exhausted my Burmese vocabulary. With a necromantic gesture, however, I removed my dental plate and let it grin on my palm for a few seconds. This impressed them so much that one of the women let out a piercing scream and overturned her cooking-pot, and, as all visitors should, we left at the height of our impact.

Next day Sandy wasn't very keen on canoeing. I wasn't very happy about going by myself, but the fascination of the islands was strong enough to conquer my timidity. I found it easier going alone, especially since there was no need to waste breath upon argument, and I bore towards the smaller of the islands. As I approached, some noises floating across the still water in the lee of the island made me hesitate, rest on my paddle, drift, then slowly, curiously, glide into the deep shade which it cast. It was very steep and rocky; a mass of trees girt by a belt of black-grey rocks.

The noises continued, defining themselves as an exasperated piping, an irritable, high-pitched chatter punctuated by a constant knocking. Visions of savage rites entered my mind, and I impelled the canoe a few nervous strokes closer. Then I saw the hordes of monkeys which clambered about the rocks, swayed and fought precariously in the trees, and squatted in gabbling groups at the water's edge. The knocking noises came from an industrious combine engaged in pounding shellfish off the rocks, beating at them with stones and pieces of wood. Each one of them was surrounded by a loud-talking group, which demonstrated to him, and to each other, the right way to go about it. While I watched, one fisherman pounded his own hand by mistake, and after the first shriek of dismay leapt on the nearest of his hecklers, and took it out on him.

They paid no more attention to me than would a Sunday-school outing to a strolling policeman, and after I'd seen their care not to enter the water, I brought the canoe right up to the rocks. Actually, the way in which they gambolled and gobbled, nattered and wrestled, in their tight-fitting suits of grey fur with black skull-caps, was strongly reminiscent of a school picnic. Two shaggy old men, sitting a little apart from the others and vigorously blackguarding the younger generation, fell silent as I slowly floated past. They watched me carefully, until, like any grumpy old man the world over, one of them stood up and shook his fist at me, and yapped curses at this new thing which was drifting across his ken.

I planned to circumnavigate the island, a project which an on-shore breeze and sea, on the other side of the island, made more difficult than I had expected. But for the first time I gained that feeling of solitary exploration—always not too far from home—which was to lend to my canoe trips their particular savour. As I forced the canoe through the choppy sea, the sun turning the wind-swept spray to salt on my tanned skin, I knew the strange exhilaration of lonely endeavour. The ships, and all that they implied, were out of sight behind me; myself and my fragile craft were the only creatures of humanity in a world of sun, wind, and sea; the islands ringing the horizon, the steep rocks away from which I coaxed the canoe, a creaming line of surf on a distant reef. I was alone, unhampered by thoughts of yesterday and to-morrow, enraptured in a moment's supreme possession of a world of my own.

Two or three days later it was even better. For the convenience of the minesweeping flotilla, we had proceeded to another rendezvous nearer to their sweeping grounds. It was a kind of great basin formed by a semi-circle of islands, with a long, placid swell coming in through the entrance to the sea. We were farther from the shore than before, but the islands had beaches which drew me irresistibly towards them. I set off in the afternoon, taking it slow and easy, and the long swell rhythmically raised me on its curving hills and lowered me into its glassy valleys. As I neared the shore, a protecting arm of the land brought me into smooth water.

Whilst still within two or three hundred yards of the shore I paused to survey the wide half-moon of the bay which I was entering. The crescent of the beach was edged by thickets at the foot of thickly wooded slopes, which rose sharply towards the summits of considerable hills. Beginning to paddle again, I glanced overside, and was at once held entranced. It was as though I floated above a garden full of colours, and as though the water beneath me were no more than liquid air. The corals and brilliant sea-flowers under the canoe looked near enough to be touched, but when I put down my paddle I could see that I was still many feet above them. As I watched, a score, a hundred small fishes glimmered rapidly over their exotic meadows, followed by a lazy group of black-and-orange loiterers. A gorgeous starfish sprawled beneath them, and they were followed by something which looked like a tatter of black velvet.

I drifted and slowly paddled towards the beach, my gaze on the sea-bed. The coral fringe gave way to a floor of sand as silvery as stardust, and the water was so clear, the light through it so strong, that I could easily discern its fine texture. At last I grounded softly on the beach, near to a tiny stream which flowed from the slopes above.

Its surface was completely unmarked, and I strolled along it with the satisfying reflection that I might, indeed, be the first white man to set foot upon it. The dubious value of this attainment was dispelled from my mind by the sudden discovery of tracks in the sand; not of men, but the deep, round imprints of some large animal. My instantaneous thought was of Burmese tigers, and I beat a hasty retreat back to the canoe. I had hardly reached it and pushed off, when I heard a crackling in the thickets along the beach. My apprehensive glance saw not tigers, but a large, black, deer-like creature—a sambur—which came to the water's edge and regarded me mildly. He was followed by two or three smaller ones, and they strayed away along the beach at a cow-like gait, pausing now and again to lick at a patch of salty sand.

But anyway it was time to return to the ship.   I began to paddle back to my floating home, and was soon swaying again to the systole and diastole of the swell.   A flying fish, disturbed by the prow of my canoe, skittered erratically over it, like the flat stones which boys skim on the water.   Its blue-mottled, metallic little body glinted in the sun ; the drops from its gauzy wings left a long brush-stroke across the polished azure of the sea.   It disappeared with a soundless splash, and the tiny ripples spread undisturbed by the bland rhythm of the swell.

III

The following evening we sailed for Port Blair, capital and chief port of the Andaman Islands.   My previous knowledge of this group, in which there are over two hundred islands, was gained from my school geography, which casually dismissed them as ' island dependencies of India ', and from one of the Sherlock Holmes stories.   I think it was ' The Sign of Four ', in which the murdered man had been a warder in the convict settlements there, and it must have been this association that gave me a mental picture of them as low and barren islands.

Our first sight of them was of a fringe of palms which seemed to grow out of the water, and which was silhouetted against an orange sunset.   They indeed grew on a low and sandy island, but when I awoke the next morning my first sight was of steep and lushly verdured hills.   We were steaming close inshore, and as soon as I went out on deck I saw the bows beginning to swing towards a narrow inlet, with a low island lying off its mouth.   It was the entrance to Port Blair, which must surely be among the most beautiful harbours of the world.

We came into the entrance round a hilly point whose slopes were planted with the slender, elegant boles of coconut palms.   The southern point, Atalanta, is a rocky and wooded cape whose trees embower the old jail, which looks more like a fort than a jail and too harmless and prettily situated to be either.   The mellowed umber stones of its

walls reminded me of old buildings in Devonshire, an association aided by the country rising behind it.   The rolling
hills, steep combes, and long seaward valleys of the countryside about Port Blair have been cleared of jungle and scrub,
and the scattered bungalows and other buildings appear to
stand on lightly wooded downs.

Port Blair is on the southern side of the entrance channel,
which, though narrow, has shores irregular with small capes
and bays.   They are used as anchorages for small craft, and
grouped about them are such stores and warehouses and
similar buildings as the port possesses.   The only berth
alongside is on Chatham Island, in the centre of the channel,
a tiny island connected to the mainland by a wooden causeway.   A sawmill stands upon it, and alongside its single
wharf was the ' Maharani ', the islands' only regular visitor,
which makes monthly voyages from Calcutta.

From the northern shore of the entrance channel the
jungle-covered hills rise steeply almost from the water's
edge, up to a thousand feet on the highest, Mount Harriet.
We passed beneath them as we slowly steamed along the
channel, past the crumbling jetty on which a Viceroy of India
was murdered by an Indian convict, past the tiny Semiramis
Bay, and into the main harbour basin.

There was room in it for a hundred ships of the size of the
' Bengal '.   The pastoral shores to the south, with their
sward-covered downs and the feathery palms by the water's
edge, were in gentle contrast to the northward hills, whose
green ridges seemed to roll back into such distance that it
was difficult to realise that the sea was just beyond them
again.   A little river wound somewhere between them to
flow into the harbour basin, between banks of mangroves.
The main harbour passes through another channel into the
farther reaches of Navy Bay, a considerable anchorage in
its own right, and another stretch which is large enough to
hold Viper Island, a turtle-backed island planted with
regimented rows of coconut palms.   The size of the
harbour, landlocked amidst these rolling hills, and yet with
easy access to the sea, would seem to make it the perfect site
for a naval base.   But perhaps one should be grateful for
whatever destiny prevented it from being thus developed
and allowed it to remain in a serenity almost unspoiled.   To

those advocates of the quiet life who wail that there is no spot left on earth in which a man can live undisturbed, I recommend Port Blair. When the echoes of our descending anchor had died away, there was no sound at all. The distant bungalows on the green slopes might have been empty of life. The only sign of industry was a motor-boat which came slowly down the little river, straining to pull three enormous logs on which a dusky figure reclined peacefully.

The Andaman Islands are a fair example of the countless corners of the world which exist in a contented obscurity. There are five islands in the main group—North, Middle, South, Little Andaman, and Rutland Island—besides about two hundred more in the rest of the group, overlapping each other down through two hundred miles of the Bay of Bengal. They include the enchantingly named Labyrinth Islands, and a volcano which still emits steam, and are separated from the Nicobar Islands by the Ten Degree Channel.

Their history is brief, accented by two bloody periods. The first was during the initial occupation of the islands, in the middle of last century, when the Onge and Jarawa tribes resisted the invaders, and the second was after their occupation by the Japanese, who treated the inhabitants with their customary barbarity. Of the aborigines of the islands, the Onges alone became reconciled to civilisation, while the Jarawas have retreated to the jungles and the outlying islands, and are still reported to kill on sight.

Apart from these savage moments, the islands enjoyed a comparatively tranquil seventy years as a convict settlement. They were mainly used as a place of exile for those who were deported from India for the country's good; political agitators, life prisoners, and such unregenerate bandits as the Shere Khan who murdered the Viceroy. The prison system was as benevolent as any such régime can be, and after a spell of confinement the convicts were put to agricultural work, allowed to have their families to join them, and eventually loaned a piece of land to cultivate as their own. The population of the islands, which is almost entirely centred about Port Blair, is mainly Indian, but there is no longer a prison settlement there, and the remaining convicts were freed in 1945. It was suggested that the

East meets West—Malayan women outside a Johore cinema

A Courtyard-block of the Cellular Jail, Port Blair

islands might be made into a colony for the Eurasian population of India, and it is certain that there is ample room for a large influx of colonists. It is difficult to say whether the Eurasians would be colonists of suitable fibre for the gruelling task of making them habitable—or whether any but pure Asiatics could be settled in them for good. Their natural resources are still almost untouched, but their climate and terrain demand tropical labour for their exploitation. The coconut and its multitudinous by-products is the mainstay of the islands' economy, besides a quantity of valuable timber, but rice, tea, maize, sugar, coffee, cocoa, and rubber have also been successfully grown.

Our first visit to Port Blair was very brief, and after a couple of days we sailed for Grand Coco, on the northernmost tip of the islands. We were fuelling Royal Indian Navy minesweepers then, and one of them piloted us into the enormous bay, surrounded by low hills lovely with virgin forest. But we were only there overnight, and sailed again for Singapore to replenish our cargo. Our next rendezvous was to be Port Mouat, and about ten days later we entered it through a narrow channel not much more than a hundred feet wide. 'Port' was a somewhat hopeful name for it, since there was nothing whatever there but forest. It was another of those huge land-locked basins in which the islands seem to abound, and the flotilla was anchored there awaiting us. At first we had thought that their patient and exhaustive search for mines about such deserted shores was purely routine business, but we learned that this and the other uninhabited 'ports' where we fuelled them were visited by timber-fellers, who towed the logs away by sea.

It was in Port Mouat that Choff and Jackson had their affray over the bar, after Choff had been on a hunting party with the Indian officers. It was there also that Sandy came out for the last time in the canoe. We had paddled two or three miles away from the ship, when the tail of an enormous fish suddenly flirted out of the water a few yards away from us, and as though this was not sufficient discouragement for him, the canoe capsized just as we got back to the ship. For these reasons, the twenty-four hours that we spent there were not uneventful, and we sailed again for Port Blair the following morning. I had just been presented with the keys to the canteen stores once more, and was so engaged in wondering how we were going to throw a party for the officers of six minesweepers that I hardly noticed the picturesque route which we were taking back to Port Blair. Instead of sailing right round to the south of the islands and up again to get at it, the Captain was taking a short cut between Middle and South Islands. It would have been impossible for a larger ship, and as we sailed through the narrow, twisting channel, it sometimes seemed that branches from the trees on the steep, rocky cliffs would be caught in our masts.

We were to have ten days in Port Blair, and Choff had erupted into a spate of organisation. On our previous visit we had made friends with the R.A.F. officer commanding the small detachment there, and when we anchored again he brought the officer-in-charge of the radio station out to see us. We welcomed them with bottled beer and unfolded our plans for a little social intercourse.

Baird, the radio officer, was an official of Indian Posts and Telegraphs; a stocky man with a sallow, good-humoured, heavily freckled face. He was an able raconteur, and, at his ease in the mess-room, was soon telling us all about life in the islands. Allan, the young flying officer, had all the casual *bonhomie* of the R.A.F., though at the moment he let Baird do the talking.

When Choff returned to the question of entertainment, both of their faces changed.

" We've been thinking of organizing one or two parties for the people ashore," he said. " How about telling us the best ones to invite ? "

Allan looked non-committal and took a silent drink, while Baird shook his head and murmured, " Not me." Then he said suddenly, " Yes, I will, though—if you're ready to invite seventy of them."

" Seventy ! How's that ? "

" That's all the white people there are in the islands, and if I give you one of their names I'll have to give you 'em all. What sort of life d'you think I'd have after you've gone, if it got about that I'd selected the ones to invite to your party ? All the ones I'd left out'd never speak to me again ! "

That side of it had not occurred to us, so the question

was left in abeyance. After lunch they invited us to visit their establishments ashore, but only Choff and I landed with them and climbed aboard Baird's official conveyance— an enormous Army truck.

The roads in the Andamans are unpaved, and those about Port Blair were obviously laid out in the horse-and-buggy days. Like Devonshire lanes, they wind and swoop erratically over the downs and into the combes, their beds worn into a deep central channel by the monsoon rains. The truck tore gallantly at them, the engine grunting and whining and the broad wheels jolting on the ruts and stones, and ground slowly down their opposite declivities. Hump-backed Brahmin cattle and grey, bedraggled water-buffalo lumbered slowly out of our way, their small herdsmen urging them on with blows and shrill insults. We entered the little town, which, with its rickety wooden houses, littered streets, open-fronted shops, and noisy pedestrians, was the replica of any Indian village, and a flock of goats, dogs, and children scattered before us as we rumbled across the market-place. Once we had passed the shacks and bungalows, gardens and rice-fields, which were sprinkled about its outskirts, the going became easier ; we thundered over a wooden bridge and entered a long, shallow valley.

For some distance, though still winding and narrow, the road was smoother ; for several miles it ran through a tunnel of grateful shade, formed by the wide-branched trees which palisaded it on either side. Their regularity suggests that they were deliberately planted to form such an avenue, and they enhanced a delightful drive through country which, except for occasional steep knolls, suggested a gentleman's park. Our noisy truck, which often had to avoid a browsing cow or drawn in to the side to allow another vehicle to pass, seemed an anomaly ; it was pleasant to imagine how a white-clad administrator may once have ridden down that shady lane, congratulating himself on the efforts which had wrested the valley from the fruitless jungle and made it resemble some green area of home. The pale, humped cattle which grazed there, and the wide-horned buffalo snorting in a deep stream we crossed, seemed out of place; when a flock of green and squawking birds swooped out of

CHAPTER TEN

ANDAMAN AND NICOBAR

I

WE TOOK BAIRD AND Allan back to the ship with us, for they had both been invited to Choff's party for the mine-sweepers. It was the first of a series which we gave, or attended, on this and our next visit to Port Blair, culminating in an entertainment for the seventy *élite*. This first one was a prototype for the rest.

Our alcoholic provisions were low, but not so low as Jackson had maintained, and Choff and I surveyed them critically.

" Some of these Indian fellers don't drink alcohol, I b'lieve," he said hopefully.

" But when they do, they *do*," I reminded him. " And there's at least ten 'r fifteen Englishmen amongst 'em, remember."

I didn't want to be discouraging, only to keep things straight, and the British officers in the R.I.N. were a formidable leavening.

" It's whisky we're mainly short of," he fretted. " Plenty of gin, plenty o' wine an' liqueurs an' slops like that, but they won't want to mess about with 'em."

It was then that he had his inspiration.

" I know, we'll make 'em an iced punch ! " he exclaimed. " Something they can dip into—then we'll only need a few bottles on the side, for them that don't like it."

" You'll need some kind of a base for that, won't you ? Lemonade, or soda-water—something aerated ? "

" H'm—there y'are ! A couple o' cases of that Yankee beer—that's aerated enough, God knows ! "

We obtained one of the great pot-bellied metal bowls from which the crew ate their communal rice, and decanted the beer into it.

" Half-a-dozen grapefruit, now—must have fruit in a cold punch. Slice 'em up into it."

I obeyed, and then emptied the bottles which he handed me one by one.

" Nobody drinks this South African wine, and it's cheap enough. Use these."

" Liqueur de Dôm," he frowned. " What the hell's this ? Ne'er mind, chuck it in. Give it a good stir, now."

" Let's have a taste at it, then."

" H'm. Bit old-maidish—must be the fruit. Give it a touch o' brandy, and some o' that old vermouth that nobody'll drink."

" Dammit, it's mild as milk," he snorted disgustedly. " Give it a *bit* of a kick—here, pour in a coupla these— stir it ! "

" Let's taste."

" Crême-de-menthe ? "

" Ah, chuck it in. Can't do much harm."

" Not bad, really," he said at last. " Got a kind of a queer taste, but it grows on you. Pity we'd got no rum to spare—just what it needs to liven it up a bit. Still, it ought to hold 'em."

It certainly did. In answer to his comprehensive invitation, about forty guests arrived and somehow disposed themselves around the mess-room, alleyways, and cabins. Some of them were British—one was a Norwegian—but they were mostly Indians, and a fair cross-section of the many types which compose that complex land. They were all out to enjoy themselves, and before long were crammed about the piano which Michael Gough was ably manipulating, and chanting the old familiar songs.

The punch was excessively popular—so much so that we had to mix a fresh supply—but seemed to have a kind of delayed action. The recollection of the evening is that it was successful, but somewhat confused. Somewhere around midnight I remember swapping blows with the Norwegian officer, who was a pale, stout man, to demonstrate the comparative resilience of our stomach muscles. He won, and whilst I was nursing myself he began a long, rambling tale about his amorous adventures in Australia.

"—an' so I put mine hand in her dress, an' som'ting bited mine fingers. It vere a ferrut ! " he concluded dramatically.

" A wot ? "

" A ferrut ! You know vot dey use to catch rappits ? Like a—like a long, t'in, skeeny, furry rat, with teeth, owndly a kinda milk colour. She 'ad one ferrut for a pet, an' kep' it down 'er dress ! "

One party is remarkably like another, and the details are rarely interesting except to the protagonists. There seemed to be some kind of party every night we were in Port Blair. The flotilla entertained us in return, we invited the hospital matron and her six nurses to dinner aboard the ship, the Bairds were frequent visitors, and an increasing circle of shore acquaintance prompted further sociabilities.

Nor were the days wasted. I spent most afternoons exploring the harbour basin in my canoe, but there were more communal expeditions. These included Choff's decision to climb Mount Harriet, in which he was joined by Michael Gough and me. At the last minute the Chief Engineer decided to come along to take some photographs, and we landed at Semiramis Bay in the early afternoon. Mount Harriet towered above us, a seemingly impenetrable cone of forest and bush, and after several false starts we managed to find the path which led upwards. A creature like a small armoured snake, with legs and crab-like claws, scuttled ahead of us, and I hesitated.

" It's only a centipede," snapped the Chief. " What's the matter ? Waiting for someone to go first ? "

He shouldered past me and strode along the path, which began to climb rapidly and soon became little more than a vague track through the trees and undergrowth. For the first time I realised that ' impenetrable jungle ' is more than a phrase ; the jungle to each side of us *was* impenetrable. It was a solid wall of bush, bound together by creepers and wedged between the trees whose branches tangled overhead. I began to realise, too, a very little of what jungle-fighting must have been like. In places the path was so steep and slippery that we would have progressed as easily on our hands and knees ; our clothes became as sodden with perspiration as though it was pouring with rain ; we panted for breath in the damp heat which hung motionless between the trees.

For the most part the path ascended erratically ; a cleared

stretch alternating with a tunnel of undergrowth, and a comparatively level length with a piece almost perpendicular ; often we had to clamber over trees fallen across the path.

" The only way to climb mountains is to keep at 'em," grunted Choff when we suggested a rest, and plodded stubbornly on. Michael, as imperturbable as ever, swung after him, but the Chief gasped and swabbed his brow. " Don' care," he gasped. " Gotta take it easy f'r a few minutes . . ."

He sat on a rotting log, and I rested on my stick near him. I watched something like a brown thread drop on to his leg from a leaf and move briefly before settling. He mopped and panted.

" Borrow my stick, Chief," I suggested.

" 's all right . . . jus' a moment . . . they go too fast. . . ."

" What's that on your leg, Chief ? " I exclaimed after a couple more minutes.

Where the brown thread had been there was an obscene maroon growth.

" Ugh ! " he said, and dabbed at it, and it burst into a crimson splotch. " Ugh, leeches ! " he said.

I was wearing long trousers, and rolled them up. A half-dozen similar obscenities were clustered round my ankles. With memories from some book of travel, I touched them with the tip of my cigarette, and they shrivelled and fell.

" Look, it's these things," said the Chief. " Millions of 'em——"

He brushed a couple of brown threads off his legs. I saw then that the leaves and grass were a-swarm with them, moving with a kind of looping motion that expressed a horrid avidity. Whatever tiny instincts impelled them were sending them towards us ; towards the sixteen pints of blood which we had brought into their domain.

" Ugh ! " said the Chief. " We'd better push on."

We caught up with the others somewhere near the summit, just about where the path debouched into a rutted, leafy lane. We walked along it a little way, and passed a clearing to one side in which a group of men were repairing a kind of barn. All the land around now showed signs of past cultivation, and a few minutes more brought us to the summit and to the large, ramshackle bungalow which stood upon it.

The men whom we had seen, and others who came out to welcome us, turned out to be the advance-guard of the Eurasian colonisation scheme. I never enjoyed a cup of tea more than the one which they gave us. But they were not cheerful. It appeared that the colonisation scheme was only semi-official, and they had begun to regard the whole project with a kind of exasperated dismay. The house and land which they had been settled on were respectively tumble-down and overgrown, and they were expected to rebuild the house and to begin producing their own food from the soil. All their materials and tools had to be hauled up the mountain in a hand-cart, and they said that they were short of most necessities.

" We wrote for nails," said a lanky, snuff-coloured youth irritably, " an' the man in charge wrote back an' said there iss a kind of thorn growing in the jungle, which can be used e-kwally well."

A wiry little elderly man, with a stubble of black beard, came and looked at us with interested suspicion, but went away again without speaking. The youngsters fell silent. We were drinking our tea in their kitchen, which was simply the space between the concrete piles on which the house was raised. The cooking-fire smouldered between two blocks of stone, on one of which stood the enamel jug in which they had made the tea. A small, coal-black youth squatted by it, making chupatties ; pouring the batter on to an iron plate over the fire, and deftly turning the wafer-thin cakes as they browned.

" Come up on the veranda an' see the view," suggested the lanky boy.

We trooped up the rickety stairway into the house, which looked like the bivouac of exhausted troops. A shot-gun lay across an unmade cot, one of several which stood about with their mosquito-nets drooping forlornly, and half a dozen cartridges were scattered on the splintered boards. Someone had begun to unpack a case of household ware, and a large teapot stood abandoned amongst a litter of straw. It occurred to me that something besides encouragement from home was lacking in these youthful colonists, but all the same I would not have cared for their task, marooned on their venomous mountain-top.

The view from the veranda swamped any such reflections. I have seen Rio Harbour from the top of Corcovado, Sydney Harbour from the Bridge, but this was infinitely more impressive. If it were more accessible it would certainly be in the tourist companies' catalogues. It seemed that the prospect was over a vast land of lakes, set in the valleys of a country of green hills, until one realised that the lakes were the sea and the hills the multitude of lesser islands. They stretched to the mists of the horizon, in a pattern of silver and every shade of green ; a picture which at once called to my mind the music of Sibelius. Beneath us, at the edge of the billowing forest through which we had climbed, lay the harbour basin, with the ships looking like toys on a piece of watered silk.

" Aren't you taking any photographs, Chief ? " I asked.

" Light's not good enough," he grunted.

I thought that if I had dragged a camera up that devilish track, to a view which I was never likely to see again, I would have exposed a reel during an eclipse of the sun. But I held my peace, and we started our return. The young men told us that we could follow the lane all the way down, although it took a wide loop round the spur of the mountain, and we found it a good deal easier going than the track.

That was the toughest of our expeditions. We spent a delightful Sunday at Corbyn's Cove, in company with the Bairds, swimming in that flashing sea and boiling the kettle on a fire of dry palm-fronds. On another afternoon they joined us and some of the flotilla officers on a trip to see the elephants working round the timber-ponds. We took our launch up the little river which enters the harbour basin, for about three or four miles until we reached the point where it had been dammed to form the ponds. The great baulks of timber were collected there to be towed down to the harbour, and from the embankment above it a light rail-track stretched away into the bush, but there was no sign of any elephants. At last the rails began to jingle and vibrate, and one of them appeared round the bend. He was towing a truck upon which lay a massive tree-trunk, smoothed and trimmed.

He surveyed us doubtfully as he towed the truck on to the embankment. His baggy grey skin made him look dusty and dishevelled, and he had the air of an elderly workman fed-up with his toil and with the idlers who gaped at him. His *mahout* released his harness and yelled self-importantly, and with ponderous deliberation he lowered his head and nudged the tree-trunk off the truck, so that it rolled down the embankment and splashed amongst the others in the pond. We all exclaimed and commented, but he simply turned his back and faced the way he had come.

" The Japs ate most of the old elephants, and the others were set free during the war," explained Baird, as the creature plodded away from us. The enormous bottom swayed in its creased grey trousers, and he flicked his tiny tail. " It was a big job catching 'em again, too. Elephants 've got plenty of sense, and they'd sooner play about than work for a living."

And so would I, but for the moment our playtime continued. A day or so later an expedition was organised to visit Ross Island, which lies about a mile from the shore, opposite to Port Blair. Oval in form and a mile or so in length, it is low compared to its parent island, but its shores slope up to a steep ridge for most of its length. The many buildings, large and small, which are prettily situated amongst the trees gave it a populous appearance, but it was actually entirely deserted.

As we chugged towards it in the launch, Baird gave us some idea of the little island's former circumstance. Before the war it had been the seat of government for the Andaman and Nicobar Islands. The Governor, who had come fourth in precedence to the Viceroy of India, had resided there with his staff, together with most of the Europeans of private or official consequence. It had been the military depot for the area, with a garrison of British and Indian troops. The colony was small, but in its minor way it had nourished the pomp of Imperial majesty.

We made fast at a splintered jetty, where the Governor's launch had once waited for him. The houses round about it were shattered and windowless, with great holes gnawed in their red-tiled roofs.

" The swimming-pool was just here," Baird commented, and pointed to a concrete enclosure with the sea washing in through its breached walls. " And here's the cricket pitch and pavilion—and over here was the power-house."

We peered in through the window at the mangled and dismantled machinery which littered the interior. Baird sighed a little and turned away, and we followed him up the main road. He gestured towards one scarred, eyeless house after another, their gardens a tangle of tropical luxuriance, and in a matter-of-fact voice told who they had belonged to, his memories of them and their owners. There was something bizarre and shocking in the contrast between " So-and-so, Police Inspector, great big feller been a Rugger Blue, and a pretty little girl he'd married on his last leave," and the deserted silence of the houses under the uncaring sun.

The road began to climb up on to the ridge, beneath the shade of massive trees. Baird paused half-way, and pointed to the shell of a large building.

" This was the Club," he said. " It had the finest dance-floor in the East. Sprung, you know, and it was kept polished like glass. The Japanese tore it up for fire-wood . . ."

My imagination pictured the arrogantly casual, self-assured, self-engrossed society which had diverted itself within those blackened walls, and which to the music of the garrison band had moved over the finest dance-floor in the East. There was something both pitiful and wistful in the reflection, in the thought of a society which, like the South before the Civil War, had unknowingly outlived its day, but still danced on beneath the shadow of its doom.

The shade became deeper, the houses more imposing and more graciously spaced amongst the trees.

" This way," said Baird, following the road's branch to the left. " The Governor's mansion—— There was always a sentry here," he added with an ironic laugh, and nodded at the mossy gateposts as we followed him up the weed-thick drive.

Government House was a great two-storied wooden

building, its paint sun-scorched and peeling. We entered through the main door, which was missing, and passed into the wide hall. It was panelled in some dark, glossy wood through which an axe had been put in two or three places, and lengths of the carved banisters had been ripped away. Almost in silence, we wandered through the bare, deserted rooms; the white-panelled drawing-room, with its tall windows like lit pictures of forest, sky, and sea; the library with its pathetically empty shelves, the bedrooms one after another vacant and befouled.

Thus passes the glory of the world. . . . I was glad to get out of that echoing, lifeless house, whose corners seemed to whisper with voices unheard to the ear; the laughter of women, the ponderous solemnities of official males. . . .

" But was there any fighting on the island ? " we asked Baird as we strolled back down the drive, and he looked surprised.

" Why, no, I don't think so. A French battleship did a bit of shelling, I believe, but their shells mostly hit the old barracks. The Japs did most of this out of spite. But look, the old church is down here——"

Except for the tropical tangle of the graveyard, almost overtopping the gravestones, the grey stones of the little church, with its slate roof and spire, made it resemble countless village churches at home. The rusted wrought-iron gates sagged on their hinges; trailing brambles caught at our legs as we walked towards the porch.

It would have been more seemly, I think, if the interior had been ravaged by fire or some such natural force, instead of by such deliberate destruction. Glass from the windows still lay on the flagstones, and a small heap of kindling was all that remained of the pews. With laborious care some creature had dismantled the organ, and had crumpled its pipes over the bare and defiled altar. On the stripped stucco walls ideographs were smeared, and in one corner, caught in a pattern of sunlight through the jagged panes, lay a Japanese helmet. None of us touched it, for fear of an old booby-trap; it remained there like the symbol of all evil power.

The island was small enough for us to roam all over it in one afternoon, but it very shortly became wearisome. The silent, shattered buildings told their own tale eloquently enough, and its repetition by the floorless hospital, the empty bungalows, the offices with ' A List of Forms for the Andaman & Nicobar Islands ' still yellowing on a cupboard door, brought an oppression to the spirit.   We returned to the boat, and made a fire for our tea upon the shore.   Life goes on, after all, and we must continue into the remainder of our portion, but as we left the island I felt as though I had glimpsed the wreckage of an age.

II

Our second stay in Port Blair was concluded by the order to rendezvous with the flotilla at Sawi Bay, in the Nicobar Islands.   Even though we would be returning, we sailed regretfully, and overnight made the passage through the Ten Degree Channel.

Such a short voyage brought us to surroundings entirely different.   The Nicobar group of islands is low and sandy, so that from a little distance all one can see is their thick growth of coco-palms apparently growing out of the water. Sawi Bay was a wide crescent of beach before a low, sandy cliff which was crowned by these palms.   It was our most open anchorage so far ; the bay offered no shelter from the smooth swell which broke in surf upon the beach, and we had to roll and pitch to our anchor some distance from the shore.

A score of canoes came out to meet us as we entered the bay.   They were outriggers, built with a high, beaked prow, and some of them were paddled by twenty or more men with the aid of a matting sail.   The rhythmically flashing blades pushed them along at a good speed, and although they came to us in peaceable hopes of selling their fruit, chickens, and nuts, one could imagine how easily they would have cut out some unwary trading schooner in the old days.

In the afternoon, of course, I had to embark in my own canoe.   It was a long way to the shore, and the distance, combined with the surf, made me think that I would just potter about the bay.   But once on the water the beach magnetised me.   Aided by the wind and swell, I found myself approaching ever nearer, until I was lying off and on just beyond the surf line. I sat in my frail craft, keeping it stern on to the swell, which lifted and dropped it with heart-beat regularity, and gazed at the gleaming sickle of sand ; at the little group of natives staring at the ships and the beached canoes near them.

What they could do, I could do. I drew upon my memories of surf-riding in North Cornwall, where the thing to do was to keep on one's board a fraction ahead of the breaking wave, between the opposing forces of the wave and of its undertow. The next time, I thought, heading the bows towards the shore, and as the curving swell lifted me I paddled frantically.

The bows left the water, the canoe was half-on, half-off the curling wave as it sucked itself inward to break. I am doubtful yet as to how it happened, but for an instant I believe that the canoe was clear of the water. The wave shot it forward, and as it slapped down again bore it onwards, foaming around it almost up to the bows, so that I was riding in the roaring, sparkling surf.

It was a moment of intense exhilaration, lasting until the bows slithered on to the wet sand, and the natives rushed excitedly in and dragged it up to the beach. They seemed to be simple, natural people—particularly in their dress—and they examined the canoe with minute care and considerable discussion. I strolled off along the beach, went up a path into the palm-groves and wandered in them for a while, and down a road whose stones were too hard on my bare feet. When I returned, a semi-circle was still squatting about the canoe, with one of them giving a lecture upon its construction.

I joined them, and handed out a largesse of cigarettes. My own did not help me to solve my problem. It had been easy enough to get ashore, but how was I going to get out again through the surf. I had some idea of swimming out, towing or pushing the canoe and then scrambling into it beyond the surf-line, and at last stood up to make the attempt. The ships looked very far away.

I thought that it was out of courtesy that the natives launched the canoe for me, but they held it in the shallow water and gestured for me to get in. I suddenly realised that they must have their own method of launching manned canoes beyond the surf, and that they were about to employ it for me. So I got in, and three of them upon each side of me half-ran, half-swam into the buffeting waves. They lifted and surged the canoe over them, until they came to the last line of surf—the most difficult, since this was the one in which the waves actually broke. But their timing was perfect. At a guttural command from one of them their glistening, brawny arms almost threw the canoe over a wave as it curved to break. For a moment I thought that I would topple backwards, and then I was sliding safely down the other side, and waving to the heads which bobbed amongst the foam of the roller. I imagine that such a method was only possible because the surf-line was not beyond their depth, and that it would be out of the question in a really big sea, but I should like to have seen one of their canoes launched in the same way.

We sailed for Singapore again the next day, to replenish stores and cargo for our final rendezvous with the flotilla. I had also been charged with obtaining sufficient NAAFI stores to re-stock the flotilla's depleted reserves, and to put a cherished scheme into effect. This was the throwing of a grand dance for the European population of Port Blair, and a party for what would be, including the flotilla officers and ourselves, over a hundred people.

This gave Choff the opportunity to rise to absolute heights of organisation, though it was certainly not done without the fullest co-operation from everyone concerned. The party was given in premises ashore, with lighting plant and music by the courtesy of the R.A.F., and it is enough to say that it crowned our visit to the islands with resounding success. And noon the next day we weighed anchor again and sailed, for the last time, for Singapore.

CHAPTER ELEVEN

TRANSFER AND PERSIA

I

I ACCEPTED OUR RETURN TO Singapore with a fairly cheerful resignation. After all, we had been ordered quite unexpectedly on to both the Batavia and Andamans voyages, so there seemed to be no reason why we should not have similar luck in the future.

But, as the tempo of our days slowed into the old routine, the prospects of wider occupation became remote. Christmas came and went, and was seized upon as an excuse for a series of uninspired parties, and after Christmas there were several changes in the personnel. The Captain, Choff, the Chief Engineer, and Michael Gough all came to the end of their two years abroad, and Rigor Mortis was transferred at his own request; the entire Indian crew came simultaneously to the end of its time, and was replaced by Singapore Chinese. In most people's opinion it was a poor exchange.

I began to feel something of a stranger by the time all the transfers were completed. I didn't get on very well with the new Captain. His opinion of me, jovially repeated to me later by another shipmaster, was that I was ' a mouthy beggar ', and it is not necessary to expound upon his reason for that conclusion. With one thing and another, I was beginning to lose interest in the ship. I was both physically and mentally fed-up with the more liquid side of our pastimes, especially after one incident in which, as ' the mouthy beggar ', I collected a considerable telling-off, and was absent from many of the subsequent parties. Most of my pleasures became solitary—reading, writing, canoeing, walking, and so on—and during the months after Christmas we seemed to get on each other's nerves more and more. Quarrels and petty disagreements became more frequent, especially now that we had lost Choff's hearty common-sense to keep us in order, and the only way to avoid them was to keep to oneself. Conversation had degenerated into reminiscences of the past, verbal fencing at each other, grousing, and reckoning up how long it was until one's relief.

December, January, February, March, April, May—each month and week, almost each day, as like another as the pages in a book. On the 16th of May we were fuelling a large, top-heavy, and ramshackle Japanese vessel, engaged in repatriating prisoners from Java to Japan. She was swarming with them; golden-brown, muscular little men with shaven heads and simian faces, crawling all over her like so many cockroaches. They were all naked except for a cotton pouch; the sickly-sweet pungency of their reek and of the messes they were cooking permeated our ship as well as their own. They piped and chattered like so many monkeys, staring at us as we sat on deck and affected to be unconscious of them.

It was evening, and the sun was going down in a final blaze after a cloudless day. A big ocean-going tanker, the 'Bath Abbey', came slowly up the Straits and anchored quite near us. She had come in for bunkers and provisions, and I watched her idly, wondering how it would feel to be aboard her.

When I went to my cabin that night the porthole was blocked by the steel side of the other ship, as it was so often blocked by the sides of ships which we were fuelling. I stared at the weeping, rusty iron, a barricade against whatever fresh air might have entered. Overhead the ventilator roared, filling the cabin with a musty draught which was further churned up by the fan. There was no refreshment in them, no freshness; only a circulation of sodden, devitalised air. I had had a row with the Fourth Engineer that morning; I was as weary of my companions as they were of me. But I had to make up my mind to live in peace with them for at least nine months more: nine months of futile pastimes and monotonous routine; of sweat-drenched clothes, lethargic appetite, and of sunshine—the remorseless, intent, and almost tangible sunshine of the equatorial tropics, which at last becomes as dreary as the darkest winter's day.

But there was nothing to do but soldier on. So I turned

in, and was awakened considerably earlier than usual by Jackson, who was officer of the day.

" Hey, Sparky ! " he bawled excitedly. " Hey, wake up, Sparky ! Hey, look at this ! I had to show it to you before I gave it to the Old Man ! Look at it, eh ! "

For some reason the message was scrawled in red crayon upon a large sheet of paper.

" Gertcher," I said sleepily when I'd read it. " Yer a bit late for April Fools' Day."

" But it's not a joke ! It's true ! Read it ! No, gimme it here—gotta take it up to the Ol' Man ! "

He snatched it before I could read it again, and departed. He seemed to be far more exhilarated by it than I was. Which was strange, for it had said briefly that the Radio Officer of the ' Bath Abbey ' had fallen ill, and that the Radio Officer of the ' Bengal ' was to transfer to her forthwith.

I perched myself meditatively upon the edge of my bunk. So paradoxical is human nature that, although yesterday I had bemoaned my fate, this morning I could only regard the stroke which was releasing me from it as a confounded nuisance. I wanted to go, but a large part of me resented this upheaval and re-adjustment. I felt, unreasonably, that I should have been given more notice of the matter, but fortunately the decision was not in my hands. I rose and started to dress.

The Captain took a poor view of the whole affair, which had the effect of submerging my reluctance and making me extremely anxious to go. However, he cheered up a little on the way to Singapore, where we were to meet the Master of the ' Bath Abbey ' at the Shipping Office. Whilst we sat and waited for him there, he chatted quite pleasantly.

A large, red-faced, white-clad, and white-haired figure entered at last, and my present Master introduced me to him. He looked at me with an instant's understandable astonishment, since not long before I had had all my hair cut off.

Recovering himself, he began, " I'm sorry about all this, but you know it's not my fault——"

" Suits me," I said, and he frowned at the interruption, grumbling :

" Suits you it's all right, then, I s'pose."

The formalities commenced, superintended by the obese Indian who was the Shipping Master. With two strokes of my pen I released my former Master from any obligations towards me, and myself from any duties towards him, and placed myself under the jurisdiction of the Master of the ' Bath Abbey '. I could now, if I wished, assault, abuse, or otherwise despitefully behave towards my old Master without being guilty of mutiny, but if my new Master forbade me to do so, then I should be disobeying his lawful commands. I had placed myself subject to them—' on board, in boats, or ashore '—until the expiry of the Articles of Agreement which I had just signed. Whilst they remained in force, he was not obliged to allow me any of my pay or grant me any shore leave, could fine or prosecute me for the use of obscene language, carrying arms, brawling, assaulting or threatening a member of the crew, and for a multitude of other offences under the Merchant Shipping Acts. He was, in return, bound to feed, accommodate, and eventually pay me, to provide me with medical attention and to allow me to make an allotment from my pay.

This compact having been entered into, we all three returned to the base. The drive across Singapore Island can be full of interest and variety however often it's been done before, and while the other two chatted in the back seat of the car I sat beside the driver and saw it all with new eyes. Now that I was departing, it was as though I saw with the sharpness of first experience the gaudy, polyglot throngs which were scattered by the reckless car; the lively, humorous face of an old Chinese, the sullen patience of the coolies and the precarious arrogance of the young men sprang back into focus once more, as though my mental lenses had been dulled by the mists of self-engrossment. I almost regretted that I was leaving, and blamed myself for not having tried to reach below the surface of this shifting, kaleidoscopic life. But perhaps too often in our lives we lose the riches of the commonplace, to which custom has blinded us, and dissipate our strength in reaching for the mirage of the future.

Returned to the ship, I found that the steward had packed all my gear except for the accumulation of odds and ends, and without time to sort them out I threw them all into two mailbags. It was time to go. The boat was waiting to take me to the other ship, and for the last time I glanced round the iron-walled cell which had held a year of my life. It was once more anonymous ; stripped and waiting for its next occupant, who would find no trace of me there. But a part of me would always be there now ; even after the ship was destroyed, that little cabin would exist as long as myself, and everything that I had done or thought whilst it was my home was now woven into the fabric of my life.

Now that I was going I could see nothing but good in everyone, and as I made my round of farewells I was pleasurably touched by the generosity with which they praised my good fortune. It was a Saturday afternoon, and the base was deep in its week-end slumber ; nothing but my boat moved on the Straits as I waved farewell to the ship. It was beginning to rain, but the day seemed brighter than during any sun-glaring spell of the last few months. I looked almost with affection at the expressionless greenery of Johore, the swamps in which I had so often drifted in my canoe, and at the dreary buildings of the base. They had no claim on me now.

They were waiting for me on the ' Bath Abbey ', and the Second Mate, a sunburned and good-humoured Welshman, stepped forward to meet me as I came over the side. " Well, how does it feel to be shanghaied ? " he asked.

I glanced round at the spacious desks. " I can't tell you how good it is," I said. " When's she sailing, anyway ? "

" Any moment now. We've just been waiting for you. Come along and I'll show you your cabin."

" Where's she going from here ? " I enquired as I followed him up on to the bridge, which was higher than the ' Bengal's ' topmast.

" Abadan from here," he replied, " but we dunno after that. Mebbe home, mebbe another trip out here. We've just come from Japan, you know. Here's your room, and the wireless room's next door. I'll tell the Quartermaster to bring your bags up for you."

I stepped into the cabin and looked about me, wondering when I should wake up. Panelled in polished wood, and with three sliding windows instead of portholes, it had a settee as big as my bunk on the ' Bengal ', and the bunk looked like a double bed. There was a desk and an arm-chair, a soft carpet underfoot, and a big wardrobe.

" Like it ? " asked the Second Officer, grinning.

I looked at him dumbly. It seemed to my bedazzled senses that it was rather like asking a released convict whether he liked a room at the Ritz. He laughed at my expression, and turned towards the door just as someone else entered.

" Pearson, Third Officer," said the newcomer, extending his hand. He was what old ladies call ' a nice English boy '; blue-eyed and open-faced, even-tempered and a little shy. His fine teeth gleamed as he greeted me, and he turned to the Second Officer. " Stand by fore and aft, Jimmy," he said. " Pilot's just come aboard. Homeward bound, eh ? "

" Aye, maybe ! See you later, Sparky. Don't get lost, now ! "

I listened to the bustle of getting under way in a kind of happy daze. As the engines sent a throb of life through the ship's fabric I roused myself to potter about the wireless room. Nothing seemed quite real ; the Second Officer's warning was more significant than he had meant it to be, since I already felt as though I had come adrift from my moorings and might be cast up anywhere by this tide of life which was bearing me on again.

II

The first meal aboard a newly joined ship is often some-thing of an ordeal, but dinner that night was an exception to my rule. I felt in place and at home almost at once. I shared my table with three of the engineer officers, all Scotsmen of about my own age, and I might have known them for months. Sometimes one finds oneself amongst company which is instantly congenial, so that life seems to flow along without a flaw, and thus I found it to be on the ' Bath Abbey '. The days passed by with pleasant speed, and although I possibly saw everything in the cheerful light of my sudden release, I don't think that it was entirely that. The officers had been together for over a year, almost the whole of which had been spent at sea, and the time had

drawn them together, instead of wedging them apart. The
ship herself was luxurious, even apart from her contrast
with the ' Bengal '; superbly equipped and fitted in every
respect, and with everything about her reflecting a sensible
discipline.

The others were all hoping that after loading at Abadan,
the oil-port at the top of the Persian Gulf, the ship would be
ordered home, but for my part I didn't much care. I was
used to the idea of a longer spell abroad, and in such company and surroundings could almost look forward to it.
For the moment, it was enough to be at sea, and I knew
again the relief of passing into the Indian Ocean out of the
Malacca Straits. As we began the long traverse across the
Southern Bay of Bengal, to round Ceylon and head north-
wards into the Arabian Sea, I revelled in the breezy, sun-
filled days. But before we had passed Ras-al-Hadd, the
cape which is the tanker-man's signpost for the entrance to
the Gulf of Oman and the Persian Gulf, we had received
radio orders to load for Kuré, in Japan.

The paradoxical thing about the Persian Gulf and its
shores is that it is not only one of the most barren areas of
the world, but also one of the richest. I've heard it said
that, in the viscous and fœtid form of crude oil and its
derivatives, a million sterling a day passes Ras-al-Hadd,
bound for all the ports of the world. The slave-dhows and
gun-runners, which His Majesty's ships once ambushed on
these shimmering waters, have been replaced by an endless
parade of tankers, under the flag of every maritime nation.

Oil seems nearly always to be richest in those parts of the
world which are otherwise most sterile, and the Persian Gulf
might be the prototype for them all. Its demoniac coasts
have been compared to the landscape of the moon, but in
truth they defy comparison. There is nowhere else like
them. The coastline of the great Arabian peninsula, for
several thousand miles from Suez down the Red Sea, along
the coast of the Hadhramaut and up into the Persian Gulf,
and down the other side and out again and along the Indian
coast almost as far as Karachi, is but an endless repetition
upon a single theme—that of a territory under the harsh
curse of the sun. It is like a land under some Old Testament malediction, which has been sown with salt and

forbidden to flourish; a country without the soul imparted
by green and growing things, and in which the sun strikes
the tinder of destruction instead of the spark of life. For
thousands of miles the coast is a maniac commotion of hills
which look as though they had been hacked out of rusty
iron; a corrugation of ridges of the colour of burnt
mahogany. There is an eerie and lifeless variety of colour
in stretches of limestone hills, the ghostly and toneless rose-
pink, lemon-yellow, silver-grey seen in the ashes of a fire;
vast drifts of sand fill the valleys between crags of brazen
rock; great canyons gape beneath cliffs striped basalt and
brimstone. The desert constantly intrudes, in impassive
and featureless stretches patched with scrub, then yields
again to massive, liver-coloured escarpments, buttressed
with coppery scree.

The incredible thing is that, along these coasts which
appear to be as dead and harsh as ashes, life does exist and
somehow flourish. Small naked villages, and even towns,
cling to the shores of many a sterile cove. Most of their
sparse livelihood comes from the sea; they are the ports
for the enormous interior, and their men are bred to a long
heritage of sea-going. For centuries the dhows have sailed
with the northerly monsoons for Zanzibar, Ceylon, and
Ethiopia, returning when the faithful wind has swung round
to the south. They are seamen, these lean and frugal
Arabs of the coast, of a type which steam has banished elsewhere, and in their antique craft they navigate the width of
the tropic seas. Within the Gulf itself a brisk coastal trade
is maintained, and often the triangular sails may be seen
gleaming against the sullen cliffs, or like a flock of birds the
myriad white flecks of the fishing-fleets. For if the land is
dead, the waters teem with life, with fish and sea-creatures
of every sort, as though those warm and enclosed waters
were the breeding-place for the world. Sometimes the sea
as far as the horizon will seethe with the jumping of colossal
shoals; sometimes a mob of porpoises arch gleaming backs
above the surface. Turtles stop paddling along to raise
their heads on periscope necks and peer at the ship with
expressions like affronted old women; sea-snakes, of
venomous yellow or barred green and purple, sidle away into
the lucid depths. Sting-rays leap from the water with a

flap of their black wings, like evil birds, before falling again
with a slapping splash; the shark betrays his presence with
a fin like the corner of an assassin's cloak, and armadas of
giant jelly-fish cruise listlessly with the tides. Occasionally,
at the mouth of the Gulf, a blue-whale humps his broad back
out of the water and gasps like a fat man suffering from the
heat.

The fish are probably the only creatures who are free of
that burden. For six months of the year the climate of the
Gulf leaves no doubt as to the reason for its sterility. The
heat is beyond description; the dehydrating winds are
comparable to nothing beyond themselves. All traces of
moisture disappear before their avid aridity; one's skin
assumes the texture of sandpaper, and everything becomes
crisp and harsh to the touch. Shoes bend themselves
double, as though they had been left before a blazing fire;
paper cracks in the folding; the tobacco falls out of cigarettes; even the eyelids feel rough over the eyes, as though
deprived of their natural lubricant. And with the wind
comes the dust from the northern deserts, seeping persistently through the slightest cracks, and colouring the sky
with a ruddy diffusion.

In such a wilderness it is a little amazing to find the
stamp of modern industry. But industry has laid waste so
many of the pleasant places of the world that it is here perhaps in its correct environment. The industry of the
Persian Gulf is oil—the oil which lies in countless millions of
tons beneath the rocks and sand, and which is drawn from
its immemorial depths to fill the needs of the world.
Abadan, the first and largest of the oil-ports of the Gulf, lies
on the River Shattal-Arab, which is formed by the con-
fluence of the Tigris and Euphrates before they reach the
sea. The coast just here is not much higher than the river
itself, and must be closely approached before it becomes
visible as a band of gamboge desert stretching across the
horizon. The river-mouth is an indistinct gap marked by
a group of tankers waiting for the tide, and the river itself
is broad and looping, the colour of milky cocoa from the
earth which it bears down to build the constantly dredged
bar at its mouth. A little way inland, the squat date-palms
ranged thickly along its banks form a welcome ribbon of

green, until they are displaced by the grim plantations of the refineries.

*Abadan is the property of the Anglo-Iranian Oil Company, held on lease from the owners of the country. It is, without doubt, a monument both to engineering technique and to financial enterprise, and a tribute to those who laboured to build it under the most discouraging conditions. No one could deny that it meets part of the global demand for oil, nor that in doing so it creates work for thousands and fuels the machinery of modern existence. And that is exactly what it looks like: the very incarnation of such uncompromising words as labour and finance. It is a sprawling camp of industry, devoted to those ends alone.

From a ship at one of the river-side berths the gaze scans a surrealistic vista of convoluted apparatus, of squat, silvery-shimmering battalions of oil-tanks and a shadeless forest of iron chimneys. From one or two of these, like devilish candles, there flares and gutters eternally a great streaked orange flame, and drifts of greasy smoke which are snatched away by the wind. Such quantities of explosive gases are produced by the ' cracking ' of crude oil into spirits and fuels, greases and lubricants, that they can only be safely disposed of by burning. Enough of this gas must be burnt every day to suffice the needs of a small town.

Amongst the giant metallic thickets of the installation there sprawls a dreary vista of buildings of a dingy yellow or lifeless brown, the colours of the desert earth. They are transfixed by glaring, dusty roads, hedged off from each other by fences of steel mesh, and in their uniform utility are as dispiriting as the barracks of a concentration camp. They include every necessity for an industrial town—workshops, offices, hospitals, stores, workers' quarters, schools and canteens—but make little concession to anything but grim utility. The bungalows and clubs of the European residential area are somewhat better, but only by comparison. The dust-smothered patches of green are as forlorn as the pictures in a prison cell; the amenities of the place are as cheerless as an orphanage playground. The very fact that there are amenities, the overwhelming fact of the whole establishment, is a tribute to the planners and

*The following three pages were written before the events of Summer 1951.

builders of an industrial area whose General Manager is, in effect, the Governor of a colony.

The parched, irritant air is laden with the putrid pungency of oil, creating an atmosphere somehow as taut and goaded as that of the place itself. Nothing matters but production ; the stinking fluid gushing from the desert must be constantly forced through the refinery and the products shipped away, in a process as urgent and inhuman as the flaring of the waste gases. There is little time or thought for anything else ; it is reflected in the strained, irritable attitude of the officials, the neurotic efficiency of underlings. About the only people who take life easily are the native soldiers whom the Iranian Government places as guards upon the ships ; ragged, languid, and underfed, rather anxious to use the obsolete carbines they are toting, but nevertheless with a good-humoured and philosophic air of being the only men around who know when they are well off.

The native town, of the same dirty fawn colour as most of the local buildings, exists side by side with the installation in an atmosphere of morose squalor. The people, who maintain life under conditions of degenerate poverty remarkable even in the East, are accomplished robbers, and a large gendarmerie is employed to keep them in their place. By way of contrast to them there is the large European population of the refinery, composed almost entirely of British supervisors, engineers, technicians, chemists, clerks, and so on. In order to make life tolerable for them, they are given the best possible living conditions, and, in the pathetic and laudable manner in which human beings will make the best of any environment, those of them whom one meets will stress the advantages of their employment whenever one comments upon its drawbacks. I talked to one of these on my last visit to Abadan : a dapper little Welshman with a Cardiff twang and a hair-cut like a sergeant-major's. He was some kind of a clerk, and we fell into conversation as he waited for the Captain. It was midsummer, and his papers crackled as he nervously sorted them through his hands.

" How much longer have you got to do out here ? " I asked.

He gave me a wistful smile, and replied, " Only one more

summer," as though the brutality of that reflection had made him forget that there were other seasons in the year.

" Is that so ? And what then ? "

" Well—home on leave, I s'pose, an' then come out again."

I looked at the buildings crouched under the remorseless sun, the haze of smoke and dust, and the quivering, streaming flames. " Blimey," I said. " It must agree with you."

He gave a kind of twitch of his face. " Well, it is not so bad, you know," he said defensively. " The wages are good, and there are nice 'ouses to live in, an' good food, an' servants, an' we 'ave the Club, with a swimming-pool, an'— why, some of the men 'ave their wives an' famil-ees out 'ere, so it cannot be so bad, can it ? Only for the 'eat, it would be nice, an' around Christmas it gets quite cold, see ? And I shall 'ave a good leave, and passage paid and everything, an' the work is not so 'ard, so long as you keeps your nose clean. Oh, there are worse places, I suppose. Think o' them pumping-stations way back in the desert, now."

" But what do you do with yourselves ? In your spare time, I mean ? "

" I told you, we 'ave the Club, see ? An' people give parties, an' so on. Oh, we 'ave everything at the Club. Billiards, bar, swimming, pictures, library everything ! "

" But don't you ever go outside Abadan ? "

" Well, there is nowhere to go, is there ? Only the desert. Basra, they say, is a nice town, or Teheran ; but I dunno. I don't fancy these native places, some'ow. Dirty, they are, an' the people so ignorant. Just as soon knife you as . . . no, we keeps ourselves to ourselves ; all at the Club, an' people's 'ouses, an' so on. Just like you keeps to your own district at 'ome, you know."

He brooded for a moment, and then murmured, " No, it is not so bad, once you gets used to it."

However, I was thankful, for my part, that the tense efficiency of the place does not keep ships in very long, and enables a ten-thousand-ton tanker to be loaded in twenty-four hours. It was June when the ' Bath Abbey ' left there for Japan, with the temperature already nudging 115°, and I did not look forward to our return in July or August.

But there was time to pass till then, and new places to see. When we got out of the Gulf, the South-west Monsoon had begun, so that we had cloudy days and damp, heavy winds for most of the way back to Singapore.   We were calling in there for bunkers and fresh provisions, and I looked at the familiar landscape with some pleasure as we sailed up the Straits.   It was good to think that I'd escaped from it, and that it had no hold over me.

It takes a week or so from Singapore to Japan, and I was looking forward to a glimpse at that strange country.   A couple of days after leaving Singapore I awoke feeling dismal and bewildered, and in the afternoon took to my bunk with a high fever.   I was annoyed, but not unduly worried, since I thought that it was a recurrence of the malaria which I contracted in West Africa, and which occasionally wakes to life again.

This time the familiar alternation of chills and fever lasted for two days, and when I dressed again I felt depressed and listless.   I seemed to have lost my appetite ; I wanted nothing to eat but dry bread and tea.   My table companions observed this with morbid interest.

" What's the matter with you, Sparky ?   You'll die if you don't eat, y'know."

" Ah, I feel kinda sickish all the time, that's all.   I've a queer kind o' lump in me belly."

" A lump !   Yer ruptured, mon ! " exclaimed the Fifth Engineer in horror.   He was a tall man with pale, wild eyes, and large cavities in his front teeth, which, since he distrusted dentists, he had himself plugged with dental cement.

" Ah, a rupture," derided the Fourth Engineer, in a throaty Glasgow drawl.   " He'd be all doubled up an' screamin' if he had a rupture.   Didn't the Second on me last ship have a rupture, an' lie on the deck of his cabin screamin' all the night with it ?   They had to take 'im ashore an' cut 'im.   Or was it an appendixitis I'm thinkin' of ? "

" I'll tell you what he's got," observed the Third Engineer calmly.   He was a dark-eyed, hook-nosed young man, which, together with his chin beard, gave him a faintly fiendish appearance.   " He's got the jarndice.   Can't ye see the yellow in his eyes ? They're like yolks of eggs. It's the jarndice you've got, b'y, an' the lump in yer belly's yer liver swelling."

" Ah, go 'way, with yer jarndice," I scoffed uneasily. " Me eyes are always yellow, ever since I had malaria."

He nodded soberly, and went on eating his dinner. " You'll see, boy," he said, with calm patronage. " You'll see."

Privately I was convinced that I was having some kind of nervous breakdown ; that I was, in fact, at last ' going round the bend ', which was so often quoted as being the ominous destination of people in Singapore. I could settle to nothing ; would read a couple of lines of a book and fling it aside ; start a letter and tear it up ; would lie on my bunk and after a few minutes rise and roam uneasily about the ship. A broken pencil-point would goad me into a silent and febrile rage. I could not start a conversation without turning it into a quarrel, it had become a tremendous effort to do anything at all, and I viewed life through a dismal fog of depression and disinterest.

When the ship arrived in the Inland Sea of Japan, and steamed between its pine-clad islands towards Kuré, I lay in my bunk and stared at the bulkhead, wondering if I could go on feeling like this until we arrived home.

Fortunately I had a toothache as well. Otherwise I should have been afraid to go to a doctor, but since I had to go to one in order to get a chit to visit the Army dentist, I thought that I might as well tell him how I felt. At least he might give me some kind of bromide which would make me feel a little less suicidal.

I was directed to go to the Receiving Post, which was a small, drab hut on one of the quaysides. A number of Australian soldiers were lounging in its shade with their hats tipped over their eyes, and arguing in bored, incurious voices.

" Down' be a silly barstud," drawled one of them as I passed. " That jock couldn't ride a ruddy rockin'-'orse dahn-'ill."

The doctor was a sharp-eyed, staccato young Indian lieutenant, who drummed his fingers impatiently as I rambled through my symptoms.

" I'd had malaria before, an' so o' course when I started sweatin' again I thought——"

" Yess-yess, yess-yess. Take off your clothes and lie on the couch, please."

He probed with hard, clammy fingers. " O-ah, yess, a spleen. Oh, my goodness, a liver. Tst-tst. And eyes, also. Tongue? Ah-ha! Kindly give me a specimen in this bottle, pleass! "

He sat down again, watching and drumming. " O-ah, yess," he said. " No doubt about it. Four weeks in hospital, on a fruit diet. I will give you a chittie, and you go at once."

" B-but what's the matter with me? "

" You have infective hepatitis. Very common in the East."

" Infectious *wot*? "

" Infective hepatitis. An inflammation of the liver."

" Like jaundice, you mean? " I asked hopefully, and he shrugged.

" Call it jaundice if you like. Anyway, you must go to hospital."

" But, doctor, I'm just going home! My ship sails to-morrow! I——"

" Do you wish to die of atrophy of the liver? No? Then hospital, if you pleass. Take this to your C/O, and this to the hospital. Sooner the better, pleass. Orderly! Next patient, pleass! "

I didn't know whether to be pleased because I had only a physical ailment, or annoyed because I was being pulled out of the ship. On the whole I didn't much care.

" My God! " said the Captain when I told him. " This ship's getting to be a regular death-trap for Radio Officers. All right, Sparky, get the Second Mate to 'phone the Navy for an ambulance to take you and your gear up to hospital. You might as well do it in style, after all."

Miya Jima

In the Junk Harbour, Hong-Kong

CHAPTER TWELVE

JAUNDICE AND JAPAN

I

"RATHER LETTING THE SIDE down, isn't it?" demanded the Sister. "Saying you'd eat your soup and then leaving it all."

I gazed mournfully at my bowl of tomato soup. Red, creamy, and rich, with golden globules of fat adrift upon its surface, in normal health I would have gulped it down with glee.

"It's too rich for me, Sister," I explained. "Besides, I'm not as hungry as I thought I was."

"You must get your appetite back sometime," she said severely, "or you'll never be out of here. Is there anything else you could eat? Even some dry biscuits with your tea?"

I looked back at her from my pillows. She was short and rounded in her grey uniform dress, and her face between the crisp lines of her head-dress was softly curved, with a complexion as fresh and tender as an April afternoon.

"Cornflakes," I answered. "Or oysters. Or some of that fruit the doctor said I should have."

"There's no fruit ration until the next boat arrives from Australia, and there aren't any cornflakes. And I've told you time and again you can't have oysters in Japan, even if you're well. You get typhoid from them. So you're just being silly."

The two naval lieutenants looked up from their interminable game of Chinese Checkers.

"He's like a pregnant woman," observed the one who had chopped the top off a finger. "The only things he fancies are what he can't get."

"That is a fallacy," remarked Sister crisply, and the Mahratta officer looked up from his plate of curry and rice.

"What is a fallacy, please?" he asked, and the Sister explained at length. "No, I meant what is the meaning of the word, a fallacy ? " he asked patiently when she had finished.

The ruptured Intelligence Officer peered over his spectacles. " A misleading argument or a mistaken belief," he said primly, and returned to his book.

" Did you ever ! " exclaimed the naval lieutenant, and his companion guffawed.

" You should try some of this curree—it is most good," said the Mahratta, looking at me across his second plateful.

His muscular, semi-nude body had the dusty bloom of a ripe plum, and I envied him his lack of perspiration, for although none of us wore anything but pyjama trousers there was no relief from the clammy heat which hung motionless in the ward. It was hotter and damper than Singapore ; the massive concrete building which had been a hospital for the Imperial Japanese Navy baked under the sun. The officers' wards were on the fourth floor, and from their windows we looked across the formless, sprawling city of grey shacks which was Kuré, towards the hills which were its landward barrier. Like extinct volcanoes, and with their sterility somehow emphasised by their wiry garment of pines, they were of that conical form which seems to find endless repetition in the landscape of Japan. The hospital stood on the lower slopes of one of them, in a hollow square about a courtyard of the same yellow, sandy soil as the rest of the terrain.

I had been in there a week, most of which had been spent in lying on my bed in a liverish daze. I had been tested for malaria, gastritis, tuberculosis, syphilis, and various other diseases ; but they had eventually decided that I was suffering from nothing more ominous than jaundice, and that I must lie there until it had run its course.

" Are you relieved now that you've started going yellow ? " asked one of the doctors cheerfully. " Most jaundice cases get pretty neurotic—think that they're going to have nervous breakdowns, until the bile begins to show."

" Ha-ha," I said feebly, to denote that I was far stronger-minded than that.

I hadn't much liked the idea of an Army hospital, imagining that it would be staffed by people as callously efficient as sergeant-majors, so that I had been pleasantly surprised by the kindly interest of the doctors and the calm friendliness of the Nursing Sisters. The best of hospitals seems necessarily to be somewhat detached and inhuman, but there was something comradely about this one which seemed unusual. The staff appeared to have a brisk cheerfulness and the power to infect their patients with something of their own vitality, which would have been remarkable anywhere, and was even more so during a Japanese summer.

" ' Stone col' dead in de market,' " boomed the radio, as we settled down to another oppressive afternoon. It was tuned to the British Commonwealth Occupation Forces station, whose operators seemed to be fascinated by a limited repertoire of records. " ' Ah'm just er prizzunuh a' Lahv,' " it crooned nostalgically through the throbbing noons, and " ' HEY, Baba-re-bop ! ' " it roared into the languid evenings.

Life assumed a placid and not unpleasant monotony. I became familiar with a new circle of acquaintances : the compact, black-a-vised Canadian chaplain who sat by my bed and talked politics ; the Night Sister, dark and slim in her khaki slacks ; the tall, fair Australian Red Cross lady, who brought me cigarettes and library-books and lingered to discuss, in her attractive Colonial intonation, the differences between Sydney and Melbourne ; the R.A.M.C. orderlies, the lethargic, melancholy Indian servants and the sleek-haired, short-legged Japanese women who polished and swept amidst hushed giggles and whispers, and the remainder of the patients in the officers' wards, with whom I swapped symptoms with the relish of old wives, and personal histories with the abandon of railway travellers.

After a couple of weeks I had regained my appetite, and was allowed to get up. In the afternoons I paced up and down the huge flat roof on which the tar was simmering in the sun, in earnest conversation with a moustachioed major of the Regular Army. We paused in our discussions of marital relationships, philosophy, socialism, and the other mysteries of life to sit on the broad coping and gaze down at the nurses sporting in their swimming-pool, or across at the tangled wreckage of the Japanese naval dockyard, or the brassy dust of the recreation grounds, where the Australians played cricket with a religious intensity.

Then one morning the little group of doctors on their
rounds paused expectantly by my bed. The lieutenant-
colonel who led them asked, " What's going to happen to
you when you leave here ? "

I had not the slightest idea. " I dunno," I answered.
" I s'pose that my skipper will have told the proper people
when I was paid off here, and they'll be doing something
about it."

" But who are the proper people ? "

" The Navy, I suppose. Their Sea Transport Officer
deals with merchant seamen—takes the place of the Shipping
Master or the Consul in other foreign ports."

" Have you been in contact with him ? "

" Nope. The Red Cross girl's been trying to get hold of
him for me, but he always seems to be busy."

" H'm. Well, we're going to discharge you next week.
We're sending you down to the Australian Convalescent
Depot at Miya Jima for a week or so, so I expect you'll be
able to get hold of him from there. Put out your tongue."

I obeyed, and subsided upon my pillows to ponder this
fresh development.

Albert, the extrovert warrant officer from the next ward,
came bustling in as soon as the doctors had gone. " Good
morning ! " he bellowed. " What are *you* looking so
cheesed-off about—got hardening of the arteries now ? "

He sat on my legs while I told him my news.

" Ooh, you're lucky," he assured me. " It's a luvly
little place, is Miya Jima. It's an island, you know. A
sacred island, sort of, what the Nips make pilgrimages to.
It's got two thousand steps to the top of it, and when you
can climb the steps they reckon you're cured. Make you
do physical jerks and all sorts there, they do, to make you
fit again. Oh, you're gonna like it there ! "

His description made me doubt it, but a few days later I
found myself dressed and ready to go, standing in the office
with a crowd of other patients waiting to receive their dis-
charges.

" Pay-shunts for Meeya-Jeema ! " roared the orderly
sergeant, and two others stepped forward besides myself.
They were a small, boyish naval rating and an equally under-
sized private in bedraggled jungle green, with a cast in one

eye and lank wisps of hair drooping from under his beret.
" 'and these to the M.O. when you gets there, and don't
read 'em on the way," the orderly sergeant warned them, as
he handed us the brown envelopes containing our papers.

" How do we get to this Miya Jima ? " I asked him, and
he gave me a blank stare.

" I dunno, sir, I'm sure," he said. " There's a ham-
bulance waitin' to take you to the ferry wot takes you across
to Eta Jima, an' I s'pose they sends you on from there.
Best ask at the Orstralian 'orspital on Eta Jima."

My two companions were apparently more used to such
vague directions than was I, for they philosophically
shouldered their kit and waited for me to lead the way.

I walked out into the courtyard and surveyed the numerous ambulances drawn up in the sun, and they followed me
from one to the other as I questioned their drivers.

" Are you the coves for the ferry ? " demanded the
Australian in charge of the last one we approached. · " Get
in the back, won'tcher ? "

We climbed in, and were driven through the winding,
unpaved streets in a cloud of glittering dust.

" Here y'are," bawled the driver as we jerked to a stop,
and we found ourselves by a long jetty with the ferry moored
at its end.

The other two tramped along to it, and then halted by the
gangway, looking enquiringly at me. I suddenly realised
that, on the strength of my shoulder-straps, they had
abandoned all responsibility for their own movements into
my charge. When I had obtained three passes for the
ferry they followed me aboard, and when we had made the
crossing they waited patiently until I made further enquiries, and obtained 'bus passes for the Australian hospital
on the other side of the island. They took their places in
the 'bus behind me, and trailed patiently after me as I was
passed on from one hospital official to another. A harried
sergeant finally informed us that there was a daily ferry for
Miya Jima, but that it did not leave until late afternoon.

" What'll we do till then ? " I asked.

I was beginning to develop something of the same
unquestioning dependence upon someone else's initiative.

" You'll just have to stick around," he replied with a

shrug. "Come back here at noon, and I'll fix you up with some grub."

I deposited my two dependents in the Red Cross recreation room, where they sank on to a sofa and immediately opened the envelopes containing their papers.

"You aren't supposed to read those, you know," I observed mildly, as they began to do so.

One of the private's eyes looked at me through his hair, whilst the other continued to regard the side of his nose.

"Thet sar'nt's allus the same way," he answered cryptically, and so I concluded that it was none of my business.

I was too restless to stay with them, and began to wander round the hospital buildings. They were enormous: colossal white cubes of concrete connected by arched walks through the gardens between them, and flying bridges from their upper stories.

A limping private in hospital blues and a slouched hat meandered towards me while I sat on a shaded bench, and after a few preliminaries burst into eager conversation.

"During the depression I near went t'sea meself," he explained, "but I went bush instead. You know— humpin' th' swag f'm one stytion to anuvver. Best years o' me life, they were. I did everythin'—shepherdin', timber-gettin', ditch-diggin', everythin'. You know what boys are."

He had a lean, angular body and a sharp, sunburnt face, accented by rimless glasses.

"Got meself lost in the desert wunst," he said proudly, and proceeded to tell me about it. "An' then I joined the A.I.F. Caw! That was an eye-opener, if you like!"

Eventually he told me that the hospital had formerly been the Imperial Naval Academy, and expounded upon the Spartan régime which had been followed by the cadets.

"No wonder their navy got beat," he said. "They wore the poor barstuds to a shadder while they was kids."

He talked on and on until noon, when I went to collect my two companions. The sergeant led us to a mess-hall as big as a Zeppelin hangar, and afterwards the afternoon yawned away until he burst upon us with the admonition to hurry up, the ferry was waiting. The hospital faced the water, and we discovered that the small landing-craft which we had watched being loaded at the stumpy pier, with sides of meat, boxes of provisions, and bags of laundry being dumped into her by trotting coolies, was also the ferry for Miya Jima. Another sergeant, who, with his superb figure and moustached brown face under his bush-hat, looked like a propaganda picture for the Australian forces, stood outside the tiny wheel-house. He spoke to us in a cockneyish whine which came incongruously from his sculptured lips.

" 'r' yeou th' noo pyshunts fer th' Depow? 'op aboard, wowncher?"

A coolie deposited the last laundry-bag at my feet, while the sergeant exchanged pleasantries with his comrade ashore. They discussed some mutual acquaintance with great heat, coming to the conclusion that he was both a wowser and a baldy-headed old clunk.

" 'e's a reel bag-snatchin', snaggle-toofed old cow," roared the sergeant aboard to the sergeant ashore above the snorting of the engine, and bracing his massive legs against the jerky departure of the craft.

The other was unable to better this description, and waved admiringly as we turned away into the Inland Sea.

II

Kuré, the former secret naval base where the two biggest battleships in the world were built, and the fated Hiroshima, and Eta Jima and Miya Jima and much else in the Commonwealth-occupied area of Japan, lies in or around the country's Inland Sea. It is not really inland at all, nor even a sea, but the broad strait between the main island of Honshu and the smaller one of Shikoku. The entrances to it are so narrow, its coasts so rugged and irregular, and it is so prolific with islands, that it does indeed give the impression of being land-locked and without connection with the open sea.

The idea of a ferry had made me think that it would be only a short trip from Eta to Miya Jima, but it took well over two hours. I sat on the side of the landing-craft, swinging my legs and singing the first four lines of " I'm

just a Prisoner of Love " over and over again, whilst the
booming engine drove us through the channels between
the islands.   The declining sun was flung back in flashing
splinters from the sea, laying an orange patina upon the
smoothly muscled bodies of the Japanese crew and lending
the scene the silhouetted, vivid delicacy of their native
prints.   The mountains of the mainland darkened against
the western sky ; on one conical island after another the
shadows lengthened in their dark crests of pines.   On their
lower slopes the tiny mushroom-hatted figures still bent
patiently in the rice-fields whose green terraces mounted
their steep sides, until they were replaced by vegetable
patches to the edge of the pines ; the scratching, patient
industry conquering the legend-haunted woods.   Behind
their impression on my mind there rose the glowing picture
of the islands of the Mergui Archipelago, lying like lush
garlands on the dreaming sea.   Here was another sea with
many islands—the Naikai, the Inland Sea—but they were
spined and harsh, fragments from the teeming land whose
soul is as sombre as the forests of pines.

Beneath me in the boat, the soldier and sailor squatted on
the boxes and discussed women with intent fascination.

" For fifty cigarettes, mind you," emphasised the sailor
in a soft Irish drawl, " for a tin of fifty cigarettes you cud do
as you pleased . . ."

I yawned, weary with the sun and the journey and the
first day out of hospital.   The landing-craft swung its
square bows round yet another promontory of tawny rock,
and another island slowly separated itself from the seemingly
impassable procession across our horizon.

" There she is," yelled the sergeant.   " That's Meeya
Jeema, an' that's the Depow."

The island's black-green coverlet of pines ascended from
the water's edge up to its twin peaks, without the hard-won
belt of agriculture which encircled the others.   Out of
them, near the strand, there rose the fretted gables of a
large wooden building.   With the setting sun there had
come rain-clouds from the sea ; they began now to clump
together, hiding the bright sky, and the grey mingling of the
storm and the evening made the house amongst the pines
resemble something from a Gothic tale.   The first drops

began to fall as we rounded a wooded point and entered the open harbour, along whose curve were huddled the houses of the town.

" Th' jeep'll bring yer kit up with the rest o' th' stores," said the sergeant as we made fast to the jetty. " We'd best go on ahead, or we'll be late for our teas."

The ragged clouds drooped low upon the hillsides, the rain teeming faster from them as we scuffled through the sandy streets of the town, between the rows of grey, ramshackle wooden houses. The sailor and the private had no coats, and their cotton uniforms soon clung wetly to them as we started along the narrow, rutted road between the beach and the hillsides, from the town to the jetty.

" There's their bloomin' sacred 'orse," said the sergeant, and nodded towards a stall out of which peered the lugubrious countenance of a dirty-grey old stallion. " The silly barstuds piy the priests to feed 'im with little saucers o' beans. Supposed to be ten thousand years old, 'e is. An' there's their bloomin' Tori, s'posed to be the biggest in Japan."

I peered through the mists of rain at the great vermilion columns of the Tori standing out of the water. Between them they supported the two scrolled and upward-curving demi-lunes, one above and larger than the other, which seem to be to Buddhism what the Cross is to Christianity.

" You shoulda been 'ere last week," said the sergeant, with melancholy enthusiasm. " They 'ad the Moon Festival then. They all put little lamps and candles in little boats and floated 'em out to sea. 'ere we are, then. Used to be a posh 'otel, this place did. All the tourist geesers stayed 'ere for their 'oneymoons and such."

The building was larger than had at first appeared, wooden-built and standing at the foot of a long, steep valley which rose up into the forest.

" Just wait 'ere, an' I'll fetch Leftenant Clint," said the sergeant, and left us standing inside the entrance hall.

From a room to one side came the tumult of voices mingled with the clink of crockery, and the other two looked longingly towards it.

The sergeant reappeared out of the rain, accompanied by a

man of about thirty-five, tall and agile in khaki drill and with a keen, tanned face.

" I'm Clint, the Adjutant," he introduced himself. " Hang on while I fix up these two, and then I'll take you round to the Mess."

A few minutes later I sprinted after him round the corner of the building, and up into a small new bungalow which had been built higher up the slope.

" Hang up yer things," he said briskly, " and come right in."

The group of men and the single woman, standing at the tiny bar just beyond the vestibule, swung around as we entered.

" Another sick man ! " cried Lieutenant Clint. " Pour him a beer, somebody ! " He gripped me by the arm and urged me inwards. " This is Mr.—— ? Mr. Page, that's right, come down to join the party. Mam'selle Canard, Mr. Page. M'sieur Lauconnier, M'sieur Dubonnet, meet Mr. Page. And this is Major Maynard and Captain Brown—both sawbones—and here's two more blokes down for a rest-cure, Squadron-Leader Falcon and Flight-Lieutenant Spain."

Captain Brown, plump, bespectacled, and affable, was presiding behind the bar. " Here's your beer, right off the ice," he said, and pushed it across to me.

" B-but I've had jaundice, you know—I'm not supposed to drink anything for three months."

" Oh, we treat jaundice differently down here. Besides, beer isn't drinking—it'll give you an appetite and tone up the system. What d'you say, Major ? "

" Oh, absolutely. It's the obvious treatment in this case."

" What's yer name, son ? " enquired the Flight-Lieutenant, lowering his glass from a large, smooth face, and I answered :

" Page."

" No—I mean yer *Name*."

" Oh—Michael."

" Pleased t' meet you, Mike. I had appendicitis—on me fortieth birthday, too. Seems like Fate or something, doesn't it ? "

The Squadron-Leader gave me a solemn stare from his rugged, brick-dust features, and an equally solemn wink. " Just disregard him," he advised. " He talks like that all day."

The Frenchwoman and the two men, who were on leave from their Military Mission in Tokyo, seemed to be compact and fragile beside these bulky, good-humoured males. But when we sat down to ' tea ' they themselves appeared clumsy compared with the Japanese women who waited on us. Their only countrywomen whom I had seen so far had been the short-legged, tittering creatures who had served in the hospital, or the sinewy and impassive women working in the fields. It was a revelation for me to encounter delicately nurtured Japanese women, even in such a detached relationship. In their white dresses, their trim, smart figures moved smoothly about the table ; a polite semi-smile hovered upon their delicate features. I had never seen complexions of such beauty ; in contrast to their blue-black, simply arranged hair and gentle almond eyes, their skin had a delicious apricot bloom, a colour as frail and entrancing as that which glows within tinted porcelain.

" *Mezu?* " they enquired softly, poising the water-jug, and laughed with shy music when the Squadron-Leader addressed them as Mary, Susie, and Kate.

The meal with which they served us was excellent, and I appreciated both the change from hospital fare and the atmosphere of simple homeliness which prevailed in the little mess. The bungalow was built in the Japanese style, but with the novel innovation of a large stone fire-place against the freezing winters.

After dinner the rain had stopped, and there was an outdoor cinema show. I reclined replete in a long cane chair, reflecting upon how strange it was to be watching Gregory Peck beneath the sibilant pines of Japan.

" I'll give you a run-over in the morning," promised Captain Brown as we consumed plum-cake and tea after the show, and the next day I lay on the surgery couch while he probed the tenderer portions of my anatomy. He finally gave it a resounding slap, exclaiming :

" You're all right ! All you've got to do now is get plenty of fresh air and sunshine. I don't care what you do

the shade of the pines curved round a spur in the hill, and joined a flight of beautifully masoned steps which led down to the town.   We paused, looking down upon the black-glazed tiles of the roofs of the grey wooden buildings, then followed the steps upwards until they led, between the pillars of a *tori* with a roof of similar black tiles, on to the wide earthen platform upon which one of the temples stood. On either side of the *tori* stood lattice-work cages, enclosing fearsomely prancing deities of carved and painted wood. They were bespattered with pellets of dried paper, and Falcon observed :

" If you want to say a prayer you write it on a piece of paper, chew it up well, and spit it on to the god.   I s'pose it kind of draws his attention to you."

The temple consisted of two bungalow-shaped wooden buildings opposing each other, painted a dark grey and with the upcurving gables which give a hint of grace and fantasy to the most commonplace erections.   Notices in stilted English requested politeness towards the temple, but though we peered into the dark interior of one of the buildings, and caught a glimpse of red and gold hangings, a whiff of incense, a chanting drone of prayers, we did not enter.   One of the paper screens that served as windows slid open as we passed, and a shaven-headed young priest, in a slate-grey silk kimono, watched us with calmly insolent appraisal until we had left the precincts.

The path continued upwards through an ugly waste of boulders and naked, sun-parched earth, washed down by a typhoon cloudburst in the previous year.   The temple had only been saved from it by the dam of logs and boulders which the torrent had piled up ahead of itself.   All the wooded mountains, on the islands or on the mainland, show the scars of similar typhoons, where the soaked earth has slipped and avalanched uprooted trees and boulders into the lower forests.

" If I was a Japanese, I'd drown meself," stated Falcon placidly.   " The whole country's nothing but ruddy mountains, and no sooner he gets a house built, or a bit o' land planted in rice and pumpkins, than along comes an earthquake or a typhoon an' wipes it all out for 'im.   He has to sell his daughters to pay his taxes, and work from dawn to midnight to get enough to eat. No wonder they're a suicidal race—it's a wonder they find living worth the bother. Leave alone Emperors, and atom bombs, and such."

The pines began again, the going became steeper, and the path became a winding flight of shallow granite steps. They vanished into the dim shades of the woods, smoothed and dully polished by the touch of countless feet.

" There's supposed to be two thousand of these, but we won't bother to count 'em," observed Falcon as we began to climb.

They wound up and up, in irregular flights, broken by zig-zags of path along the hillside, recommencing with spirals around some steeper spur. Sometimes they climbed narrowly between the gnarled, dark-amber trunks of the pines, whose branches met in a dark canopy and whose roots ridged the gritty path ; sometimes entered a slanting trough in which the sun lay thick and golden, rippled only by the quivering dart and hover of insects. We looked down into the still, lifeless shade between the labyrinths of pines, in which no birds sing and the forest seems to await true darkness before it stirs, or from some promontory gazed over the sheening billows of the tree-tops, descending to the match-box town and the twisted azure channels of the sea in arrested surges of dark, sun-glossed green.

Although we wore only shorts and sandals, we were soon sweating profusely in the heavy, devitalised atmosphere between the trees.

Falcon planted his staff a little more heavily as we progressed, grunting, " I'm a bit past the age for this caper—it's all right for you young fellers."

Watching, as I followed, the muscles ripple smoothly beneath the fair, trickling skin of his wide back, the alternate tension and relaxation of each vigorous calf and thigh, I reflected that he was probably at least as robust as myself. But when the steps climbed beside a slanting outcrop of smooth rock, across whose face a stream had worn an angular cleft, he ordered a rest. I scrambled down the rock to dip a handful of water, and found it icy and delicious, but as I climbed back Falcon said conversationally, " Don't put your hand there."

Beneath my palm a whipping flick disturbed the friable compost of earth and pine-needles.

"Someone told me about the snakes up here," said Falcon. "Said that there's only two kinds—brown with yellow heads and brown with yellow markings. It's the yellow-headed ones are poisonous—or perhaps it was the yellow-marked one. I didn't see what kind that was, did you?"

I have an atavistic horror of snakes, but although I now gaped dry-throated up into Falcon's ruddy, quizzical features, his placidity forbade expression of my fear.

"Let's hike, son," he suggested, and I heaved myself up on to the path beside him.

A little farther on we emerged from the pines to find that a long stretch of both steps and forest had been torn away by the landslide; where they had been was a wide, diagonal gully littered with boulders, with the stream trickling beneath them. It rose steeply to a raw, reddish cliff, but the plodding feet of the pilgrims had already worn a tortuous new path amongst the rocks. We passed a party of them resting, sturdy young men and women with brown, jolly faces and smoothly moulded limbs. They were dressed in grubby white cotton; the men in knee-length trousers and the girls in curiously old-fashioned sailor blouses. One of them was relieving herself with frank nonchalance; an older woman with a crinkled, humorous face was persuading a doll-like infant to eat scraps of raw pumpkin. Perched on a rock, an old man in a frayed straw hat preached vigorously to a youth drinking out of a bottle, his voice see-sawing in time with his flourishing, scrawny arms.

"I dunno just what they make this pilgrimage for," said Falcon as we entered the shadowless shade of the pines again, and found the continuation of the steps. "I s'pose it's because the whole island's sacred, and they acquire merit just by climbing to the top. I never could figure out these people's religion, anyway."

As we neared the summit the path and steps mounted and dipped over steep folds in the hillsides; into deep glades and on to steep ridges. The harping of the cicadas had faded as we ascended; the air was cooler, and its muted

St. Andrew's Cathedral, Hong-Kong

'Fatty'

stillness caused an involuntary drop in the voice. In that deep hush there was the sense of an intangible omnipresence amongst the irregular aisles of the pines ; a sense which had doubtless inspired the erection of the numerous shrines by the edge of the path. Like little wooden houses, they held inscrutably smiling figurines of the Gautama Buddha, before which had been placed tributes of faded paper flowers and worthless money. Here and there were clustered little piles of stones, beneath a jutting rock or between the roots of a tree ; the tiny cairns which are the tokens of prayers for lost children.

The round, humming chime of a bronze bell quivered between the trees ; we passed beneath another *tori* flanked by grotesquely capering deities and entered the precincts of another temple. A very casual, semi-derelict temple, this ; two or three priests lay gossiping on their mats within the doors, and a woman tossed a bowl of dish-water out of one of the windows. We were very near the summit, could see nothing above us but the sky, and passed the great bell hanging on a beam between two trees, with the log used as a striker swaying by its side. An old man in shorts and elastic-sided boots, and his wife in a grey kimono, stood politely aside to let us pass ; bowing rigidly and hissing with formal courtesy. The steps climbed between two great rocks as grey as weathered canvas, and then wound erratically amongst an upheaval of huge, smooth-faced boulders, which we discovered to be the island's crest. The grottoes between them sheltered more figures of Buddha and more prayer-cairns ; paper flags and streamers printed with prayers were stuck into their clefts, and some ardent devotee had placed a beer-bottle holding a paper chrysanthemum on a higher pinnacle.

We emerged between the rocks to find ourselves on a levelled space, the summit of the island. A couple of ramshackle pavilions had been erected to rest and shelter the pilgrim, whilst he admired the swooping, sun-glossed vista of the forests through which he had climbed, the avalanche-scarred mountains of the mainland, and the islands scattered upon the kingfisher-blue of the Inland Sea. In the one which we entered were already seated a young man and half a dozen children, whom Falcon surveyed with

L

rugg' d benevolence. The children were eating ra
kins as though they were apples, and the young ma
so reticently wistful at sight of our cigarettes that
him one.

He held out his cupped hands for it, with an
clamation of " Sank you, sair ! "

" You speak English ? " I asked, and he looke
blank.

His flat, shallow eyes shifted uneasily, and like
boy who knows that he cannot answer a questio
peated temporisingly, " Chew . . . spik . . .
Angris ? "

Knowledge suddenly illumined his aquiline feat
he cried, " Angris! Yiss, sair, I am spik Angris
bit, ownree. I am . . . I am . . . h'm . . ."

He frowned, shook his head over several words
tasted to himself, then muttered a sentence seve
beating out its cadence with a forefinger before tr
us. " I—am—a—schoorteesher. Yiss ? "

" Ah! A schoolteacher! And is this the scho
We indicated the children, but he beamed and
head.

" No, sair. Theer is me—my—brollers an' si
am same . . ." He relapsed into whispering ex
again, but finally asked humbly, " Fam-ree ? " an
at our approval.

" Were you in the Army ? " I asked.

This he recognised at once, and nodded vigorou

" You liked it ? Good ? "

" Good ? No-no, not good ! "

He quickly pulled open his shirt and unbut
trousers. On his smooth citron skin were t
puckered scars, one below the breast-bone and the
the curve of the belly. He shook his head, displa
to us. " Not good ! Not good ! "

The children watched as though they had hear
too often before, their faces assuming the *blasé* i
which typifies Mongolian features in repose.

Soon afterwards we started back, and Falcon
" Thank God it's all down-hill. There's another
that we might as well take, if we can find it."

stillness caused an involuntary drop in the voice. In that deep hush there was the sense of an intangible omnipresence amongst the irregular aisles of the pines ; a sense which had doubtless inspired the erection of the numerous shrines by the edge of the path. Like little wooden houses, they held inscrutably smiling figurines of the Gautama Buddha, before which had been placed tributes of faded paper flowers and worthless money. Here and there were clustered little piles of stones, beneath a jutting rock or between the roots of a tree ; the tiny cairns which are the tokens of prayers for lost children.

The round, humming chime of a bronze bell quivered between the trees ; we passed beneath another *tori* flanked by grotesquely capering deities and entered the precincts of another temple. A very casual, semi-derelict temple, this ; two or three priests lay gossiping on their mats within the doors, and a woman tossed a bowl of dish-water out of one of the windows. We were very near the summit, could see nothing above us but the sky, and passed the great bell hanging on a beam between two trees, with the log used as a striker swaying by its side. An old man in shorts and elastic-sided boots, and his wife in a grey kimono, stood politely aside to let us pass ; bowing rigidly and hissing with formal courtesy. The steps climbed between two great rocks as grey as weathered canvas, and then wound erratically amongst an upheaval of huge, smooth-faced boulders, which we discovered to be the island's crest. The grottoes between them sheltered more figures of Buddha and more prayer-cairns ; paper flags and streamers printed with prayers were stuck into their clefts, and some ardent devotee had placed a beer-bottle holding a paper chrysanthemum on a higher pinnacle.

We emerged between the rocks to find ourselves on a levelled space, the summit of the island. A couple of ramshackle pavilions had been erected to rest and shelter the pilgrim, whilst he admired the swooping, sun-glossed vista of the forests through which he had climbed, the avalanche-scarred mountains of the mainland, and the islands scattered upon the kingfisher-blue of the Inland Sea. In the one which we entered were already seated a young man and half a dozen children, whom Falcon surveyed with

ruggd benevolence. The children were eating raw pumpkins as though they were apples, and the young man looked
so reticently wistful at sight of our cigarettes that I offered
him one.

He held out his cupped hands for it, with an eager exclamation of " Sank you, sair ! "

" You speak English ? " I asked, and he looked politely
blank.

His flat, shallow eyes shifted uneasily, and like a school-
boy who knows that he cannot answer a question, he repeated temporisingly, " Chew . . . spik . . . Angris ?
Angris ? "

Knowledge suddenly illumined his aquiline features, and
he cried, " Angris! Yiss, sair, I am spik Angris. Smawr
bit, ownree. I am . . . I am . . . h'm . . ."

He frowned, shook his head over several words which he
tasted to himself, then muttered a sentence several times,
beating out its cadence with a forefinger before trying it on
us. " I—am—a—schoorteesher. Yiss ? "

" Ah! A schoolteacher ! And is this the school ? "

We indicated the children, but he beamed and shook his
head.

" No, sair. Theer is me—my—brollers an' simsters. I
am same . . ." He relapsed into whispering experiment
again, but finally asked humbly, " Fam-ree ? " and beamed
at our approval.

" Were you in the Army ? " I asked.

This he recognised at once, and nodded vigorously.

" You liked it ? Good ? "

" Good ? No-no, not good ! "

He quickly pulled open his shirt and unbuttoned his
trousers. On his smooth citron skin were two great
puckered scars, one below the breast-bone and the other on
the curve of the belly. He shook his head, displaying them
to us. " Not good ! Not good ! "

The children watched as though they had heard the tale
too often before, their faces assuming the *blasé* impassivity
which typifies Mongolian features in repose.

Soon afterwards we started back, and Falcon grunted,
" Thank God it's all down-hill. There's another way back
that we might as well take, if we can find it."

From the temple we walked a path running along the saddle-back between the two peaks of the island, until we came to the top of another flight of steps descending into the pines.

" These should bring us out on the other side of the Deepo, unless I'm much mistaken," said Falcon. " What're you waiting for ? "

I had hesitated two or three steps behind him, and I pointed with my stick at the long snake writhing down the needle-covered bank towards the steps.

" 'strewth, it's got a yellow belly and a yellow head," said Falcon with interest. " It must only be poisonous on Tuesdays."

The slim chocolate-and-yellow body made for a step half a dozen below us, and paused upon it. Its head appeared, and it gazed at us in silence over the rim of the step, with its little forked tongue flipping nervously in and out of its mouth. For some moments we regarded each other, men and snake, its eyes as expressionless as two drops of ink. For my part, if the snake had stood there all day, so also would I, but Falcon suddenly rapped smartly with his staff. It drew back as though affronted, and then squirmed unhurriedly away up the opposite bank.

" God bless you, you don't want to be afraid of a little old snake," exhorted Falcon heartily as we descended. " Why, y'oughta see 'em in Awstrailyer. Thick as yer thigh, some of 'em, an' the blackfellers eat 'em as though they were chicken."

But we saw no more snakes, though Falcon once guffawed heartily when I started back from a movement at my feet, which turned out to be a large ant carrying a piece of twig.

" Crocodiles, snakes, and ants—the whole ruddy insect world's against yer," he chuckled.

The steps became a path which groped between tree-tops on one side and a great overhanging escarpment of lichenous grey rock on the other, with a fantastically twisted tree growing out of a cleft in its face. There were more rocky outcrops on this side of the mountain ; the steps squeezed between them, and mossy boulders were scattered thickly amongst the trees. Once we had to pass beneath a rugged tower of rocks, from a hole in which a cool, damp breeze constantly and unaccountably blew. It gave Falcon the opportunity for some ribald speculations concerning the anatomical arrangements of Japanese deities, but, all the same, it was strange. The cold, steady stream of air which flowed silently from a hole in the rock, fluttering the prayer-streamers hung about its mouth, must have had some natural explanation, but there was something a little eerie about it.

So also there was about the whole descent on this side. The mossy steps and paths gave no sign of the constant use of the others; we met no one; the stillness between the more thickly growing trees was absolute. In the twilight beneath the dark canopy of boughs, between the gnarled, contorted trunks so close on the hummocked hillside, the expectant hush was not brooding, but tense; keyed, as it were, to a personality which was inhuman but not divine. In such places the mind is tuned at once to the forest fear which thrills out of some memory older than time; the shuddering knowledge belonging to every race and age of the things only to be glimpsed from the tail of one's eye, which only rustle in the dead leaves behind one's back. The dryads of the Greeks, the gnomes and trolls of Norway, and the soul-less, ageless creatures which inhabit the Gothic tales of the Brothers Grimm, the ancient and universal worship of hills and groves were all inspired by places such as these, where the imprisoned life of the trees seems to diffuse a taut malevolence against those who can move freely amongst them. It would not have been difficult for senses under the spell of the pines to conjure grasping, woody hands and sly old faces from their twisted branches and knotted trunks; to glimpse a tawny, shaggy body vanishing amongst them, nor to hear the click of a hoof on stone and the trill of a pipe of reeds.

III

I climbed the mountain several times during my stay on the island; once more with Falcon, once or twice by myself, once with one of the W.V.S. girls who had been sent to open a canteen on the island, and who had joined our mess. Alternatively I swam or sun-bathed, explored the narrow, rugged road which ran between the hillsides and the cove-indented shore, or sometimes spent a morning strolling about the little town. Like similar towns the world over, its proximity to a shrine ensured its devotion to a kind of trashy commercialism. The sandy streets of weather-silvered wooden houses were mostly composed of shops dealing in flimsy toys and mass-produced souvenirs, and filled with aimlessly drifting groups of pilgrims and sight-seers. Photographers abounded, standing hopefully in spots where the Tori, the sacred horse, or the stone lanterns along the shore road might be used for their backcloth, or in shops whose displayed samples were a yellowing sartorial history of several decades; European visitors posing in rigid Edwardian waists, the skittish frocks and skin-tight trousers of the 'twenties or the shorts and halters of the 'thirties, and shown feeding the sacred deer which once roamed about the island. The blockade destroyed their sanctity, and their dappled bodies and meek, slender necks have gone the way of every other living creature in Japan, with the exception of humans, insects, and snakes.

I had been a month on the island, and, though not exactly anxious to go, was no longer sufficiently charmed to wish to remain. Besides, I was nearing the end of the two months' paid sick leave to which I was entitled. Presumably on account of the jaundice, I was still subject to moods in which I experienced the same kind of complicated, conscience-stricken unhappiness of a character in a Graham Greene novel, but apart from them I could count myself as having recovered and enjoyed my stay. Anyway, it was difficult to be liverish in the company of the Australians, with their unsophisticated humour and naïve self-esteem, and the more I saw of them the better I liked them.

I had tried several times to contact the Sea Transport Officer, but without success, and the eccentric telephone system did not make the effort any easier. I reconciled myself to the idea that someone, after all, must know who and where I was, and that in the fullness of time I would be dragged out of my retreat. And then one day Captain Brown came in to lunch and said: " This came in to-day, Mike. I suppose it's about you ? "

He passed the mimeographed slip of paper over to me,

and under the long preamble of figures, initials, service advices, and repeat addresses I read 'Inform whether Radio Officer Page M.F., ex-" Bath Abbey," able to resume duty. Passage to Hong-Kong to join " Bulbul " arranged on " Lochannan " ends.'

I looked over it at Brown.

" D'you think that you're fit to resume duty ? " he asked. " No reason why you shouldn't have a couple more weeks if you don't feel up to it, y' know."

" Well . . . I dunno. Not much sense in hanging around, I s'pose. When does the ' Lochannan ' sail ? "

" To-morrow evening, from Kuré. Sure you won't stay a bit longer ? "

We looked at each other, and he shrugged. " Okay. I'll fix up transport for you to-morrow afternoon, and you can go straight aboard. We'll be sorry to see you go."

And when it came to leaving I was sorry myself; to leave a place in which in so short a time I had made good friends, and to embark again into the unpredictable. I had no idea as to what kind of ship the ' Bulbul ' might be, except that she would be under the same ownership as the two previous ships, and hence probably a tanker.

It was arranged for me to be given a lift on a boat which was going right up to Kuré, and the next afternoon Lieutenant Clint drove me down to the landing-stage.

It was evening before I arrived in Kuré anchorage, and saw the ' Lochannan ' rising out of the dark water in a towering pattern of lights. As my boat arrived alongside it jostled numerous others clustered about the accommodation ladder, beneath the yellow square of the boarding doors. A burly quartermaster bellowed profane directions to their pilots, and somehow I got myself and my bags on to the jerking grating of the ladder, and dragged them up into the safety of the ship.

I found myself in a kind of vestibule with glass doors on one side and a wide staircase on the other, and occupied by a gloomily subdued crowd of officers and women. The reason for their gloom I never knew, but they stood there with the hopeless expectancy of children at the beginning of a party. I looked helplessly at them through the drifting clouds of tobacco-smoke, and they looked back at me out of the corners of their eyes. My imagination faltered at the idea of asking directions from any of that hushed, despondent throng.

Suddenly I felt my arm gripped from behind, and turned to see a craggy-faced, red-haired naval officer staring at me.

" Hallo," he said pleasantly. " I thought I knew you, but I see that I don't. My name's Bustard. What are you doing ? "

" I dunno—I—just came aboard . . ."

" So did I. Have you had any dinner ? Neither have I. Come along, we'll find some."

" But what about reporting aboard ? Our berths, I mean, and——"

" Oh, never mind that. We're aboard, that's the main thing. They'll bed us down somewhere, don't worry. In the meantime——"

He piloted me firmly through the crowd and the glass doors, which opened into the dining-saloon. Still gripping my arm, he signalled to one of the stewards hurrying between the tables.

" This officer's had no dinner," he said sharply, as though it was the steward's fault. " See to it, will you ? And you might as well bring me some while you're about it."

With startled deference the steward ushered us to a table.

" What're all those people hanging about outside for ? " I asked as we began our soup.

" Them ? Oh, Army types," said Bustard. " They'll stand there until someone tells 'em what to do. Quite clueless, you know. Amazing."

After dinner he helped me to carry my bags up to the purser's office, where he was immediately pounced upon and borne away by another officer, who exclaimed with some exasperation, " I've had to talk myself hoarse to wangle a double-berth cabin, and you hang about all day——"

" All right, old boy. All things come to him who waits, y'know——"

They departed, and I tapped at the door of the purser's office. It was opened by an elegant individual wearing a cigarette-holder, white trousers, a singlet, and a monocle.

" Excuse me—are you the purser ? "

" Yes ? " He surveyed me sympathetically through his monocle while I explained myself, and then said, " Oh, of course—there was a signal about you. Well, you're only going to Hong-Kong, I believe ; there's an empty berth in E.1—just along the alleyway there. Quite all right, old chap—glad that you got here okay."

I carried my bags along to Cabin E.1, and clumped them heavily down within. It contained six bunks in three tiers, and was occupied by four men who were huddled about an old, half-naked character seated on a lower bunk. They were dressed in such a mixture of army and civilian clothing that I thought they must also be merchant seamen, but as they all turned to look suspiciously at me the old man cackled :

" 'allo ! Come along in, Mister ! Just room for one on top. Heh-heh ! 'ere, jevver see this before ? "

He held out a broad, soft palm upon which lay three pennies. While I stared at them he turned his hand over, but the pennies did not drop. He flicked his palm upwards again, and it was empty.

" See ? Just a matter of 'ey presto, and 'ere they are ! "

He thrust forth his other hand, and the three pennies lay ranged upon it.

" Kid stuff, that is," he derided. " Jus' t' keep in practice. Y'oughta see me wiv all me props. Fahsands o' pahnds worf. 'course, I don't carry 'em on this Forces entertinement caper. Make yer fink I would, you bet. Ikey Peck's th' nime. Ike Peck, Illusionist. Fahsands o' pahnds we've mide, me an' me bruvver. An' spent 'em. You bet. Heh-heh ! "

He smacked his crumpled lips. He had the emptily sagging obesity of age, the lifelessly blanched hair and drooping jowls, but his formidable nose had a gallant gleam and his eyes held a kind of sly humour—the expression of one who has overcome a great deal by the strength of his wits.

" Ow, yer a mervellous owld barstud, Ikey, an' no error," commented one of his audience, with a wink at me.

Encouraged by this, I asked if they were also merchant seamen.

" Wot, us ? Crikee, I should say not. Saowljers, we

are—till diy before yisterdee, anyway. Gintlemin o'
leesure naow. Fust-clawss passengers. Gov'ment gives
yer a choice, see—ship back to Awstrailyer, or a passage
anywhere else y'wanna gow. We thought we'd try our
chawnse in the Owld Countree. A shiff, that's me.
Oughta be plenty o' jobs for a shiff in Britain now, didn't
there ? "

" For a wot ? "

" A shiff! Bloke wiv a tall 'at an' a sweat-rag. You
know."

" A grub-spoiler," commented one of the others drily.
" Well, I'm gowin' t' bed. Owld Ikey's fair wore me out
with excitement."

They commenced to unpack, and the Chef produced a
pair of glittering, sharply-pointed shoes, and offered them
proudly for inspection. " Proper spider shoes, aren't
they ? " he asked.

" ? "

" For kickin' spiders' eyes out with," he explained, and
gruntingly squeezed a large foot into one of them. Admiring the effect with the pride of Cinderella, he asked,
" How far 're you gowin', chummie ? "

" Only to Hong-Kong."

One of the others, a dark young man with a Latin
arrogance of expression, dropped a sock back into his kit-
bag. " Hong-Kong ? How far is that from here ? "

" Only about three days."

" Ah, d'you hear that, Jack ? I reckon I'll 've had all I
want of this tub in three days. I reckon I'll have a look
at this Hong-Kong. What're we gowin' all th' wiy to
Britain for, anywiy ? "

" Yair," said the Chef, still admiring his shoes. " We'll
jine th' Chinese Army, eh ? We'd be gin'rals, sure. Mike
them chow-chow barstuds jump lively, my oath."

" You reckon they got any cabaretts in this 'ong-Kong ? "
appealed old Peck at large. " You know—night-clubs,
theayters, essetra ? I never bin t' Chayna. Mebbe's I
could git a contrack there. Eh ? What siy ? No sense
in gowin' to Colombo if I c'n git a crib in Chayna. Eh ?
You'll see, b'ys, you'll see. You watch owld Ikey.
Fahsands o' pahnds worf o' props I got there——"

He rubbed his hands briskly, removed his teeth and placed them on the wash-stand, and gave a shrill cackle of excitement.

I began to undress, listening idly to the discussion which my destination had provoked.

A lanky young man with yellow hair worried, " But s'posing we don't get work, and are stranded there—what then ? "

" Ah, that's nothin'," scoffed the Chef.   " All you needs 's a thick skin an' plenty o' cheek, an' you can git outa anythin'."

I pulled myself up on to my narrow top bunk, and lay staring at the rivets a few inches from my head.   Ikey succumbed upon his pillow, protesting against the heat, while the others wrangled and laughed and bumped about the cabin.

" It's rowmance that you want," the Chef explained. " Where's the rowmance in gowin' t' Britain ? Tell y' what, we'll see owld Three-eyes there in th' mornin', an' see if they'll give us back the passage-money to Britain if we gits off in Chayna."

As my eyes closed I felt a vague envy of their initiative and self-dependence, and the last thing that I heard was a voice saying, " We've only got three diys, so mike up yer bloomin' mind by Saturdee . . ."

CHAPTER THIRTEEN

ACROSS TO HONG-KONG

I

IT WAS THE FIRST time that I had travelled by trooper, or indeed by any passenger ship of that size, and I sincerely hope that it will be the last. The British and Indian units which she was carrying did not half fill her trooping capacity, but already there seemed to be barely room to move. It was bad enough for the officers and the so-called first-class passengers, but in the troop-decks they were packed as tightly as biscuits in a box.

There were approximately six feet by three of the ship which you could call your own—the bunk which was allotted to each passenger. In our cabin we were fortunate; it accommodated only six of us, and the forward-facing portholes admitted a constant breeze. Farther down the alleyway fifteen naval officers shared an airless hutch, and to one side of us the alleyway was blocked by the kit of a seasick party of Indians, whose orderly squatted amongst it with his head in his hands. On the other side a dozen or more women wrangled continuously in resolutely reasonable tones, and invariably left their more intimate garments behind them in the bathrooms.

Apart from the bunks, there was nowhere to go but the boat-deck, which in every respect—the quantity of displayed flesh, the catch-as-catch-can flirtations, and the uproarious parties determined to get their money's worth—had the atmosphere of a Bank Holiday beach. There was also the smoke-room, which might have been transferred direct from some provincial hotel. There were the same pillars, apparently fashioned out of solidified brawn; the same mud-coloured carpet and the same liver-coloured maidens supporting Byzantine lamps; the same mausoleum of an empty fireplace, and the same stiff, characterless furniture. Only the stewards were different: big, vigorous young men in

a sulky rain. Through it the conical ranges of the mainland loomed darkly, and the huge ship slid cautiously through a pock-marked, pewter-coloured sea. She seemed to be heading directly for a coast without an entrance, and I stood amongst a damp, chattering throng watching it approach. Lieutenant Bustard strolled by and nodded to me, and I asked him where the entrance was.

" Oh, we're heading for the Lye Moon Pass, I expect," he said. " Hong-Kong's an island, you know, and you have to go round the side of it to get into the harbour. You won't see the entrance until we turn to go through the Pass."

He leaned beside me on the dripping rail, and in a short while the vessel began to turn ponderously to port. She throbbed slowly towards an entrance channel between steep dark hills, their crests obscured by the clouds which clung greyly to their sides. It was still raining in a drearily determined manner, and a square-sailed sampan with a slim, varnished hull scudded out of the mist towards us.

" Here's the pilot," said Bustard. " Now we shan't be long. This is the island on your left," he explained. " And these are the New Territories to starboard."

As we began to move more rapidly along the channel the right-hand shores became more level and then curved round into a deep bay, with scatterings of buildings beginning to clump together about shipyards and dry-docks, from which the metallic clamour of rivet-guns drifted through the sodden air. They gave way to more buildings which developed into an irregular crescent of European-style apartment-houses, stretching around the shores of the bay until they were dominated by a colossal square building, whose huge and many-windowed walls loomed darkly through the veils of rain.

" The Peninsula Hotel," said Bustard. " And that's the Star Ferry—you use that to get to Hong-Kong from Kowloon. That's what they call the part of Hong-Kong that's on the mainland."

An oval craft, with a slim funnel protruding through its canopied top deck, had fussed around our stern, taking on an alarming list as its passengers crowded to the disembarking side. It groped its way alongside a covered jetty on the blunt horn of the bay's curve, about which we were now majestically turning to enter the broad, shipping-scattered reaches of Hong-Kong harbour.

" Pity it's such a mucky sort of day," said Bustard. " This is a wonderful harbour when you can see it properly."

The great vessel proceeded in a cautious semi-circle, until its bows pointed towards the liner berth ; a wooden pier several hundred feet long and two or three score wide, but not much more than a man's height above the water. Accustomed to the more intimate uproar of a smaller ship's berthing, to me there seemed to be a remarkably impersonal efficiency about the way in which the great ship was manœuvred alongside.

Only a few people were scattered upon the rain-glistening planking of the pier, mostly officials and Service people, who shouted greetings to their friends along the rails.

" They won't let me aboard," cried an Army officer with a drenched spaniel on a lead, and the dog moved its tail in mournful agreement.

As the gangway was run out, a tall figure in gleaming oilskins, sea-boots and sou'-wester moved out of the group and took up a commanding stance at its foot, and the officials hurried past him to come aboard.

" You'd better get busy now," said Bustard. " Cheerio —see you again sometime. Look after yourself . . ."

The purser's office was already busy with khaki-uniformed, leather-holstered police when I reached it, and they very quickly checked my credentials and gave me permission to land. I jostled the Chef as I turned away, and asked, " Where'll you be staying ashore ? "

" I dunno, Slim ; gotta get there first. At the Why, I guess, if there is one. See you around, anywiy. Be good, cocky."

I turned to the task of wrestling my baggage ashore. The stewards had all discreetly disappeared, which at least obviated the necessity for tipping them, but it was an arm-breaking job to wrestle my bags the length of the ship, from the forward cabin, which had been a blessing but now became a curse, down three flights of stairs and along seemingly interminable alleyways to the gangway, which had been put out right aft. I had no idea as to what I was going to do once I got ashore, beyond some vague scheme for finding a

taxi and then hunting for my ship.   I manœuvred my first
two bags down on to the jetty, and as I was about to return
for the others an oilskinned figure stepped forward and
asked :

"Would you happen to be Mr. Page ? "

I looked up in surprise. " Why, yes.   And you're——"

" Atkins is the name.   Chief Officer o' the ' Bulbul '.
I've got a boat waiting on the other side o' the pier."

We shook hands before the vast grandstand of the ship's
side, and I looked into a face deeply scored with weather and
experience, the rigid, uncompromising features of a man
whose code is narrow but precise.   His sun-wrinkled, grey-
green eyes looked coldly into mine as he said :

" Fetch the rest o' yer gear, and I'll give ye a lift over to
the boat."

We carried the bags across the pier and handed them
down to the Chinese sailors in the boat.   Standing on the
thwart beside Atkins, with our elbows resting on the hoop
of the canvas hood as the thin rain beat into our faces, I
learned that the ship was employed on duties similar to the
' Bengal's ', and also that she was smaller and newer.
Another glorified lighter, I thought, and asked hopefully :

" But doesn't she ever make any voyages outside Hong-
Kong—coast-wise or anything of that sort ? "

" Not since I've been in 'er, and that's a year agone," he
grunted.   " Look, there she is ahead."

Looming through the rain-drift I could see the rounded
stern of a small ship, of about 1500 tons.   She was of the
type to which we used to refer as ' galleons ', because of the
fancied resemblance of their high sterns and low prows to
those of the Elizabethans.   It is a handy and efficient
design for that class of ship ; the bridge, engine-room, and
accommodation are all situated in the stern, so that the main
deck is quite clear for working.   A raised cat-walk runs
from this after-part to the tiny fo'c'sle head, and as we came
alongside, a large, khaki-clad figure walked out on to it,
and stood there filling a pipe and solemnly regarding us.

" That's the Second Mate," said Atkins.   " I'll tell
someone to take your gear to your cabin, and take you up to
meet the Old Man."

It was no trouble to get aboard, since her main deck had

little more freeboard than that of the launch which Atkins now dismissed. I followed him up the ladder to the cat-walk, exchanging wags of the head with the Second Mate as we passed into the accommodation.

" This is your room," said Atkins proudly. " It's a bit small, but I had it painted out for you."

" It's jolly good," I said appreciatively.

It was very little larger than my cabin on the ' Bengal ', but the modernity of the ship made a vast difference.

" Let's go and see the Old Man now, and then you can settle in," urged Atkins. He was still wearing his oilskins.

The deck officers' and my own cabin were in a short alleyway on the starboard side of the saloon, and the engineers' quarters were on the port side. Astern of us were the petty officers' accommodation and the galley, below on either side of the engine-room were the crew's quarters, and above us were the Captain's cabin, the bridge, and the wireless room. Everything was as neat and com-pact as a box of matches, and it was always a little surprising to realise how many men were housed in such a limited space.

I followed Mr. Atkins up the companion-way out of our quarters to the next deck, and he approached an open door. " New Radio Officer reporting aboard, sir," he said gruffly, and stood back to let me enter.

A dark and alert-looking man was rising from his desk to greet me, his white uniform gleaming in the cool gloom of his room. My spirits rose as we shook hands and ex-changed a few words.

" Well, I expect that you want to get your gear stowed away," he concluded. " I'll see you at dinner."

II

There were only seven of us at dinner in the little mess-room. I was introduced to the Second Mate, who seemed even larger at close quarters than he had done from a distance. He was a massive Scotsman by the name of Mackenzie, with lively blue eyes and hair of the pale straw colour into which red hair fades. There was another of the same clan, Archie Mackenzie the Third Engineer, a

CHAPTER FOURTEEN

JUNKS AND SAMPANS AND NATHAN ROAD

I

My own life began to settle down into a somewhat improved replica of the Singapore existence. We were engaged upon duties similar to those of the 'Bengal', spending similar periods of inactivity at anchor or alongside, but not such lengthy ones as did the former ship. Hong-Kong was a busier port than Singapore, and our entire time was spent within the confines of the harbour; ourselves a part of that endless spectacle which has the harbour for its background.

Hong-Kong is an islet of sanity and order upon the fringe of the vast maelstrom of chaos which is China. As though symbolic of this, the great harbour and the small strip of coastline known as the New Territories are barricaded against the remainder of the mainland by a fanged range of hills, rising here and there to a sharply peaked mountain, boulder-strewn and tinted ochre and saffron and rust. The road to Canton runs along the looping coastline between these hills and the sea, and the fleets of trading junks come leaning up before the wind between the myriad islands, large and small, which stud the coastal waters. It is as though they were themselves the peaks of a drowned territory of mountains, and they have the same tawny hues, the same dark, purplish-green clothing of scrub as have the coastal ranges, with the bright emerald of rice-fields close to the water's edge. The island of Hong-Kong, the seaward barrier of the great harbour which lies between itself and the mainland, also resembles nothing more than another mountain range. Its dominant feature is the Peak, the huge dark hummock whose crest the southerly winds wreathe in mist, and with the city of Victoria piled upon its precipitous lower slopes and curving around its feet.

Formerly, a resident of Hong-Kong moved farther up the Peak as his social status ascended, and it is inevitably the point towards which the rest of the colony tends. The remainder of the chain of hills which composes the island rises towards it. It is the highest point of the tail of islands which straggles away to form the westward barrier of the harbour, and the tongue of land which is the Peninsula of Kowloon points towards it from the New Territories. When you take the ferry across from Kowloon to Hong-Kong you land not far from the station of the Peak Tram-way, the funicular which will take you almost to its summit.

The city of Victoria, invariably referred to by the island's name of Hong-Kong, lies at the foot of this minor mountain, rising so steeply from the water's edge that it appears as though each house were built upon the roof of the one below it. From the many-roofed Aw Boon Haw pagoda, standing above its pavilions amongst the ridges and foothills tumbled about the northern slopes of the Peak, the water-front curves round a long, shallow crescent in a succession of dingy tenements, whose flat roofs sprout a forest of laundry poles. They are interrupted by the custard-yellow and terra-cotta blocks of the China Fleet Club and the Mission to Seamen, followed by the grey barracks and red-brick workshops of the naval dockyard. After this the city proper begins in an equally dingy but more impressive belt of office buildings, hotels, department stores, public buildings, and apartment houses, packed closely together and terraced above each other, and presided over by the great white tower of the Hong-Kong and Shanghai Bank. They form, as it were, the sub-strata for the remainder of the city, piled up the steep hillside behind them, with larger buildings isolated upon knolls or promontories and with a dark surge of tree-tops amongst the abrupt folds of the mountain-side. The city eventually degenerates into a long line of warehouses stretching along a water-front bristling with the masts of sampans and junks, behind which the Chinese quarter arises like an ant-heap of stone. At night-time the city arises out of the dark waters in a pyramid of lights, beneath the huge bulk of the mountain against the sky.

It is against this background of the island of Hong-Kong, the built-over peninsula of Kowloon with its protective mainland ranges and the lesser islands to the east, that the spectacle of the harbour life is displayed. The deep-sea ships which enter for a few days, the freighters and coasters which discharge their cargo at anchor or at the Kowloon wharves, are somehow the intrusion of an alien modernity into this panorama; the tugs and lighters and bustling ferries and motor-launches which besprinkle the waters of the harbour, and the grey-green arrogance of the anchored warships, only serve to emphasise the quaint grace and decorative utility of the swarming native craft.

Among all the demonstration of commercial ardour the slim sampans flit over the waters in wind-blown flocks, with a staccato of fire-crackers to discourage the sea-devils; the fleets of junks come parading up through the channels from Canton, their painted eyes staring into the harbour which opens before them and their russet sails taut-stretched. For craft which appear so enchantingly grotesque, living antiquities with their caravel-shaped hulls, great carved rudders, and overhanging stern cabins, they are remarkably agile and responsive under sail. See them becalmed in a windless sunset, and they are like vessels from a painted screen, the last rays coating their varnished hulls with gold and warming their sails with an orange-and-amber glow. Decorative, mediæval; but even as you admire them you think that they are surely too clumsy and awkward to have any other merits.

The first sight of them under way destroys this illusion. We used often to be anchored close to the Kowloon junk port, the typhoon shelter formed by enclosing the angle of the peninsula with the mainland behind an elbowed sea-wall, and the junks would have to cross our stern before coming round on to the tack to take them into the entrance. In late afternoon squadrons of them would be making towards their haven, clustering together as they approached from various parts of the harbour, or racing in scattered line ahead through the channel between Stonecutters' Island and the mainland. With a kind of bizarre urgency they would race towards their tacking point astern of us, but as they approached, with a precision as definite as though obtained by a code of signals, they would assume station astern of each other; each after each would reach the favourable moment, the helm would go over, and almost without loss of way the high-pooped, archaic craft would wheel as sweetly as a polished yacht, to lean over upon a tack at right angles to her previous one and dart towards the harbour entrance.

It is always a little startling to realise that events which to oneself appear exotic are homely and commonplace to those who are familiar with them. As the junks passed around our stern, close enough to distinguish the caulking on the smooth, varnished hulls the colour of pale tea, we could look down on their decks and see the matter-of-fact way in which the crews were handling the whole picturesque performance. The helmsman, as likely as not a trousered young woman with a baby slung on her back, would be standing at the great tiller on the steeply slanting poop, with an old man squatting beside her puffing at his long pipe, and watching the manœuvre with sardonic reserve. Two or three more women would be cooking over fires in earthen pots, an ancient sprawled asleep on a mat and a bunch of children playing with a litter of puppies, whose Black Chow mother sat sentinel over them all. Upon the cargo high-piled in the waist some of the crew would be gambling or gossiping, with a couple of orange-skinned, black-trousered sailors hauling upon the sheets and a boy clearing away the boat slung over the stern. They are family affairs, these junks ; many of their captains have a double authority in being head of the family as well as the master of the vessel. And the family will have descended from generations which knew no other life ; one unit in the vast sea-going peasantry of China.

In their smaller way, the sampans are also family affairs. In these little craft, with their square sails and their cabins made from matting stretched over bamboo hoops, a man and his wife and children may eat and sleep and earn their living. They ferry passengers and small cargoes about the harbour, fish, dredge for mussels from the mud-banks with baskets lashed to fifty-foot poles, peddle fruit and curios about the anchored ships and act as floating brothels ; the ' beef-boats ' which creep alongside ships at night with their painted, melancholy freights. The boat-women and their children are as adept with sail and oar as are their men ; frequently the husband seems to be the business partner only, taking his ease in the cabin while his wife

stands and swings at the oars with sturdy rhythm, or
handles tiller and sheet, with her plump, ruddy face
crinkled against sun and spray. The ambition of the
sampan-owner seems to be to attach himself as permanent
retainer to one of the ships stationed in or frequently
visiting the port. We ourselves had one which spent its
time trailing astern, proudly flying a blue flag with ' Bulbul '
worked upon it in crooked white letters, and waiting for
commissions : to ferry our Chinese sailors ashore or to be
engaged upon one odd job or another. Its owners were a
young man and his wife, a slim, sprightly girl with a gold
tooth and a twisted foot ; always as clean in their faded blue
pyjamas as was their little floating home.

They were some kind of relations to our Amah, who was
a portly young woman something under five feet high. Her
real name was Chan Chok, but we always called her Fatty,
on account of her corpulence. She had a chubby face
the ruddy-orange tint of a ripe pippin, with shrewdly gay
brown eyes and hair which was the coarse sepia of tarred
rope.

She did all our washing and mending for us, for which
we each paid her a pound a month, and as the months
passed so did her girth increase. We wondered whether
there might not be some good reason for it, but when taxed
upon the subject Fatty would say only, " Bad talk ! You all-
time speak big lie ! "

She went about her work with her accustomed zest,
swapping back-chat with the sailors in Cantonese and with
us in pidgin-English, and every evening bearing the results
of her day's labours about the cabins with cries of " Cap-tin !
Washin' ! Chiefy Offisah ! Washin' ! Sparkay ! Oppen
door ! Sew-sew ! "

And then, shortly after Christmas, the sampan was
whistled up in a hurry, and our clothes went unwashed for a
few days. Unusually slim, but as chirpy as ever, Fatty
returned with a shawl-wrapped bundle slung between her
shoulders, and told us that she had bought it for a hundred
dollars from a woman who did not want it. And with her
customary shrewd, sparkling grin, she distributed amongst
us the little red envelopes in which, she said, it was proper
to make an offering to a baby boy.

II

I did not go ashore at all for the first week I was aboard
the ship.   I contented myself with watching the life of the
harbour, as one watches a busy loom and sees how it gathers
all the threads into one bright design.   My only excursions
outside the ship were on the Wednesday and Sunday
evenings, on which nights we had a permanent invitation to
visit another ship, the ' Baltic ', and watch the cinema shows
which they gave aboard.   It was from our hosts there that I
learned that the ' Brahmin ', a ship of the same company
which was due to return home in the New Year, was lacking
a radio officer.   Her previous one had been flown home on
compassionate leave, and I at once applied to be transferred
to her for the homeward voyage.

My first trip ashore was when Costello invited me
ashore for an afternoon's ' shopping '.   We landed at one
of the Kowloon wharves, whence we walked along the long,
straight road behind the warehouses to the Star Ferry
terminus.   It was the dock coolies' dinner-hour, and they
sat in ragged lines against the warehouse walls, gobbling
bowls of rice purchased from the street-kitchens and
littering the pavement with fruit-skins and the fibrous wads
of chewed sugar-cane.   Their bamboo carrying-poles, as
thick as a man's arm and seasoned to a dull bronze, leaned
against the walls, and intent groups who would rather
gamble than eat squatted about a game played with inch-
wide cards.   Their round, hard faces, coppery with grime
and sunburn, peered under shapeless hats at the fall of the
cards ; the muscles bulged on their brawny backs and
thighs as they shifted impatiently ; they burst into a sudden
harsh caw of protest or elation as the stakes were gathered in.
The street was filled with the spicy redolence of camphor-
wood, from the shops which made boxes and chests, and a
few maimed beggars in the remnants of National Army
uniforms extended their bowls for alms.

We came out into the main water-front road, streaming
with vehicles and pedestrians making towards the ferry
terminus.   This is a covered pier with several turnstile
entrances, and we joined one of the queues being shepherded
through by uniformed inspectors.   Costello paid our fares

with four of the filthy, tattered ten-cent notes, and we passed through to join the throng which awaited the ferry. The Star Ferry is such an essential link between the two sections of the colony that it forms something of a link between all sections of the community as well. There are two classes, the upper and lower decks, and the coolies in their almost uniform dress of black trousers and tunics usually save their cents by travelling second-class. But on the upper deck you may rub shoulders with Chinese gentlemen in pastel-tinted silk gowns and felt-soled boots, domestic servants in crisp white tunics and office-girls in high-necked, form-fitting gowns; National Army officers in jaundiced khaki, European business-men in crumpled tropical suits, soldiers and sailors from the Imperial establishments; travellers and visitors of every kind, from dungareed merchant seamen to loudly exclaiming Americans. Nervous, cadaverous Chinese clerks sit next to plumply suave young Chinese merchants, with their haggard wives and droves of beady-eyed children; brazen-voiced and brassy-haired Anglo-Saxon matrons sit with their despondent, expressionless menfolk.

The oval craft cants steeply as it comes alongside, with the passengers crowding to be first on the gangway, which falls with a rattling crash. As they stream ashore, those waiting to embark crush against the gates, and as soon as they are opened charge aboard in a race to obtain a seat on the slatted benches or in one of the glassed-in cabins. I sat beside Costello in the bows, watching the city approach as we sailed across the mile or so of water; we were hardly half-way across before people began to cluster about the gangway, and when the ferry bumped alongside we wedged ourselves into the crush.

"Watch yer pockets," warned Costello. "There's some of these fellers'd strip you naked, and you'd not know they'd laid a hand on you."

I obeyed him, but we were lifted with the forward surge and eventually decanted into the water-front road with our possessions intact.

"Okay, now," said Costello. "I'm just going up to the Bank, if you want to come along."

We walked along the arcaded sidewalks past the plate-glass windows of the shipping companies, dodging the clamouring shoe-shine boys and the sellers of the oiled-paper umbrellas which cost fifty cents when the sun is out and two dollars when it is raining ; waited to cross the road until a column of great glossy American automobiles had passed by, and continued until we came out into the main street with its grubby-green, jangling tramcars and tangled traffic. The streets of Hong-Kong are far too narrow for the amount of traffic which they have to bear, but the authorities do not seem to deter the introduction of unlimited numbers of unwieldy American cars.

Costello turned left towards the fluted white tower of the Hong-Kong and Shanghai Bank, and I followed him between the great bronze lions and the armed police which guard its entrance. I exclaimed with surprise as we passed through the revolving doors and were translated in an instant from the clammy heat outside to the cool freshness of the air-conditioned interior.

" It's great, isn't it ? " asked Costello. " Just like going home for five minutes to come in here."

He led the way up the marble stairs into the main banking hall, and I sat on one of the benches while he transacted his affairs. I gazed about the massive hall, which dwarfed the impatient swarm of clients upon one side of the counters and the deliberate clerks on the other : a veritable palace of finance, a temple whose great polished stone surfaces and opulent wood-work and polite clamour were all dedicated to the power of gold ; whose priests were the prim young European and Eurasian clerks, and whose devotees stood in jostling groups before the tellers' cages, with the loitering, holstered police as symbols of its sanctity. I looked up into the blue-and-gold panorama of Commerce worked into the mosaic of the central dome, and reflected upon what a sermon one of my anarchistic friends might have preached upon such a text as this.

Costello rejoined me, stuffing a wad of the big green ten-dollar notes into his wallet. We left by another door, and I looked up at the rocky faces of the Peak, towering above the tree-tops amongst the buildings across the road.

" How d'you get to that railway up to the top ? " I asked, and he raised his benign gaze to follow mine.

" Watch yer pockets," said the Chef. " One o' these little rooters near got my wallet the other diy."

We discussed going to the pictures, and stood for a while outside the brilliant caverns of the cinemas, looking at the cardboard cut-outs advertising the shows, and having peanuts, sunflower-seeds, and chewing-gum thrust at us by the child hawkers outside. We were attracted by the shrieks and rumbling from a roller-skating rink, but decided that it was too energetic. We stared into shops full of the gleaming black and gold of lacquer-ware, received inviting smiles from the wenches who already paraded upon their beats, watched craftsmen making model junks and women embroidering table-cloths stretched upon blackwood frames, with their eyes a couple of inches above their rapid needles and bright silks.

" Well, it's a pity to see all these pretty grog-shops gowin' to wiste," said the Chef. " An' it's nine o'clock. I reckon it's about time I sampled some o' that stuff I been sellin'."

He led the way into the glaring interior of one of the cafés, and we passed through into the back room. Small tables were set about the dance-floor, and against the irregular, whitewashed walls, which were decorated with clumsy murals, yawning groups of Chinese and half-caste girls awaited partners. A waitress came towards us, dressed in sprigged pyjamas and walking with that peculiar awkward swagger, belly stuck out and arms dangling and heels trailing, which many of the Chinese women develop through wearing wooden sandals. The sound of these sandals, the click-clack of their beat on floors and pavements, underlies all others in Hong-Kong, and since they are held on only by a single strap across the instep, their wearers have either to shuffle or swagger.

" Wha' d'you wahn ? " she asked. Her face was the colour and texture of yellow soap, framed in lank black hair ; her flat black eyes regarded us with that blank stupidity which is akin to insolence. She gaped at us with adenoidal disinterest.

I made some comment about her when she had gone to fetch our beer, and immediately found myself involved in an argument about Chinese women. The Chef was already so

A Tong-Kang (small junk) at Hong-Kong

The Steep Streets of Hong-Kong

enraptured by the doll-like creatures, painted and satin-clad, who represent one portion of Chinese womanhood, that he would hear no word against the whole. It is that same artificiality and fragility which fails to attract me, but it seems that it is only possible to be violently partisan or completely disinterested about Chinese women; I don't think that I met any European who was neither one way nor the other. In any case, it is impossible to generalise about them, any more than about the women of any nationality. The clinging, feline daughters of joy have no more relation to the particularly insipid type represented by our waitress than have the sturdy, ruddy-cheeked boatwomen to the white-powdered typists and shop-girls in their European clothes.

Like all café arguments, mine with the Chef came to no conclusion, though he did admit that " The Chows ain't a patch on the Nip sheilahs." He changed the subject by ordering a dish of crayfish, which we ate with our fingers.

" There's nothin' in the world gows together so well as crayfish an' beer," he explained, cracking a claw between his teeth, " unless it's more crayfish an' more beer. Less have another gow."

The back room was beginning to fog with smoke, and by this time was well filled with soldiers of various ranks, sailors, merchant seamen of numerous nationalities, and civilian clerks and technicians of the type who form much of the European colony. A curtain had been drawn back from a kind of large niche in the wall, and the pianist and fiddler who were somehow crammed into it were engaged in a feverish contest with each other. Some complicated dancing was in progress to the result, with the girls who had been sitting idly when we arrived being violently escorted around the floor. The Chef was especially entranced by one of these, a plump and flimsily dressed semi-Portuguese who was displaying all of her national talent for the dance.

" Caw, look at 'er waggle! " he exclaimed. " Look at 'em bounce! She must be a cross between a rubber-plant an' a yo-yo! "

Horrie had left the table, and had been absent for longer than seemed necessary, so I went to look for him. I opened the door through which he had gone, and found

N

myself in a tiny courtyard which stank like a stable.   Someone was retching noisily in a corner, and in another Horrie
stood pinned against the wall by a large man in a sleeveless
shirt.   He supported himself against Horrie's shoulder
with a hand like a boxing-glove, while with the other he
held up the dungaree trousers which had slipped under his
ponderous belly.   A shaft of light from the doorway was
reflected upon the naked dome of his skull.

" Like I was tellin' yer," he stammered, and paused
reflectively.   " Where d'ya say you come from ? " he
asked.

" Awstrailyer," said Horrie patiently.

" Yurr . . . thass right . . . yurr, like I said . . .
d'ye see, now ?   When I were . . . d'ye see wha' I mean ?
I were jus' gonna tell yer . . . d'ye unnerstan' me ?   Some
kine a' furriner, ain'cher ? "

Horrie saw me watching them, and nodded.   His
captor slowly turned his head, revealing a glistening, small-
featured face.

" 'air's anuvver of 'm," he grumbled, and shouted,
" Jor-day ! "

The figure in the corner, now bent almost double, gurgled
and spat.

" Jor-day ! " roared Baldy again, and then cajoled thickly,
" Geordie, yer little hooer, come ovver 'ere."

" Go an' root yerself," retorted Geordie briefly, and
gurgled again.

" Yer wha' ! " bawled Baldy incredulously.   " Say tha'
again, will yer ?   I dares yer !   G'wan, tell me ! "

" Gerroo," moaned Baldy, and repeated his request.

Baldy let go of Horrie, and weaved into the centre of
the yard.   His massive, pear-shaped figure swayed in uncertain silhouette against the whitewashed walls.

" Roight," he said portentously.   " I'm gonna fix yer
for that.   Jus' say it again, that's all, an' I'll fix yer."   He
gestured ferociously with both arms, and his trousers began
to slip.   " Jus' lemme fine me belt, an' I'll fix yer. . . ."
He bent over to peer about for his belt, and waddled slowly
over to where Geordie still propped himself against the
wall.   " 'ave yer seen me belt, Geordie loov ? " he enquired, and slumped his arm about the other's shoulders.

" Whassamatter, hinny ? " he crooned. " Are yer feelin'
pooerly ? "

We left them to it, and returned into the café. Affairs
were equally unsettled there. The music had stopped,
and the players gazed, with deprecating smiles upon their
flat brown faces, at a group in the centre of the floor. It
consisted of a soldier and a civilian, two policemen and two
girls. The latter screamed persistently at each other,
while the soldier gazed with a sheepish smile at the civilian,
who held a handkerchief to his mouth and mumbled
angrily from behind it. A trickle of blood ran down from
beneath it, hung for a moment upon his chin, and dripped
on to his white shirt. The policemen watched them
stolidly, thumbs hooked into their gun-belts, or gazed
wonderingly about the others in the room.

As we regained our table a fresh commotion heralded the
return of the manageress, a globular little woman in a
magenta gown, with a face like a yellow bladder, and thin,
painted lips. She was dragging a European police officer
by his sleeve, glaring at the combatants, and gibbering a
frenzied garble of English and Chinese.

" Chun wah t'zee ah amma ah zee 'rrest 'um! " she
squealed. " Mau'ah ! Respeckable 'ouse galoo toong mai
ah oo ! Yip kalee ach bloddy bostuds fightin' ovver gels
onk sip gum meow allacha sup ! "

The civilian turned to the police officer, revealing a
mouth like mashed raspberries.

" 'e started it ! " he yelled. " I calls anyone to witness
as 'e 'it me first ! "

" All right, come along out o' this," the policeman
growled, and jerked his head at his men.

The five of them left in a sullen group, while the two girls
continued screaming at each other until the manageress
hustled them away.

" Oh migawd, I 'aven't laughed so much since the
sergeant broke 'is leg," said the Chef as the music started
again. " Seems like yer wise to pick one gel an' stick to 'er
in this boozer."

A fifth person had joined our table since I'd been away :
an elderly man with a fiddle-shaped face, covered with
irregular wrinkles like the rain-marks on a dusty wall. He

had been impatiently watching the argument, and as soon as the girls left, turned to Bluey and said, " Like I was sayin', I got this little ship tradin' up an' down the coast. All sorts she carries—chewin'-gum, motor-cars, proper lucky dip. But I c'n no more get an engineer to stay with me than fly in the air. If it's not booze, it's women ; if it's not women, it's booze. Go adrift soon as look at yer, they will. . . ."

Bluey was grunting in abstracted agreement, his bright eyes scanning the girls still left against the wall, and he suddenly left the table.

The other man cut himself short and fidgeted with his glass. His brown, hairy arms were blotched with faded tattooing, and he wore four or five ornate rings on his stubby fingers. He glanced shiftily at me, from weak, bloodshot eyes under a grey tangle of brows. " 'r you an engineer ? " he murmured.

I shook my head, and he shrugged.

" Young fellers——" he began, and started to cough. It was a whooping cough which seemed to churn up out of his depths and fight its way out of his throat ; his face began to look like a pale prune, but he still struggled gamely to complete his denunciation. " Young fellers," he gasped, beating himself on his chest. " Haroo-har-har-harch . . . young fellers nowadays . . . haroo-harch-haraaah . . ." He choked for a few moments, bent double, and then straightened himself with a great effort, gripping the edge of the table and staring at us with bulging eyes and the tears hopping in and out of his empurpled wrinkles. " Young fellers nowadays don't never——"

We never learned the truth about the younger generation, however, for his congested eyes took on an abrupt expression of surprise, and without another word he got up and wandered away to join a group at another table. Horrie and I looked at each other. Bluey and the Chef seemed to be committed elsewhere, and by now the room was a welter of disorganised bodies. The atmosphere was a humid soup of smoke and perspiration, laughter and argument and song, through which the strains of music pulsed feebly. A couple banged against our table, the man's face sweating and avid, and the girl uttering small, unconvincing screams as he snatched at her, and as they passed two newcomers swayed over and stood solemnly looking down at us. The taller of them clutched at the back of a chair and asked, " D'you mind—d'you *mind*?—'f me an' my mate siddown zis table? Th' joint's a li'ul crowded, d'ye see? Wur not try'n'a bum anythin' off you. We got money—my mate's got plenny'a money. 'avencher, mate? "

His mate threw back his head and gave a long, quavering howl, staggered for a moment, and then fell backwards across the knees of the party at the next table. In the confusion Horrie and I got up to go, colliding with the manageress as she bounced back into the room.

The rickshaw men squatting between their shafts looked hopefully up as we pushed through the bat-wing doors. " 'sha? 'sha? " they suggested, and then with a rushing patter of bare feet we were surrounded by ragged, shaven-headed urchins. " Cumshaw? " they wheedled urgently, pushing their begging-bowls against our legs. " Cumshaw, Johnny? Cumshaw? "

It was past midnight; the neons and signs were extinguished and the street was a broad, dim canyon of masonry. From one or two of the cafés we passed a gaudy light still streamed; from a parked police-car came a metallic crackle of radio instructions and it slid away from the kerb with its aerial whipping gently to and fro. A group of military police bantered cautiously with a simpering girl, and two or three children hovered around a stumbling drunk. One of them made a darting snatch, and in an instant they had flitted noiselessly into the black slit of an alley; the drunk reeled and tottered, slobbering obscure curses and plucking at his pockets. The windows of the unlit shops reflected our passing; in their doorways a huddled sprawl of figures crouched or slept. The street was quiet, yet alive; asleep like a man with a dark conscience seething beneath his dreams.

" We're too tired, ducky," said Horrie to a couple of girls who crooned suggestively at us, their white dresses a blur in the dimness.

They giggled uncomprehendingly, and we turned the corner to pause outside the austere precincts of the Y.M.C.A.

" Ah well . . ." sighed Horrie. " If that's it, we've 'ad it, I s'pose. Doin' anything t'morrah? How about coming up the Peak with me? "

" Okay," I agreed. " I'll call round for you. G'night, now."

I walked away towards the wharves, where I could hire a sampan to take me out to the ship. On the steps above the dark, lapping water a couple of Frenchmen supported each other; one very short and stout and the other equally short, but as nip-waisted as an ant.

" *N'oubliez pas!* " he repeated again and again to his companion, one arm about his neck and the other hand clutching his lapel. " *N'oubliez pas, n'oubliez pas!* "

Equally often, the other grumbled, " *Jamais . . . jamais . . .*" until in a sudden passion the thin one shook at his coat, and they swayed perilously close to the water's edge. As they recovered themselves he prodded his nose at the other like a striking snake, and hissed viciously " *N'oooo-bliez pas!* "

" *JAAAAM-AIS!* " bellowed the other, throwing back his head to project the sound out over the swaying black mirror of the harbour. They clung together, breathing heavily, and the sampan-wallahs tittered as I edged past them to reach the boat. The thin one swung around and saw me.

" *N'oubliez pas, m'soo——,*" he requested me thickly, and I assured him " *Jamais!* "

Which seemed as good a word as any other with which to conclude a night's drift.

CHAPTER FIFTEEN

WALKING AROUND THE ISLAND

I

I CALLED FOR HORRIE AT mid-morning the next day, and we crossed to Hong-Kong. We wasted some time in looking for the Peak Tramway station, not knowing that it was quite close to the ferry. We wandered uphill, past the chair-carriers squatting by the bamboo sedan-chairs, for hire to anyone who cannot face the steep slopes, and found ourselves walking through the streets incongruously like those of an English seaside town; the terraces of little, peak-roofed houses grey and prim and lace-curtained. Then, somehow, we arrived in the precincts of the small, demure Cathedral, standing in a hollow surrounded by grassy banks and trees and slender palms, the walls a cool wheat-colour under the flooding sun.

Eventually we discovered the station, a square white modern building beside the steeply slanting rails. One of the cars was standing at the platform, and we entered it to find it already well occupied by a party of tourists, and by some European housewives returning from a morning's shopping to their homes on the Peak. We started smoothly, the wheels grinding over the rails and the thick, greasy cable lisping over its runners; soon we were being pulled up a deep trough lined with bushes, with a glimpse into the back-windows of the houses standing above it.

Our backs were pressed hard against the seats as the gradient increased, there was an uneasy feeling of being impelled backwards as the car carried us forward. The women with their shopping-bags chatted as unconcernedly as though they were in a suburban 'bus, without sparing a glance for the tree-tops and house-tops and rock-scarred, grey-green slopes which fell away on either side of us.

" I hope that ruddy string don't break," murmured Horrie, echoing my thoughts.

The wire with its dull shimmer of black grease did not appear to be nearly so sturdy now, but I said hopefully :

"'Oh, I s'pose it's a funicular, you know—there'll be a gadget underneath to brake it if it starts running backwards.'"

He grunted doubtfully, as the car stopped at a tiny station bowered in tamarisks. Some of the women got off, crying farewells to their friends ; the wheels began grinding again, and most of the tourists clung grimly to the seats in front of them. We reached the top before we expected it, after two or three more halts, and suddenly found ourselves in another white-concrete station. The remaining passengers all seemed to know where to go, and walked briskly away along the road. We were still not right at the summit, and after a moment's hesitation we began to walk along the road which curved up towards it.

It was pleasantly cool, for the thousand-odd feet which we had ascended seemed to have taken some of the sting out of the sun, but it was still warm enough to make us walk slowly. We passed a couple of blocks of flats and some large grey buildings which appeared to have been barracks, with the courtyards before them littered with broken masonry amongst the weeds, the windows blank and staring, and a gaping shell-hole here and there.

The road began to climb more steeply, we passed some smaller houses standing behind their gardens, and then dipped in and out between conical hummocks, smooth and grass-covered, as though the mountain had made several attempts at reaching its highest point before contenting itself with the scrub-covered hillock which surmounted all the rest. We left the road and followed a path which wound around it, leading to a grassy platform upon which an ancient cannon silently menaced the harbour. For a while we sat there, gazing out over the hills of the mainland, the colour of camel's hair and of purple grapes, the sheening island-sprinkled figure-of-eight of the harbour, and the cascade of buildings below us which was the city.

" Smashing, ain't it ? " asked Horrie. " Don't suppose there's any kind of a kayfe laid on up here, do you ? Must be very nigh on feeding time."

We started back to look for somewhere to eat, passed the

Tramway station again, and then paused in our search, for a long admiration of the seaward view. From the low wall on which we sat, the slopes fell away towards the sea in sweeping dips and curves like the careless folds of an olive and sage-green drapery brushed with mauve and lavender. In the long combes and seaward-sloping glens dark thickets slumbered under the sun of noon ; far below us, the slopes were checked in their descent to the sea by an undulation of round green hills. Amongst these hills, from the band of turquoise dividing the shore from the blue of the deeper ocean, the sea intruded in a jigsaw pattern of coves and inlets ; in one place a pool of turquoise was set amongst the emerald hummocks of the hills. Around its rim we could perceive a tiny bristling of masts, and a miniature junk was motionless upon its surface.

" I think that must be the place that they call Aberdeen," observed Horrie. " Looks nice down there, don't it ? That road down the hill back there," he continued. " Wonder if it goes right down to the bottom ? "

" I guess there'd be a road right around amongst those hills as well," I answered. " Long walk, though."

" Get a 'bus back from Aberdeen, maybe ? "

" But what about grub ? "

" Oh, there'll be somewhere we can buy a snack. What d'you say ? "

" I'm willing."

We got off the wall on which we were sitting with our legs dangling amongst the bushes, and made for the descending road. It was more like a lane ; asphalted, but narrow and overhung with bushes, and so steep that we had to lean backwards as we walked. Soon it modified the gradient a little by zig-zagging down the hillside, and as we descended I was reminded of Cornwall by the slopes of wiry, grey-green turf, the outcrops of flinty soil and lichenous boulders, and the constant tinkle of little streams amongst the thickets.

" Someone told me that Hong-Kong means ' Island of Sweet Streams '," said Horrie. " Must be poetical geesers, these Chows."

The way turned out to be even longer than we had expected. We met no one, and passed nothing of greater interest than some abandoned and bullet-scarred block-houses by the side of the road. After half an hour or so of walking the going became more level and the slopes gentler ; we descended beside a gully in which the streams came together to form a noisy cataract, and when we reached the bottom found that it flowed into a reservoir whose waters were the same translucent turquoise as the sea. Under a sign which forbade bathing a bevy of naked Chinese children were splashing merrily, but as soon as they saw us they left the water and scampered over the grass with cries of " Cum-shaw ! "

We only escaped them when we got on to the main road, and if they had been dressed they would have followed us there. As it was, another gang of them left a desultory game of football to take up the pursuit, and were only scattered by some vivid Australian threats. We were passing through a kind of village in which the houses hid behind high walls, with flowered boughs drooping over them to shade the road. On the other side there was a tree-filled glen, with women washing clothes in a little stream and spreading them out to dry on the grass. Somewhat farther on there was the nostalgic sight of a herd of plump cows grazing complacently on the hillside. I stopped to look at them ; they were the first cattle that I had seen since leaving home, and their sleek hazel hides against the green hill made me think of Devonshire farm-house teas. They were the Dairy Farm herd, and a moment later we passed the farm buildings.

The road switchbacked over the coastal hills, with every dip angling around a rocky little cove ; the greater slopes of the mountain towered against the sky and poured the after-noon heat back down on us. Trucks and cars whizzed by, almost bouncing as they hit the bottoms of the dips ; our only company was trotting lines of coolies carrying bolts of cloth.

" Gee, it's kinda warm," panted Horrie. " D'you s'pose anyone would object if I took me shirt off ? "

Shirtless, we trudged onwards ; past a bay out of which the funnels and masts of a sunken ship protruded with an air of rakish bewilderment, and a Chinese graveyard on the hill-side with the graves marked by semi-circles of stone like protecting arms. A coolie came towards us up the hill, at the unvarying jog-trot which they maintain however hard the going; the ragged drawers which were his only clothing were soaked with sweat, and every surface muscle visible upon his fleshless body. The baskets on his carrying-pole were heaped with oranges, and Horrie's face lit up at sight of them.

" I'll have some o' those if I've gotta brain 'im with 'is own pole," he exclaimed.

He held out his arms, and the coolie swerved to go round him, stopping only when Horrie swerved too. He looked at us impatiently, without speaking; his chest heaving slightly and the baskets swaying on the ends of their pole. Horrie held out a dollar bill and pointed at the oranges, and the coolie shook his hand, palm outwards, in the gesture of negation.

" Uh! " he said. " Uh-uh-uh! "

Horrie pointed to the dollar bill and to the oranges again, but the coolie still shook his hand.

" You," said Horrie earnestly, " sell me," pointing to himself, " oranges for one dollar ? " pointing to the basket and the dollar bill.

" Uh-uh," said the coolie. " Uh-uh-uh."

He held up two fingers to his lips, pursing them and making kissing noises.

" Cigarettes ! " exclaimed Horrie, and fumbled for his packet.

The bargain was struck, the coolie departed before a trail of smoke, and we perched on the roadside wall to suck our oranges and take off our shoes.

" Wisht my wind was like that coolie's," grumbled Horrie. " Run like that an' smoke a fag as well—blimey ! "

After a brief rest we plodded on again ; up and down the switchback of the hills and in and out of the jigsaw of the creeks and coves. At last we surmounted a long incline to see below us the harbour of Aberdeen : the turquoise poo which we had seen from the top of the Peak, lying between a hump-backed island and the shore. Before long we were walking along the sea-front, halting frequently to peer into the shavings-littered sheds of the sampan builders along the stony beach. They worked stolidly at their traditional

contrast to the paunchy men and over-trousered females, a
kipper-coloured Chinese woman as lean as a whip came up
from the beach with a bundle of dripping rags in her hands.
She began to hang them upon the rail to dry, and we saw that
they belonged to the infant who was slung upon her back :
a miniature shirt and jacket and pants like a grotesque,
tattered travesty of the ' tiny garments ' of sentimentality.

Climbing the rise out of the valley, we gazed enviously at
the numerous fine homes which stood on either side of the
road, amongst the conifers above us or on the brink of the
cliffs.   The hill which we were climbing was longer than
most of the others we had passed, for the countryside had
changed.   We had left the slopes of the Peak itself some way
behind us, and were walking at the feet of the long range of
hill which rises towards it.   From this backbone of the
island long ridges ended in rocky capes, with steeply rising
gullies between them.   These gullies, with the sharp escarpments of the range frowning above them, are wide and
irregular, broken up and confused by terraces and smaller
ridges which end in abrupt spurs.   But where they reach
the sea they form the succession of lovely bays which are
the most attractive feature of this side of the island.   Their
beaches have unfortunately received the corporation stamp
of promenades and sea-walls, and houses and hotels perch
upon the hillside spurs, but without much affecting the
grandeur of the dark tumbling of the hills down to the sea.

All the same, it is a long tramp along the road which
climbs over the hills separating the bays and borders their
crescent beaches.   By the time we were walking down the
winding slope into Repulse Bay it was early evening, and
at last we heaved ourselves up on to the railing along the
sea-wall and sat there looking down upon the people on the
beach.   With the ruminating contentment which follows
physical exertion, we watched the Chinese family parties :
the trim girls with their skins like gold-dusted ivory and the
young men with high-pitched voices and their ponderous,
complacent parents.

The queues were already forming for the 'buses back to
the city, and, groaning at the renewed effort, we finally
strolled over to join one.   It was an Orientalised replica
of any suburban group returning from a day's outing ;

fretful children and snappish mothers and giggling, yawning couples supporting each other, and exasperated fathers pretending to read the paper. Perhaps the main difference was that they abandoned any pretence at civic courtesy as soon as the 'bus arrived, and with abusive gusto engaged in a free-for-all to fight their way aboard. We missed the first 'bus on this account, but as soon as the next arrived wielded our elbows with the best of them and got a place.

The ride back to Hong-Kong from Repulse Bay is an inspiring journey in itself, with the road winding upwards to the pass in the escarpment and then swooping down again in a series of long loops.

The 'bus dropped us close to the ferry, we relaxed on the slatted seats with a feeling of conscious virtue, and sauntered towards the Y.M.C.A. from the Kowloon pier.

" Come up an' have a shower, an' then we'll go an' eat," suggested Horrie. " I could eat one o' these rickshaw coolies, straw hat an' all."

Splashing about in the dank concrete gloom of the showers, we complimented ourselves on our feat.

" Jus' wait till the cool weather comes," prophesied Horrie. " We'll walk all round this little ole island then."

CHAPTER SIXTEEN

STREET SCENES AND PICNICS

I

BUT BY THE TIME the cool weather came, at the end of October, Horrie was on his way back to Australia. In the meanwhile we had explored yet more of the city and island together. We had visited the Aw Boon Haw pagoda, that strange erection of a patent-medicine king who, the story goes, has been told that he will live as long as he continues to build. We searched for a friend's grave amidst the wooden crosses in the cemetery for those who perished in Japanese captivity. There is something simple and intimate about this cemetery, as though those who lie there in that little plot which overlooks the sea, beneath the brooding shade of the trees and the Union Jack fluttering on its staff, had somehow inspired into the very atmosphere the sense of their ageless companionship. Reading the inscriptions which recorded the resting-places of men and women of every age and degree, it was impossible not to contrast the peaceful beauty of the day with the scenes of courage and savagery which those surroundings had once witnessed. Children and soldiers, women and seamen, the old and the young, are joined in a kinship to which their countrymen can never attain, and which they can only regard with an awed humility.

Horrie and I also spent a great deal of time in a search for ' Cat Street '. We had been assured that in the street of that name we should be able to pick up some astonishing bargains, since all the shops in it were alleged to deal in stolen goods. I heard the same legend again and again, but never succeeded in finding the street. During our search we climbed up the alleyways which are like angular ravines in the mountain of masonry, so steep that they often become steps just as they are about to attain the perpendicular. We wormed through the teeming, raucous, jostling streets which terrace the hillside; lost our way in undulating, elbow-

Sampans at Aberdeen—Hong-Kong

The 'Bulbul' going into dry-dock at Kowloon

width lanes which led nowhere. We were in that part of the city which, from the harbour, is seen as a featureless mass of buildings above the water-front warehouses.

While I suppose that it is incorrect to call any section of Hong-Kong the Chinese quarter, since in every part of it the Chinese vastly outnumbered the Europeans, we found ourselves in a world very remote from the Hong-Kong Hotel or the cafés of Kowloon. The hillside streets, and the alleys which cross them, compose a city in which European influence struggles but feebly against that of the Chinese. When you are being crushed amongst the dawdling, gabbling swarms in the garbage-littered streets it is difficult to remember that it exists at all.

Not one thing, or a few things, are different, but everything. The senses are assaulted by an entire cosmos of new impressions, which are resisted at first in the same way as you attempt to make an individual path through the crowds. You are buffeted, jostled, sweating, irritated progressively by the loitering swarms who block your passage and the hurrying coolies and messengers who weave in and out of them without regard for anyone who stands in the way. At last you learn that you must drift with the crowds or elbow and sidle through them. Loiter with the myriad idlers and with their own engrossing interest in the passing show, or remain as selfishly intent upon your own progress as those who have business to attend to. Useless to expect the automatic minor courtesies which smooth your way in a Western city, and useless to expect to adjust yourself other than gradually to the chaos of exotic impressions.

The Chinese have an enviable ability either to concentrate exclusively upon the business in hand, or to relax utterly and enjoy the process, which the Americans call kibitzing; taking part in all that is going on while remaining a spectator. Every craftsman seems to attract his own circle of kibitzers; watching with appreciative interest whatever he happens to be doing, discussing the finer points, occasionally handing him something, passing the time with gossip whenever he reaches some routine process. Cobblers, tailors, carpenters, tinsmiths, motor mechanics, butchers— no trade seems to be too commonplace or too humble to lack its *aficionados*. The coppersmiths tinker and hammer

o

and the tailors pedal away at their machines and the watch-makers squint and the butchers chop and saw with frowning concentration and the kibitzers stand or squat and watch with as much interest and discussion as though they were seeing it all for the first time.   Not only the craftsmen, but every shop and booth and little stall seems to retain them ; sitting outside if there is no room inside, gossiping across the street or to the people next door if there is nothing going on ;   when you enter a shop they will be there, chattering with the attendant, and falling silent when you enter, watch-ing every detail of the sale being made and erupting into comment immediately you turn to go.   I imagine that the Chinese can very rarely be bored ; life, simply as life, appears to contain such an endless parade of interest for them.

It is the contrast between the workers and the lookers-on which gives the streets their disjointed atmosphere ;   it is disconcerting, somehow, to realise that when you have yourself come to stare, there are scores of people who ask no better diversion than to stare right back at you, while the busy ones ignore you completely.   They are used to being stared at, you are not ;   whilst you are staring you are being scrutinised, criticised, dissected, by people to whom staring is one of the fine arts.   The only thing to do is to enter the game, abandon self-consciousness and reticence, and hope to attain something of the same proficiency.

It is no use hurrying over it ;   the kibitzers take their time, and so must you, allowing the gaze to rest first upon the surface and then to penetrate more deeply, examining the bulk, the round, the texture, and then more slowly savouring the finer shades and subtleties.   The seal-maker sits in his little booth, carving upon wood or ivory the ‘ chops ’ with which all business documents are stamped, and only by accomplished kibitzing can you appreciate the strength and delicacy with which he carves a complicated ideograph upon a surface as small as a sixpence.   A woman is sitting by a letter-writer, hugging her black-pyjamaed knees and casting her gaze upwards whilst she dictates in a monotonous sing-song ;   neither of them seems to object to the appre-ciative listeners, nor to the eyes which watch how the black ink-stick is rubbed upon a moistened stone, to charge the brush with which the skull-capped scribe writes his columns of characters.

Imperceptibly, the bedazzled senses commence to respond. We no longer attempted to trot through the streets like the coolies, but loitered and stared. At the fortune-tellers, stocking-menders, lantern-menders; into the coffin-maker's, whose wares were piled up like brightly painted boats; at the huge sets of false teeth advertising the dentist's, the lurid illustrations of horrifying diseases outside the medicine-shops. Climbing the hillside alleys we passed between orange and jade heaps of pumpkin and water-melons, flaming hillocks of tangerines, the sprigged and candy-striped bolts of cloth to be made into pyjamas; examined the coarse porcelain bowls, ornamented with dragons and butterflies, from which coolies would one day eat their rice; the red and green and blue clusters of wooden sandals, hanging like bunches of gay fruit; tried on cheap clothing and haggled over the price of suits which we did not intend to buy. We discussed buying a fluffy and waggish Chow puppy from a kerbside vendor, gaped at the pressed ducks and whole roast pigs which had been brushed with some dressing which gave them a patina like an old violin, and held our noses to peer in at the barrels and boxes of dried fish. Braving the almost tangible stench of the fish market, dodging the charging porters who shrieked at us in the Chinese equivalent of Billingsgate, we admired the pink hummocks of prawns and the regiments of fish for which we had no name; bluey-brown monsters and weird metallic creatures and slimy objects like overgrown green slugs.

If I had had all the money I've ever earned, and more, I could have spent it on the things I saw which I wanted to buy: lacquered cabinets with red and gold dragons sprawling across the gleaming midnight of their surfaces; heavy silken tapestries embroidered in crimson and gold; grotesque and ribald carvings of gods and demons and bewhiskered sages; cloisonné vases with a glaze as pure as a pearl and as subtly shaded as the evening sky; bronze Buddhas and silk Palm Beach suits, snakeskin shoes and a jade amphora; a nest of carved boxes, in which every one you opened revealed one smaller until the tiniest of all; a model junk and an ivory fan and a transparent porcelain tea service; an opium-smoker's equipment of chased silver,

and a lapis-lazuli bowl.   But I was beginning to discover
what seemed to be the secret of the Chinese : the things
which I could not have and could not do I could enjoy
vicariously, looking at them and admiring them and in
some sense taking them into myself, and so possessing
them.

Out of the ululating streets and precipitous alley-ways we
brought a motley of memories.   The intense aliveness of the
Chinese, the way their features vary from the plump and
bland to the finely-chiselled, aquiline, and haughty ; their
expressions from downright stupidity to the shrewdly
sardonic, from gaping innocence to the ironically gay ; their
complexions from the greasy yellow of cheese to the golden
bloom of apricots, from ruddy orange to a coppery tan,
greenery-yallery to a rose-flushed primrose.   We remem-
bered the chanting clash and squealing dissonances of
their music, the hysterical frenzy of their arguments, and the
laughter-accented gossip.

We recalled the clack-clack of the painted wooden
sandals ; the clicking of beads on abacus wires as the shop-
keepers reckoned their bills ; the children scurrying in
ragged freedom or engrossed in solemn apprenticeship to
some trade ; the old-young, knowing faces of the child
beggars ; the infants sleeping through all the turmoil on
their mothers' backs ; the wailing cries of hawkers and the
grunted warnings of rickshaw-coolies ; the street vistas
barred with sunlight, flamboyant with the reds and golds of
shop-signs, and vociferous with life.

Our search for ' Cat Street ' was unsuccessful, and we came
out at the wrong end of whatever bargains were made, but
we enjoyed ourselves all the same.   Horrie's money,
however, was running low, and before long I joined him on
another exploration—that of the shipping companies'
offices, where he tried to obtain a passage back to Australia.
The answer was everywhere the same—all booked up for
months ahead.   He was becoming anxious, for staying in
Hong-Kong much longer would mean that he was spending
his fare in keeping himself.   But at last he managed to find
a vacant berth on a passenger-carrying tramp, bound for
Australia via the Philippines, and in a few days he was
gone.

II

The days began to lengthen into weeks, the weeks into months, until I could look back with surprise that I had already been there so long, and look forward with increasing anticipation to the day of my departure. Within a single night the weather had changed from steamy summer to crisp, sunny autumn, and the evenings were often chill when we were returning from the ' Baltic's ' cinema shows. Our boat was very small, and we envied the powerful Diesel cutter attached to the ' Baltic '. Especially since they spent most of their time alongside, and rarely seemed to use it.

But the succession of warm and brilliant days, which we were to enjoy through November and much of December, inspired them with the idea of a more congenial occupation for their boat than carrying mail and stores.

One evening when we went across to their pictures, their Second Officer greeted us with the question " Who's coming for a picnic on Sunday ? "

" *Pic*-nic ? " repeated Atkins incredulously, as though he had never heard the word before, and gave a scornful laugh.

The Chief Engineer made some wisecrack, and the Second Officer shrugged tolerantly. He was a powerfully built, apple-cheeked young Cockney, completely devoid of self-consciousness, and he would have asked the Governor of Hong-Kong to his picnic if he had thought it a good idea.

He was joined by Sandy, their Fourth Engineer, a bandy and barrel-chested young Glaswegian with a humorously determined face and a mane of tawny hair.

" Mah Goad, them bums is here again," he chuckled hoarsely. " A-hey, are ye comin' to our picnic on Sunda' ? Are ye on, Erchie ? "

Archie and I accepted at once.

" Mind you, it's to be a real do," warned Bridges, the Second Officer. " Start early and get back late——"

" Three bottles o' whusky an' four o' gin and a few cases o' beer——"

"——shut up, Sandy. We are laying on the grub and stuff, and we'll probably be asking a few other people, so if you wanna bring any friends, tell 'em to roll up. The boat'll hold about thirty, I think."

Further arrangements were made after the cinema show, and for some reason I was elected to be captain of the expedition.

" For," quoted Bridges, " the sake of good order and discipline. There's got to be someone in sole charge on a do like this, otherwise it ends up with an argument about where to go, or what time to go back, and things like that. Everybody that comes on the picnic'll have to agree that Sparky's in charge, and I'll be second-in-command to see that they do."

Sandy snorted disdainfully, and I accepted the position with somewhat uneasy foreboding.

Archie and I turned up at well before the appointed time on the Sunday morning, and found Sandy and Bridges engaged in provisioning the boat.

" Hey, Archie, what'd you do with Sandy last night ? " cried Bridges. " He woke me up at two this morning and said we were going on a picnic. Ph-ew ! We shouldn't't've needed any Diesel oil—we could've run the engine on the smell of his breath."

" He was all right when he left me," said Archie, and Sandy added indignantly :

" Aw reet ! 'course I was aw reet. Take no notice o' yon blithering deck ornament—I just wakened 'im to ask if he was sleeping well."

" I slept all right after I got a whiff of that portable distillery o' yours. You were as tight as a mackerel's ear'ole, and that's water-tight."

" A-hey, never mind the wisecracks—get this boatie loaded. Whaur's all them other useless beggars hidin' theirsel's ? "

He heaved himself up out of the cutter, and out of the clutter of gear about the gangway selected an oil-drum filled with coal, and pierced brazier-wise with holes.

" What on earth are you going to do with that ? " exclaimed Archie.

" That's Sandy's patent stove," jeered Bridges happily. " He's practising to be a night-watchman when he leaves the sea."

" Ach, yer verra funny.   Ye should be on the fillums—
no one 'ud go to see yer except yerself.   Wull ye please give
me a hand wi' this gear ?   Hond me doon me jaiket, if it's
no' too heavy for ye."

Those of their shipmates who were joining the expedition
drifted up one by one : Telfer, the Third Officer, whose
shaven head and broken nose made him look like a fair-
ground boxer, and the lanky Third Engineer, and the
Second Engineer, Ralston, a scrawny and silent little man
whom Bridges teased unmercifully.

" What's the matter, Sec' ? " he cried as soon as he
appeared.   " Did she kick you out of bed, or something ?
Not often we see you about on a Sunday morning."

Ralston sniffed in an unamused fashion, while Sandy
climbed back aboard and roared :

" A-hey, wull ye feenish yer gowsipin' an' naiterin' an'
get yon boatie loaded ?   Wull ye bear a hond here th'
noo ? "

" What's that in English ? " enquired Bridges, but began
to work upon the pile of gear by the gangway, and we
passed it down into the boat.

Sandy began to check it off on a tattered scrap of paper :
" Water—oil—sangwiches essetra—firrst-aid kit—kettle—
taypot—a-hey, whaur's th' taypot ?—cups an' glawses——"

The cutter was rapidly beginning to look as though we
were abandoning ship, but he was finally convinced that we
had everything aboard.

" Aw reet, Spairky, take command," he ordered.   " Engine signals is one bell for start, two for stop, and three for
go astern.   If you want anything else, just shout.   Take
her to the Kowloon jetty first, tae pick up the others, an'
then ye can go whaur ye please."

He ducked into the engine compartment, and I jerked at
the bell-cord.   The Diesel whined and thudded into life,
and as I leaned on the tiller and we churned away from the
gangway I asked Bridges :

" Who're these others we're collecting ? "

" Oh, just some bits and pieces the lads invited.   I was
gonna ask a couple o' people myself, but I thought I'd see
how this one goes off first."

He gave some raucous toots on the klaxon as we

approached the Kowloon pier, to scatter the usual shoal of sampans which were waiting about for patrons. Tilfer clutched at the splintered woodwork with his boat-hook, and out of the crowd of idlers on the pier a little group climbed gingerly down the steps. It included three Chinese girls attired in slacks and blouses, who were helped aboard with much squealing and giggling and immediately appropriated by their hosts.

"Wance aboard th' lugger," shouted Sandy joyfully, poking his head up through the hatch. "Yoo-hoo! Annie! Lucy! You remember me?"

"As if anyone could ever forget him," said Bridges, as I rattled a fusillade on the bell to recall him to his duty.

But as soon as we had manœuvred clear of the jetty he scrambled round to join the group in the forward cockpit. The engine needed no attention in open water, and I steered south-westwards for the channel between Stonecutters' Island and the mainland, and settled down to enjoy myself.

The torrents of sparkling air which were pouring south-wards before the approach of winter ensured that it was perfect weather for our picnic. The harbour had a Sunday morning calm, with the ships smoking peacefully at anchor and the junks and sampans purling smoothly through water like ruffled azure silk. The mainland ranges stood out in sharp relief, tawny and olive, against the serene clarity of the sky, and as we passed the radio towers and rocky, snuff-coloured hillocks of Stonecutters a tocking of rifle-fire drew our attention to the ranges near the beach, where the targets moved up and down like derisive eyes above the puffs of sand.

Archie and Bridges and I gossiped above the steady thudding of the engine, which was punctuated now and again by a shrill outcry of laughter from the bows. We could see Sandy's tawny crest bobbing up and down beyond the cabin roof, and after a while he scrambled aft again. He was in bubbling spirits, talking and laughing incessantly as he dragged off his clothes and pulled on his swimming-trunks; the sun glowing over the smoothly fleshed muscles of his shoulders and back.

"Oh-oh," said Bridges when he dived into the cabin, and we heard the clink of glass. "Here it comes now."

He emerged hugging an armful of bottles, and Bridges asked, " Leave some for dinner-time," as he began to pass them round.

He beamed back at us as he edged back along the gunwale outside the cabin. " Och, a short life an' a gay one," he replied.

We drank our beer, chatted, and admired the scenery. The channel which we were taking past Stonecutters' opened out into a broad reach, which offered a diversity of channels between the islands beyond it. A few junks were sailing towards that closest to the mainland, and I followed and passed close to them. Their crews watched us incuriously as we outstripped one after another of them, and gazed blankly at Sandy standing up and gesticulating in the bows.

" The puir heathen ! " he shouted scornfully, and devoted himself to tossing the empties overboard.

At once two or three little boys leaped from the junks and swam towards the floating bottles, engaging in a splashing squabble as they reached them together. I watched them doubtfully, wondering how they would get back to their craft, but the wind was light and the junks were no more than ghosting along. As we passed the last of them we saw that she was being helped along by long sweeps, with a woman tugging at each oar.

" That's what I like to see," said Bridges approvingly. " I know a few women it'd do a power o' good to pull on a junk oar for a few weeks."

The boat pounded on ; we passed through a scattering of small islands and found ourselves entering a long strait between a column of islands and the mainland. We could see the cars speeding along the Canton road at the foot of the rocky hills, and on the beach which it bordered were pleasant little summer-houses and beach-huts, parties of people a-sprawl on the sand or frolicking in the sea. On our port hand the islands were growing steeper, with little coves indenting the low cliffs above which the slopes of brown-green turf ascended to their conical summits. Each of these coves was pointed out to me as we passed them, and suggested as a likely picnic place, but I rejected them all because their beaches were too small, or there was a rice-field behind them, or the approaches were too rocky. I wanted to get out of the strait between them and the holiday panorama of the mainland beach, and see what lay beyond.

At last it came to an end. It opened into a broad stretch of water with the next group of islands across its outer rim, far enough away for their details to be indistinct. The sun shone and the sea sparkled and the engine drummed; a babble of voices and laughter came from forward, and Archie leaned on the cabin-top, smoking reflectively, while Bridges stood beside me and kept up a constant flow of wisecracks and unrepeatable anecdotes and scraps of ribald song.

"This is a bit of all right," he remarked. "Did you ever hear the one about the curate and the barmaid?"

For my part, I was utterly content; the moment contained all the ingredients which make up my idea of a good time: superb weather, a small boat, good company, somewhere new to explore—there is nothing else in the world which has a flavour quite so candid and fresh.

Our low 'height of eye' had made the islands seem farther away than they really were. We had reached them by noon, and it became apparent that they were the first of another long group running roughly parallel with the mainland. They were bigger than the others we had passed, and their hilly backbones were higher and more sharply peaked, but on the nearest of them there was a sickle-shaped bay containing an inviting beach.

"D'you know how the tide's running?" I asked Bridges.

"It should be about high tide now, I think."

"We'd better not beach 'er, then, or we're liable to be stranded. What d'you say we anchor just far enough off so's we can wade ashore?"

He agreed, and began to scramble forward to stand by with the anchor and look out for rocks. Dead slow ahead, we crept into the bay, with Bridges taking soundings with the boat-hook. The shore came closer, and he shouted:

"Soundings! Carry on—you've plenty of water. Take 'er as close as you can."

I glanced over the side, seeing the deep green of the water lightening and becoming transparent, the sandy bottom shimmering through it. "This'll do," I shouted to Bridges, and jerked at the bell-rope. "Leggo yer anchor ! "

Sandy came out of the engine-compartment, his face alive with excitement. " Och, tae hell ! " he said when he saw our position. " Whit way didna' ye take 'er up to the beach ? "

" The tide's dropping—she'll go aground if we take 'er in much closer."

" Aye, it's aw reet for you—ye can swim, I canna. What about the lassies ? An' a' thon stuff to be carried ashore ? "

" Blimey, there's no swimming in it. The water won't come up to yer navel."

He refused to be convinced, until the three girls, like fragile ivory dolls in their swim-suits, had jumped one after the other with giggling shrieks.

" Here goes nothin'," he cried, holding his nose and jumping with closed eyes, and opened them with a startled expression when he found himself standing upright. " A-hey, it's grand ! " beginning to splash the others. " Hey, don't just stand up there—hond doon some o' that gear, an' let's get crackin' ! "

The beach was a deep half-moon of smooth sand, with a stream trickling through the rocks in one corner, and the ground behind it rising to the scrub-covered hills. But it seemed that the island was not so uninhabited as had at first appeared, for in one corner of the beach was a kind of hay-stack of grey-green grass, and beside the winding gully of the stream's course down the hillside there were numerous little biscuit-coloured patches of ripe rice. And then a chicken-chested urchin, in ragged jacket and pants, appeared from nowhere and squatted upon the rocks to watch us.

We camped beside the stream, and Sandy trotted about finding stones big enough to support his stove.

" Watch this," murmured Bridges. " It's gonna be good. How d'you reckon to light it ? " he asked and Sandy looked at him scornfully.

" Whit d'ye reckon I brought that can o' Diesel ashore for ? " he enquired. " Just a wee sprinkle of ile an' it'll be away with the mixer."

He doused the coal liberally from the jerrican of Diesel oil, which looked as harmless as dirty water, and touched a match to it.   It flickered for a moment, and then, with a gust of sooty smoke, streaked with violet flame, the oil caught fire.

" That's better'n a' yer messin' around wi' paper an' sticks ! " crowed Sandy triumphantly, and tilted the can to give it a livener.

The flame leapt up the tea-coloured trickle and touched off the gas, so that a long, wavering jet of mauve fire hosed forth from the bung-hole of the can.   We scattered to the accompaniment of loud shrieks from the girls, but by some miracle the oil in the can did not catch.

" A-hey, whit's biting yees ? " asked Sandy in surprise. " Fill the kettle—I'm thusty ! "

We approached somewhat cautiously, but the fire had subsided to a mere guttering furnace.   And before long the kettle had boiled and the tea was made, and we were ploughing through the robust assortment of victuals provided by the ' Baltic's ' pantry.   But even the after-effects of the feast, which left me wanting to do no more than lie on the sand and admire the sky, could not weigh down Sandy's ebullience.

" Ye came to enjoy yourself, didn't ye ? " he roared, stirring me with his toe.   " Waken up, and look cheerful ! "

" Oh, go an' chase money-spiders," I moaned, and was bombarded with sand and stones.

There was no escape : we had to join him in round games in which the main object seemed to be escaping from Sandy jumping on your back and ramming your face in the sand.

" Did ye never see 'em putting the weight at the Hielan' Games ? " he yelled.   " Watch yerselves, then ! " and a boulder weighing about half-a-hundredweight would sail past your ear and splatter against the rocks.

Eventually we rounded upon him and drove him into the water, farther and farther out, until his guffaws became uneasy, and he reminded us ever more despairingly :

" I canna swim, ye daft feuls ! A-hey, a joke's a joke— d'ye want me to droon ? "

We spared him at last, and as we waded back ashore I had a look at the boat.   " Hey, there's not much water left here," I called.   " The tide's running out fast—what about taking 'er out a bit ? "

" Ach, dinna haver. We can aye push 'er off if she gets stranded. Awa' wi' us noo and explore the island."

Brimming with doleful prophecies as to what would happen if the boat were stranded, I accompanied them upon the exploration of the island. We followed the course of the stream, which very shortly tumbled over a series of steps which were probably artificial, since on the same level as each of them was one of the terraced rice-patches, with the grain brown and mature above the dried yellow mud. Rice grows under water, so there must have been some way for the muddy little shelves to be flooded when the seed was planted.

Soon we heard voices and saw movement above us, and came upon three or four women who were engaged upon harvesting the crop. Their tanned, simple faces, under the flat, round hats, viewed our invasion with a kind of bland consternation ; they stopped work and huddled together, whispering a little and twisting at the corners of their black cotton tunics. Standing near them was a small ox, tethered by a nose-ring, and the patchy grey colour of a street drying after rain.

" A-hey, look at the wee bulluck," said Sandy, patting it on the back. " Whit d'ye say we buy it and take it aboard for a pet ? "

One of the girls said something to the women, who giggled nervously and started work again. They were winnowing the rice into a sack : stripping the ears from the stalks and shaking it through a sieve to separate the grain from the chaff. Two of them had small, broad-bladed sickles thrust through their belts of plaited straw, and soon they got into the rice-patch and crept along the rows, hacking off handfuls of stalks and tossing them aside for the others to garner. There could have been nothing more primitive, and yet it had the authority of all elementary things. We watched them solemnly, a strangely con-trasted group, and the three slim, delicate-handed girls looked with a kind of wondering amusement at the peasant women.

Sandy soon tired of watching the reaping and the Biblical technique of separating the ears from the chaff, and strolled up to the ox. " A-hey, did ye ever see them rowdeow monkey whilst one of the girls endeavoured to convince him that our intentions were harmless. Eventually he recalled his retainers, and with whispering grins and sidelong glances at Sandy they tucked up their trousers and waded out to the boat.

" Hee-yah ! " they cried. " Ah-hee . . . ah-hoi . . . ah-hee . . . yah-hey . . ."

" Hee-yah ! " echoed Sandy. " Heave, ye yalla scovengers ! Hee-yah ! "

The boat stirred uneasily, and they increased their efforts and their song. Supported by his attendants, the old man shrilled excited instructions from the shore, and they stepped up their tempo until with a final triumph chant of " Hi-yaaaah ! " the boat abandoned resistance and began to slide astern. They let her go, and gasped with self-congratulation as she glided back into deeper water.

" Hey ! " shrieked Sandy. " Stop 'er ! "

Three or four of us churned after her and managed to check her escape.

" Be gees, let's get tae hell oot o' this," grumbled Sandy. " Whit wi' savage beasties an' pushing the boat oot for ye, I'm sair frae tip to toe."

The islanders helped us to reload the boat, and stood waiting expectantly as we prepared to depart. The old man chittered urgently at them from the beach, and Lucy explained :

" He is telling them to ask for cumshaw."

Sandy exploded. " Dinna tell me they've the confoontit impairtinence tae ask for payment ! Hanna we gi'en 'em free entertainment th' whole o' the afternoon ? Awa' wi' yees, yer yalla blaygairds, till I take th' toe o' me boot to ye ! "

" Oh, fair play now, Sandy," expostulated Bridges. " We'll give 'em these scraps that're left over, and a few fags—that'll be enough."

Sandy subsided muttering, and we gave the islanders the remnants of our feast. They seemed well satisfied, and when last we saw them were trying to keep their wages from being commandeered by the old man.

We planned to circumnavigate the island and to try returning through the western seaboard entrance to the harbour, instead of by the Stonecutters channel. The afternoon was fairly well advanced, and the combination of sun and air and exercise made us all pleasantly languid, content to loll about and watch the scenery go by.

" It's no' sundown," said Sandy, " but anyway we've had our teas. So we'll have a wee drappie to keep us going."

The island turned out to be considerably larger than we had expected, and we could discover no navigable channel between it and the next in the group. But there was no hurry; there was plenty of time to go right round the next, and the next after that, if necessary.

However, this next island proved to be bigger still. We kept thinking that when we rounded the next cape the hills which we could see beyond it would be those of another island, but every time we discovered that there were still more in that seemingly interminable chain of hills. They were very nearly mountains; steep and conical and with smooth cinammon slopes, monotonous and complacent in their regularity.

The launch drummed on, and the others sat talking in drowsy undertones, punctuated by Sandy's hoarse chuckle and the clink of bottle against glass. Ahead of the boat the water stretched away into the reflective placidity of approaching evening, already touched with ruddy undertones from the declining sun ; on our starboard hand the mountains of the mainland were in silhouette against a lambent sky. Far away in the distance I could see a mountain in the shape of a perfect cone ; poised and serene and somehow intangible.

I steered closer inshore, in the certainty that rounding the next point would bring us into the channel between this island and the next, and that we should be able to start on the return trip. But it brought us into nothing but another broad bay, hardly distinguishable from the others except that a sizeable house, red and white in the fading light, stood on a level space between the hills and the sea. It looked lonely and inviting, as houses do in otherwise deserted places, and was an unexpected reminder of humanity against the darkening background of the hills. I wondered idly whether it were no more than a farm-house,

P

CHAPTER SEVENTEEN

HOMEWARD BOUND

I

WE CONTINUED THE SUNDAY picnics until the weather grew too cold, and the days and weeks passed until Christmas. This was a brisk, sunny day, in pleasurable contrast to my previous Christmas in Singapore, and after it the days slipped by faster and faster until the expiry of my two years' contract and the celebration of Chinese New Year. It was the middle of the brief winter, with lowering skies and the temperature a couple of degrees above freezing, and throughout the day the colony erupted in a bombardment of fire-crackers. Along the water-front it was as though the city was besieged; all the morning we could see the twinkle of explosions through the drifts of blue smoke, and a constant crackling roar drifted across the harbour. It was quieter in the afternoon, but began again in the evening; I was ashore in Kowloon with Bridges and some of the others, and the broad length of Nathan Road tattoed and banged as though with street-fighting. Fire-crackers were being thrown from upper windows to explode in mid-air, or about the ears of anyone not wary enough to dodge; parties of urchins were flinging them from alley-ways and doorways, and the pavements were littered with the split paper cartridges. It was both a celebration and an assault; a fiesta in honour of another year successfully overcome and a warning to the devils to stay away from the new one.

We had intended to go to the pictures, but the others found this opportunity for general hell-raising too good to be missed; the sport did not appeal to me, and I went to see Bob Hope by myself. Turning away from the cinema ticket-office I bumped into the Chef.

" Give you two dollars for yer tie," he said.

It was a yellow silk affair of which I was rather proud, and I ignored his offer.

"Thought you'd be out celebrating on a night like this," I said.

"Blimey, I only just finished celebryting Christmas. Comin' in?"

"Come an' have some supper," he invited when we emerged again into the still eructating streets, and we went to Tkachenko's. Over a potent curry I asked how he was getting on.

"All right, boy, all right. Well in with the boss I am now. Give me a new suit for Christmas, 'e did. Thinks the world o' me."

"I s'pose that you'll be settling here for good?"

"Naow! Not on yer life! I got itchy feet, b'y. I've 'ad this plyce. I've seen it, see? I'll be on the move agyne any time naow."

"Where to, then?"

"Oh—I dunno. Anywheres. Bangkok, mebbe—or Saigon." He sipped his beer, and said caressingly, "Sourabaya . . ." and then with his normal briskness, "Yer only young once, y'know."

"I sh'd think you'd be afraid of getting stranded somewhere," I said, and he repeated the remark he had made aboard ship:

"With a thick skin an' plenty o' cheek you can get out of anything."

He was well supplied with both, and I wished him luck in his employment of them. He bade me good night outside the restaurant, and walked away towards the Star Ferry as brisk as a fiddler's fingers.

I was not to see him again, but I was soon engrossed in the cultivation of a new circle of acquaintances—the officers of the 'Brahmin', the ship to which my transfer had been arranged for the homeward voyage. She was undergoing a leisurely refit, and after Christmas her sailing date was postponed from week to week. I spent a good deal of time aboard her before I actually joined; setting my own department in order or idling away the time in conversation with her officers. She was an old ship, built during the first world war, and there was a lot to be done to patch her up for the voyage home; no sooner was one repair completed than it seemed to give rise to another.

bellow from the bridge, and the Third Officer came down the ladders in a couple of jumps.

" Man overboard ! " he shouted. " Old Man says to clear away the starboard boat, Mr. Casey. He's turning the ship round, but don't lower away until he says."

" Bloody fool of a sailor rushed up on the bridge and started pulling at the telegraphs," he explained to us. " I thought he'd gone barmy, and kicked his bottom out of it. They've wasted about ten minutes jabbering until they got enough sense to say there was a man in the drink."

" Who is it ? "

" One of the cooks, I think—I dunno for sure——"

He departed to his boat station, and we called to the chief steward. He was a little shuffling, grinning old man, as bent as a question-mark, and he came up with his usual apologetic smirk.

" Who's overboard, steward ? "

" Dunno, seh. I t'ink it 'im second cook. Yiss. Very silly man, all same. T'is sailohman, e' say 'e see 'im bend over aft-side for drop bucket, catch'm foot, pretty quick fall down. Yiss. Bi'm'by finish, I t'ink. Heh-heh ! "

We gathered that the second cook had been dumping a bucket of garbage over the stern, and had overbalanced and followed his bucketful overboard. Even allowing for the delay, during which the panic-stricken sailor who had seen him fall had attempted to stop the ship by himself, the man could not have been far astern ; we steamed in slow circles about the spot where he had disappeared. There was nothing to be seen but the rhythmic blue heaving of the swell, mocking and impassive, swaying and sparkling in careless reminder of the vastness of the sea and the insignificance of man.

There was a shout from the men watching in the bows, after a moment repeated from the bridge.

" There 'e is ! Just about a point off the bow. Lower away, Mr. Casey ! "

" Aye-aye, sir——"

The boat-falls squeaked and protested in the blocks, the davits shuddering as they took the weight of the boat ; after a moment we could all see the yellow blur beneath the surface which was the shirt of the drowned man. The ship was stopped, and immediately drifted broadside-on to the swell ; the boat took the water with a squattering splash, and leaped upwards again as the roll of the ship tautened the falls. She swung like a pendulum on the end of them, and it seemed that she was bound to crash into the ship's side when the returning roll dropped her into the water again.

" Slack away ! Slack awayyy ! " bawled the Chief Officer, half-way down the ship's side and hanging on by one hand to the boat-ladder. " Leggo yer blocks ! For Chrissakes give 'er some slack ! "

The heavy steel blocks through which the boat-falls are rove are hooked on bow and stern to the boat ; it is no easy matter to release these when one moment they are pulling tautly upwards and the next bashing down on to the thwarts. The men in the boat were tumbled helplessly as the roll of the ship snatched her upwards and dropped her again, and, with ready fatalism, they looked up to the Chief Officer for guidance. He clung to the foot of the swaying ladder, watching his chance to drop into the boat ; he missed it once, was dipped up to the waist by a heavier roll than usual, and with a crackle of imprecations let go his hold and was dragged into the boat.

He got the blocks unhooked and the motor started, only to find that ship and body had drifted apart ; some minutes were consumed in searching for it, directed by signals from the ship. They found and grappled with it ; in the obstinate manner of the dead, it resisted upheaval, and the boat careened sharply as her crew dragged it over the gunwale in a sprawl of arms and legs.

Lifting the boat out of the water was an even trickier operation than dropping her ; the ship was brought head-on to the swell, but still plunged so badly that hooking the blocks on again seemed almost impossible. At last the forward block was hooked, and the fall immediately tautened so that it might not work loose ; this raised the bows too high out of the water, and on the next surge the stern dropped and the sea licked aboard. The body, which had been stretched face downwards across the thwarts, swayed idly to and fro as the boat's crew scrambled and tumbled around it.

Finally they managed to get both blocks hooked. The

The ochre and citron and orange blocks of the waterfront tenements sank below the Mediterranean horizon, and we received orders to proceed to Leith. It developed into an indirect procedure, since we had to radio to Malta for a replacement part for the engine, and go in to pick it up. We expected only a couple of hours in Valetta harbour, with the sand-coloured forts and the houses terraced upon its rocky sides, and the bells of all the churches sounding together upon the hour; but when we came to weigh anchor there was an unfortunate accident, and although the anchor cable came up, the anchor remained on the bottom.

We were forced to remain in harbour long enough for the spare anchor to be unstowed, lightered round to the bows, and shackled on, and those of us not engaged in the process were quick to seize the opportunity of a night ashore. I went with Vakil, the Fourth Engineer. We hailed one of the gaudily painted little boats with the unpronounceable name of '*dghaisas*', and were ferried ashore for sixpence. Malta is a place which I never much wanted to visit, conceiving it to be a kind of Latinised Portsmouth, and so I found myself unexpectedly charmed with the winding streets of steps, the tall, secretive buildings with their hint both of Morocco and Spain. There was some kind of political campaign going on, and the walls were patchy with posters vehement with exclamation marks; loudspeakers blared in the little cafés with their bright windows full of bottles, and scarlet-sashed groups of priests gesticulated at each other on the steps. We found what we supposed to be the main street, and strolled along it amongst the evening crowds: soldiers and sailors jostling the black-suited, crinkly-haired islanders, and high-wheeled pony-cabs whip-cracking and jingling amongst the automobiles.

The sound of music attracted us to a kind of plaza facing a space which had been cleared by the bombardment; under the dusty trees before a café, chairs and tables were set about a little pavilion, in which a trio played excerpts from the operas. It was pleasant to drink our beer under the cool stars, with the bulk of some official building standing in unlit dignity against the sky; Vakil stared about him as though with the reflection that Europe wasn't going to be so bad, after all.

"Iss tsere anytsing like tsis in England?" he asked hopefully.

I was watching the 'cello player, a broad-chested man with spindly legs, who strummed upon his instrument in an abstracted manner and revolved slowly around it, as though to give everyone the benefit of his performance; while he played, he stared out over the crowd at the wire-legged tables with a kind of dreamy complacency. They took no notice of him, but consumed their coffee and ice-cream and liqueurs almost absent-mindedly, as though they were but a relish to their talk, with only the brown-legged children staring about with wide, wondering eyes. At most of the tables there was a family group, the elders square and im-mobile except for their mouths, the young matrons broad-sterned, heavy-bosomed, fecund, the girls languid and darkly voluptuous.

"Tsey soon seems to get verree fat, don't tsey?" re-marked Vakil. "Tse young ones is nice, all right, but all tse ossers is like baybee elephunts."

"Women with mixed blood soon go to seed," I said idly, but as soon as I had repeated the platitude I saw that I had said the wrong thing.

I hastily suggested that we should go to the pictures, which we had discussed earlier. It was almost time for the last house, and when we entered through the low-browed foyer we seemed to step back a century in time. It was like entering one of the playhouses in a Cruickshank illustration to a Dickens novel. The building was tiny, and almost cylindrical; row upon row of little boxes rose to the ornate ceiling, with their fronts each painted with a different picture in oils: a landscape, or swans on a lake, or a dramatic sunset. We took our cramped seats in the stalls, and it seemed incongruous to be waiting to see Shirley Temple in surroundings which would have been instantly familiar to the Muggles' and the Infant Prodigy.

The music had finished when we came out, and most of the cafés were closed. Doubtless we could have discovered further entertainment, but were not much disposed for any-thing but a return to the ship. We found the steps again, and were half-way down them when we were halted by the sound of a peculiar rapid pattering behind us. Round the

corner came a young man scurrying downwards at a break-
neck speed ; his feet were flickering like a dancer's, as though
independent of his body, and as he passed us he gave us a
sharp, disdainful look, that of the professional for the amateur.
"Tsey must start mighty young to learn tsat caper,"
remarked Vakil mildly.

We were aboard by midnight, and had sailed again by
noon the following day.

We were very lucky in our weather ; all the way from
Hong-Kong we had had nothing but calm seas and gentle
winds, when anything stronger would have made our progress much slower. Even the passage across Biscay was
calm and mild, and we came up Channel and into the North
Sea in weather that was smooth with spring. The old
familiar landmarks appeared again : the wallowing red
hull of the Sunk lightship, the gull-circled drifters off
Grimsby, Flamborough Head ; the squadrons of grubby
colliers bound southwards from the Tyne, Lindisfarne,
patches of ploughland on the green-and-lavender downs of
the Lowlands. And then, in the still of a late afternoon,
we were steaming past the islands in the Firth of Forth,
with the smoke hovering unstirred above Burntisland and
the great bridge straddling across the western sky.

We had arrived ; the voyage was at an end. All at once
it seemed as though I had never been away. Upon returning to things and scenes which were once familiar,
somehow one expects them to have undergone a change
similar to one's own change during the absence from them ;
to find them unaltered gives a tinge of unreality to the time
of separation. I did not know how much I had myself
changed ; I only knew the contentment of home-coming,
the satisfaction of another voyage safely completed. I was a
little older, and perhaps a little wiser, than when I went
away ; more cautious in some things, more careless in others.
Even if I had not learnt a great deal, I knew that at least I
was beginning to learn how to learn. And above all things,
I was discovering that life itself is a sea with many islands ;
an ocean always uncharted, often ominous, and upon which
each of us must voyage alone, but never out of sight of the
islands of hope and friendship, achievement and laughter
and love.